Youth Justice
and
The Youth Court

An Introduction

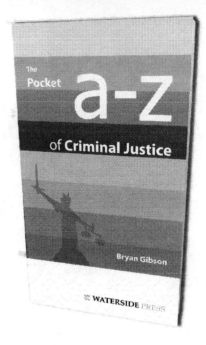

Youth Justice
and
The Youth Court

An Introduction

Mike Watkins and **Diane Johnson**

Edited and with additional material by **Bryan Gibson**

Foreword **Chris Stanley**

WATERSIDE PRESS

Youth Justice and The Youth Court
An Introduction

Mike Watkins and Diane Johnson
Edited and with additional material by Bryan Gibson
Foreword Chris Stanley

Published 2010 by
Waterside Press
Sherfield Gables
Sherfield on Loddon
Hook, Hampshire
United Kingdom RG27 0JG

Telephone +44(0)1256 882250 Low cost UK landline calls 0845 2300 733
E-mail enquiries@watersidepress.co.uk
Online catalogue www.WatersidePress.co.uk

ISBN 1904380 530 (Paperback)
ISBN-13 9781904380535 (Paperback)

Cataloguing-In-Publication Data A catalogue record can be obtained from the British Library.

Cover design © 2009 Waterside Press.

UK distributor Gardners Books
1 Whittle Drive, Eastbourne, East Sussex, BN23 6QH.
Tel: +44 (0)1323 521777; sales@gardners.com; www.gardners.com

North American distributor International Specialised Book Services
920 NE 58th Ave, Suite 300, Portland, Oregon, 97213-3786, USA
Tel: 1 800 944 6190 Fax 1 503 280 8832; orders@isbs.com; www.isbs.com

Printed by the MPG Books Group, Bodmin and King's Lynn

e-book *Youth Justice and The Youth Court: An Introduction* is available as an e-book and also for subscribers of Myilibrary and Dawsonera (eBook ISBN 9781906534813)

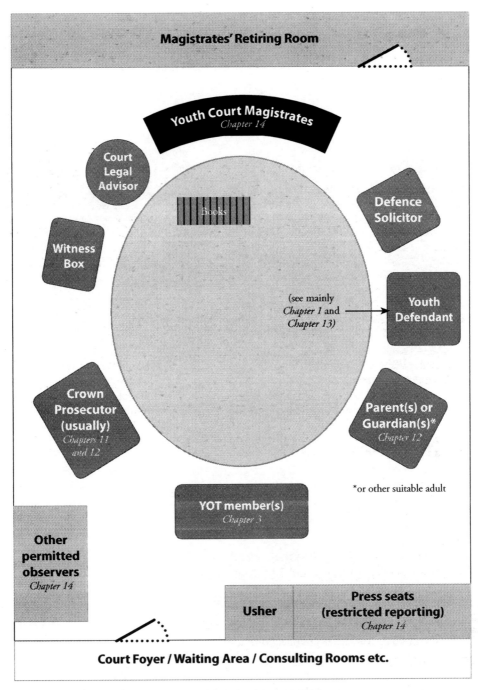

Magistrates' Retiring Room

Youth Court Magistrates
Chapter 14

Court Legal Advisor

Books

Defence Solicitor

Witness Box

(see mainly *Chapter 1* and *Chapter 13*) → Youth Defendant

Crown Prosecutor (usually) *Chapters 11 and 12*

Parent(s) or Guardian(s)* *Chapter 12*

*or other suitable adult

YOT member(s) *Chapter 3*

Other permitted observers *Chapter 14*

Usher

Press seats (restricted reporting) *Chapter 14*

Court Foyer / Waiting Area / Consulting Rooms etc.

Example of a youth court layout

Contents

Please also see the important notice about the contents on page xx

THE YOUTH JUSTICE SYSTEM (YJS) AT A GLANCE

THE YOUTH JUSTICE BOARD

Gives general direction and guidance but is essentially independent and non-executive: *Chapter 3*
Can make grants or facilitate other forms of support to youth justice services: *Chapter 5*
Oversees the 'secure youth estate': *Chapter 17*

Event	Main case outcomes (in addition to any informal support)	What part of statutory system is engaged	Voluntary sector bodies that may become involved
A child under 10 years of age **is involved in what would be criminal offending or anti-social behaviour** if he or she happened to be 10 or older: see mainly *Chapters 1, 6* and *10*	Acceptable behaviour contract (ABC) Child safety order Parenting Order	Local authority children's services Police Education/school	SureStart Family centres Youth groups Charities as per *Chapter 3* and the examples in the *Glossary* may become involved *at any age*
A youth aged 10-17 years inclusive **is at risk of offending**: *Chapter 6*	ABC Anti-social behaviour order (ASBO) Other appropriate crime prevention measures.	Youth offending team (YOT') Police Community safety teams Local youth service Education/school	Youth groups Advice centres Substance misuse, sexual health and other points of referral may be used *at any age* Sports/leisure provision
A youth aged 10-17 years inclusive **has indulged in anti-social behaviour (ASB)**	ABC ASBO Restorative justice approaches: *Chapter 4*	YOT Community safety teams Local youth service Education/school	Youth groups Advice centres Sports/leisure provision
A youth aged 10-17 years inclusive **is under arrest** for an offence: see mainly *Chapter 10*	Police detention pending investigation or release on bail to return to police station or if charged with an offence the youth court	Police Crown Prosecution Service (CPS) Criminal Defence Service (CDS) (or privately funded lawyer) YOT Appropriate adult	Youth groups Advice centres and, e.g. Citizen's Advice Bureau (CAB)
A youth aged 10-17 years inclusive has committed an offence but **may not need to be prosecuted**: *Chapter 11*	ABC Restorative approaches 'Telling-off' Police reprimand Police final warning Youth conditional caution	Police CPS YOT	Youth groups Advice centres

Event	Main case outcomes (in addition to any informal support)	What part of statutory system is engaged	Voluntary sector bodies that may become involved
A youth aged 10-17 years inclusive has committed an offence and **is to be prosecuted**: see initially *Chapter 12* and for the range of possible sentences *Chapter 15*	Summoned to appear at a local youth court (or adult magistrates' court:) *or* Released on bail to attend such a court, *or* Held by the police (or local authority where longer periods are involved) and produced directly to the court. Certain cases can progress to the Crown Court. For all of the above, see *Chapter 13.*	Police CPS YOT Youth courts (mainly: see left hand column) Youth offender panels (YOPs) to deal with referral orders in respect of (mainly first offenders: *Chapter 3*. Sentencing guidelines Council (SGC) Note the momentum for alternatives to custody: *Chapter 17.*	Youth groups Housing/ accommodation providers Advice centres Representative bodies such as the magistrates' Association Youth Courts Committee and penal reform groups
A youth aged 10-17 years inclusive **is remanded on bail or in custody** during a court adjournment to await the next stage in criminal proceedings against him or her	Remand on bail Court ordered secure remand (COSR) Remand in custody: see mainly *Chapter 17.*	Bail support schemes Specialist foster carers Secure children's homes Secure training centres YOIs Note the anomaly whereby 17-year-olds treated as young adults for remand purposes.	Advocacy services Voluntary sector bail support and visiting schemes.
A youth aged 10-17 years is subject to a community based sentence: *Chapter 16.* See the chart at the end of that chapter for the 15 basic requirements.	YRO with 'basic requirements' YRO with added features: *Chapter 16* Transitional 'old-style' community orders where the offence was committed before 30 November 2009	Police YOT Community safety teams Health providers Substance misuse or mental health services	Accommodation providers Youth groups
A youth aged 10-17 years is subject to a custodial sentence: *Chapter 17*	Detention and training order (DTO) Various Crown Court custodial orders	Youth secure estate YOT Mental health services Post-custody supervision on release	Advocacy services Prison visiting Accommodation providers upon release e.g. YMCA Rehabilitation charities

Government Departments involved
(frequently at one remove from independent, sponsored or supported services)

Ministry of Justice with regard to justice-related provision
Department for Children, Schools and Families concerning children's services
Home Office which sets criminal policy and has policing and public safety oversight
Cabinet Office (and other departments), including re social exclusion/inclusion.

AGE AND TERMINOLOGY: A NOTE

The age of criminal responsibility (also known as 'criminal capacity') in England and Wales is ten years[3] (having been increased from eight years in 1963): see *Chapters 1 and 7*. As with the standard age of majority, 'criminal majority' is reached at 18 years of age. For a long time, those in the 10-17 (inclusive) age range were, for criminal justice purposes, called 'juveniles' (partly allied to the then juvenile court). With the launch of the youth court in 1992 under the Criminal Justice Act 1991 and the emergence of 'youth justice', the term 'youth' came into common use. Readers should also familiarise themselves with certain other legal, formal or colloquial terms:

- **adult** normally means anyone who is aged 18 years of age or over unless the term is qualified in some way, e.g. **young adults** are usually those aged 18-20 inclusive
- **young adult** may also be used informally to denote older youths not yet 18
- **young offender** is a term used in sentencing law in particular to mean those aged 18-21 years inclusive, but informally it may also include older youths not yet 18
- for youth court and youth justice legislative and associated purposes, **children** are those aged 10-13 years inclusive
- for the same purposes a **young person** is someone aged 14-17 years inclusive[4]
- with regard to many welfare provisions, the term **child** is used in blanket fashion to mean all people of whatever age who are under 18
- with regard to child safety orders, **child** means someone under ten years of age who (among other things) is alleged to have committed acts which, had he or she been ten years of age or older might have amounted to criminal offences: see *Chapter 7*
- Police and Criminal Evidence Act 1984 (PACE) codes use the now mostly redundant term **juvenile** for those aged 10-16 years inclusive: see *Chapter 10*
- for PACE and court remand purposes 17-year-olds are **treated as adults** even though not 'adult enough' for the magistrates' court: see *Chapters 10* and *13*.
- the Criminal Procedure Rules 2005 use not just the terms **child** and **young person** but also **relevant minor**, the latter to signify people aged 10-17; and
- for those aged 16 or 17 years, legislation sometimes provides that they can be considered as **older children** or **younger adults** depending on their circumstances.

These are just some of the twists and turns of age-related terminology that youth justice practitioners and others need to be aware of. Usually, the context in which

---

3. October 2009
4. Here, the plural is 'young persons' not 'young people'. The latter term is, like 'youngsters' or (as some people prefer) 'kids', simply one used in ordinary speech or writing to signify people still in their youth but without any precise, particular or technical reference to age.

words are used will automatically trigger recognition of the sense in which a term is being used and of the age group in question. Context is the main key to understanding what is intended if matters are not immediately clear. The same individual may, e.g. be a 'youth', 'juvenile', 'young person' or 'child' depending on:

- the exact stage in the youth justice (or child welfare) process;
- the nature of what is occurring; and
- the perspective of the practitioner or narrator concerned.

Young defendant
Readers should also note this term which is relatively new, but which has a particular meaning by virtue of a *Practice Direction* of February 2000 following a decision of the European Court of Human Rights in the case of *T and V v. United Kingdom*.[5] The ruling states that children and young persons (above) tried at the Crown Court (*Chapter 13*) are 'young defendants'.

Use of the term youth
This book uses the term 'youth' (rather than the former term 'juvenile') to mean someone of an age appropriate to the youth court and associated purposes such as the work of youth offending teams (YOTs) and youth offender panels (YOPs), i.e. someone aged 10-17 years inclusive. If further distinction needs to be made, he or she will be either a child (10-13, inclusive) or young person (14-17, inclusive). Where there is any deviation from this, or from the descriptions given on the previous page, this is made clear in the text. Readers will also find the *Glossary* towards the end of the book useful in placing many matters into context.

Inclusive age-ranges
Readers should also note what is in effect a convention of stating age-ranges on the basis that they are 'inclusive'. This should be assumed throughout the book unless otherwise stated, although as a precaution the word inclusive is liberally added.

How old are young people anyway?
So far as court proceedings are concerned, section 99 Children and Young Persons Act 1933 provides that the age of any person appearing to be a child or young person coming before any court (other than to give evidence) can be enquired into by the court in question. A determination can then be made concerning his or her age for the purposes of those proceedings. The court will proceed on the basis of any available evidence, such as a birth certificate or the word of a parent, or failing that by considering the appearance and characteristics of the individual concerned.

5.[2000] Crim. LR 187 ECtHR

About the authors

Mike Watkins is solicitor (now non-practising) and freelance training consultant. He worked for over 33 years in the Magistrates' Courts Service, 22 of these years as a justices' clerk and (latterly), Director of Legal Services for Warwickshire, where he also had lead responsibility for the training of all of the magistrates in that county.

He has written national training materials for the Judicial Studies Board, the Magistrates' Association and the Universities of Birmingham and Cambridge. His other involvements with Waterside Press include contributing to or advising on the *Magistrates' Bench Handbook*, *The Sentence of the Court*, *Criminal Justice Act 2003: A Guide to the New Procedures and Sentencing* and *The Magistrates' Court: An Introduction* (5th. edn. 2009).

Diane Johnson is head of service for Warwickshire Youth Offending Team. She has an extensive background in children and family services, youth justice and the development of multi-agency partnerships

The editor

Bryan Gibson is a barrister, author and editor-in-chief of Waterside Press which he founded in 1989. His involvements in youth justice extend to the development of multi-agency groups and networks in the 1980s. Whilst working at Basingstoke, Hampshire as justices' clerk, he helped to establish the country's first 'custody-free zone' for youth offenders which was maintained for over three years.[1] Details of his books appear at WatersidePress.co.uk

The Foreword

Chris Stanley is chair of the East Kent Youth Court, chair of the Kent Magistrates Association, a Council Member of the national Magistrates' Association and of that body's Youth Courts Committee. He is a former Head of Policy and Research at Nacro and now advises the Prison Reform Trust on youth justice matters.

---

1. For an account of the phenomenon whereby alternatives to custody completely replaced detention centre orders, see *Growing Out of Crime: The New Era* (2nd. edn., 1992), Rutherford A, Waterside Press, *Chapter 5*.

Foreword

CHRIS STANLEY

The youth court is 100 years old. It was established by the Children Act 1908, which was implemented in April 1909. For the first time the Act, in justice terms, separated children and young people from adults appearing in the courts and established the juvenile court where specially trained magistrates sat, dealing with the youngsters' criminal behaviour and welfare needs.

The developments that led to this fundamental change can be traced to the beginning of the 19th century. In 1833, Nicolas White, a nine-year-old, was sentenced to death for theft of items worth two pence. This was commuted to a whipping and transportation. Reformers such as Mary Carpenter proposed reformatory schools and a range of other institutions such as industrial schools that were set up to deal with children and young people who had offended. By 1870 there were 65 reformatories holding 7,000 young people. These 'schools' later became approved schools under the Children and Young Persons Act (CYPA) 1933, then later still, under the CYPA 1969, they became community homes with education.

In 1881 the Lushingham Committee was set up to examine reformatories and industrial schools. It questioned the wisdom of placing young people in institutions at all. At the time, they held 24,000 young people. Lushingham wanted alternatives to incarceration: remedies for youth crime within the home and the school.

It took the reforming Liberal Government of 1906 to make the fundamental changes. It introduced the Children Act 1908. This barred under 14s from custody and only 14 or 15-year-olds were sent there under unruly certificates. The new Act established the juvenile court which had powers to hear all offences except murder. The court had to separate its business from that of the adult magistrates' court. It took a more holistic approach to the children and young people appearing before it, dealing with welfare matters as well as criminal cases.

Over subsequent decades the pendulum swung between welfare and punishment in dealing with juvenile offending. In 1933, the CYPA of that year pointed to welfare and treatment as the way forward, creating, as the authors of this book explain, the principle that the court should have regard to the welfare of the child (see *Chapter 1*). The key provision is section 44 of the 1933 Act. It remains with us today, reinforced by later statutes and now sitting alongside the new youth sentencing purposes of the Criminal Justice and Immigration Act 2008, the assessment of 'seriousness' as introduced by the Criminal Justice Act 1991 and the principal aim of the Youth Justice System which is to prevent offending and thereby re-offending.

During the mid to late-1930s the clamour for punishment increased, and it continued to grow after the Second World War. The first detention centres were opened in 1948. The 1960s saw the return of welfare and treatment approaches. The CYPA 1969 would effectively have abolished criminal proceedings against younger children but key provisions were never implemented by the incoming Conservative Government in 1971, so that the age of criminal responsibility stays at ten years, which is low by the standards of many countries. The common law *doli incapax* rule as it affected those aged 10-13 was then abolished and younger children are now treated like older ones in terms of their basic criminal capacity (see *Chapters 1*).

In the 1980s we see another swing. The Criminal Justice Act 1982 replaced borstal training with youth custody, and restricted custodial sentences. The Government made £15 million available to fund alternatives to custody and care. During that decade, the holistic approach continued, often under local (and what were among the first multi-agency) initiatives, and with the then juvenile court as the venue for both care and crime cases. The Children Act 1989 changed this, splitting the jurisdiction into the juvenile court (crime) and the family proceedings court (care).

The current youth court dates from the Criminal Justice Act 1991 which was implemented in 1992. It deals with 10-17-year-olds inclusive. Youth court magistrates sentence youths for all but a minority of (often) serious crimes (see *Chapter 13*), and have a maximum custodial sentence, the detention and training order, of two years.

Our youth court has some of the most complex legislation of any jurisdiction. Much of the law is adult law passed down, often inappropriately, to the youth court. One academic commentator, Lucia Zedner, suggested that:

> ... the sentencing of young offenders continues to enjoy (or, perhaps better, to endure) a rapidity of change and innovation not found in the rest of the system. It is as if the sentencing of young offenders represents an experimental laboratory where new ideas flourish with little regard to research findings, still less to any theoretical or conceptual framework.[1]

Some of us working in the youth justice and family systems think there need to be changes. Some argue for a joining of the youth and family jurisdictions to form a Family Justice Court, dealing with children holistically, with care and crime handled together. This is how the Scottish children's hearing system has operated for over 40 years. Children and young people who commit crimes are often the same children who are abused and neglected. Why not deal with them in one jurisdiction as we did for 80 years following the implementation of the Children Act 1908?

The issue for me as a youth court magistrate is that, week after week, I sentence children and young people for their criminal behaviour. Often they come from very dysfunctional families with a multitude of problems. The main principle of

---

1. 'Sentencing Young Offenders', Zedner L, in *Fundamentals of Sentencing Theory* (1998), Ashworth A and Waskik M (eds).

sentencing in the youth court is to reduce offending. How can a criminal court tackle the underlying problems that are the main contributor to the offending? Only by addressing these issues can we hope to start reducing offending. If youth courts had powers to transfer cases of children and young people with overwhelming welfare needs to the family proceedings court, where family issues could be addressed, we would get some way towards solving this.

Is the youth court an inappropriate venue to deal with children and young people whose criminal behaviour has brought them to the notice of a Criminal Justice System that cannot then address the underlying causes of that behaviour? Much of Europe has a holistic approach to dealing with children who are troubled or are in trouble. Some countries have inquisitorial systems. Would this approach be more suited to young people in England and Wales?

This book will help readers to understand the complexities of the Youth Justice System of England and Wales as it stands, following the reforms of 2009. But need the law really be so hugely complex? And why do we still insist on criminalising young people? The diversion systems, referral order and restorative approaches described in this book are perhaps a step in the right direction, but go nowhere near far enough. Why, when youth crime is top of most politicians' agendas and is featured in the media every day, has the way we deal with young people not been more closely scrutinised (and in a systematic and non-party political way)?

As the authors suggest, the Youth Justice System, so long seemingly in one sort of crisis or another has at least arrived at a watershed and there appear to be some real changes afoot. But in truth the Cinderella of the courts system needs a complete health check and overhaul, since, in some respects, we have gone backwards. 'Crime prevention' needs to be viewed as something more fundamental than can be achieved by punishment and criminal records. A Royal Commission should be set up to examine the way we treat our children and young people under 18 years of age and also perhaps to reconsider the various age thresholds and how chronological age and levels of maturity are balanced. Drawing on the experience of Scotland and Europe, that commission could propose a more appropriate system for the 21st Century.

Chris Stanley[2]

---

2. Chris Stanley writes in a personal capacity. Details of his career in youth justice appear on page xiv.

Acknowledgements

In co-writing this book I have drawn on over 38 years involvement with the Magistrates' Courts Service, although the pace of change in youth justice is now so fast that historical experience can sometimes be a handicap. Thanks are due to all colleagues who, past and present, have endured my questioning and demands. In particular, I must thank Pete Owen, an experienced and accomplished youth court specialist legal adviser, who has given so freely of his up-to-date technical and practical knowledge to try to keep my contribution accurate and relevant.

I have also imposed on the goodwill, in particular, of Gill Harris at the Judicial Studies Board and Joanne Savage at the Sentencing Guidelines Council.

Thanks are due to Bryan Gibson and all at Waterside Press for again helping to transpose my outpourings into cohesive text. I am also grateful to Chris Stanley for his comments on our drafts and for contributing a comprehensive *Foreword* that reassured me that I was not alone in thinking that it might now be time for a fundamental review and simplification of youth justice.

Thanks are also due to my co-author Diane Johnson who doubtless very quickly realised that I had drawn her into far more work than was initially disclosed. All errors, omissions etc in my contributions are mine alone although I welcome receipt of contrary views and interpretations. Finally, and by no means least, my great thanks to my wife and PA Ann who, despite having previous experience of the rather self-indulgent nature of my writing books, has again supported me all the way.

Mike Watkins October 2009

In order to contribute to this book I have drawn on over 30 years experience of working with young people in the youth justice field, both directly and as a manager of children's services. For the last ten years I have managed a youth offending team, working in partnership with other agencies and I thank all my colleagues across this field for their knowledge and experience which I have drawn on in the book.

The Youth Justice Board has provided vision and direction for those practicing in this field, balancing the demands of promoting the welfare of young people with the important role of public protection. Much of their guidance is referred to and can be accessed on their comprehensive website.

Thanks go to Mike Watkins and Bryan Gibson for the opportunity to include some broader issues relating to our our roles in the Youth Justice System. I am heartened by the interest many graduates and others show in working in the youth justice field and I hope that it fuels their interest and enthusiasm.

Diane Johnson October 2009

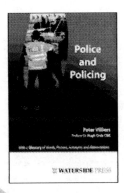

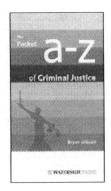

Important notice

In an attempt to publish this book to coincide with the anticipated commencement of the relevant parts of the Criminal Justice and Immigration Act 2008 (CJIA 2008) it was necessary to work to the officially intimated commencement date for those parts, i.e. 30 November 2009 (but see also *Chapter 9* for certain other implementation dates). However, at the time of going to press, no official confirmation of the commencement provisions had yet been made public.

The definitive version of the Sentencing Guidelines Council's document *Overarching Principles: Sentencing Youths* was also due to be issued so as to link with the new statutory provisions but, due to circumstances beyond their or our control, that version had to be reserved just as this book went to press.

Rather than defer publication, some early prints of this book therefore do not contain the definitive version, but that upon which the SGC consulted (which we might hope will not be radically changed in its subsequent definitive and ultimately published format). Consultation Guidelines are reproduced in their entirety at page 229.

The definitive version will be available for download free of charge in a format to match this book as soon as it is available: see www.WatersidePress.co.uk for further details concerning this. Its content will, inevitably, depend on when and if relevant parts of the CJIA 2008 come into force.

Although plans are well advanced at local level to operate the new youth rehabilitation order (YRO) provisions for offences committed on or after 30 November 2009, no statutory instrument had, at the time of going to press, yet been seen which would, in particular, bring into force section 9 of the 2008 Act (the four new statutory purposes of youth sentencing: see *Chapter 15*).

Without section 9 of the 2008 Act being in force, courts would nevertheless still have to take account of the existing 'principal aim of the youth justice system' (the prevention of offending) and longstanding 'welfare' considerations in section 44 Children and Young Persons Act 1933.

But, subject to any general guidance from the SGC, there would be no obligatory reflecting of four of the five statutory sentencing purposes for adults set out in section 142 Criminal Justice Act 2003 (punishment, reform/rehabilitation, protection of the public and reparation). Even *with* section 9 of the 2008 Act in force in relation to youths, there will still, as that provision currently stands, be no statutory inclusion of the fifth adult sentencing purpose, namely the reduction of crime (including by deterrence). It could be that the government is reconsidering the implications of this.

Every possible effort has been made to check the accuracy and currency of all the information in this book. Readers of early versions should, however, read it in the light of the contents of this notice and the hopefully transitional situation which it describes. They are advised to check if in any doubt, particularly where dates are concerned.

CHAPTER ONE

Perceptions of Youth Crime

How society portrays young people forms a convenient backdrop for any discussion of youth justice. Images of youth crime, accurate or otherwise, can have a powerful impact. How people believe that the police, courts and other parts of the Youth Justice System (YJS) 'measure up' to events as these are depicted, is bound to affect public opinion. One result can be an urge to punish, 'crack down' or take strong action.

Getting to know more about young offenders

Formal and professional responses are inevitably more measured, based on frontline experiences, solid information and evidence. They should be free from misleading preconceptions or prejudice (*Chapter 2*). There can be tensions, as when there is a mismatch between the general public's fear of crime and the risk of it actually occurring to individuals (see *Some Facts and Figures* below); or when media panics or loud demands for 'something to be done' are at odds with the merits of an actual case. This is one problem which those seeking to present a more rounded picture come up against.

Neither do such outcries usually take account, as this book does, of the characteristics or vulnerabilities of individual offenders, or from an equally important standpoint the views or expectations of victims of crime who may be more concerned with the question 'Why me' and a need for closure than outright retribution.

A wise commentator once remarked that 'the better you get to know people, the harder it is to be punitive towards them'. Media images are usually not about getting to know young people. Rather, they tend towards dramatic events, damning the nation's youth and alarming people. 'Bad news' and morbid curiosity have always been media hooks ever since the days of broadsheets and penny dreadfuls.

In contrast, modern-day youth justice processes involve courts and practitioners in carefully managing cases. There is a 'simple, speedy youth justice' initiative. Information is tested against criteria, checklists and guidelines. Decision-making structures may be used and the whole process is enhanced by reports, assessments and ongoing practical training. Reasons must be identified to support outcomes. This book is about a less publicised side of youth justice which is only now, in the 21st century, beginning to 'open up' under Government-led initiatives.

A more objective standpoint

In an age of accountability and scrutiny it is impossible for the YJS to disregard public opinion and the 'temperature' of youth justice' is unavoidably affected by what people read in their newspapers.[1] But many members of the general public should perhaps be credited with a better understanding of the kind of issues in question. They know that youth crime, when it does occur, can be a sign of some other malaise. Youth offending is also often pathetic or a sign of immaturity rather than dangerous or worrying. When, in a minority of cases, it is the latter there are provisions to deal with this as described in *Chapter 13* in particular.

In more run-of-the-mill situations, very many members of the public would be likely to support departures in restorative justice as described in *Chapter 4*.[2] Properly explained, measures to divert youngsters away from prosecution (*Chapter 11*) or custody (*Chapters 15 to 17*) are likely to be welcomed. Similarly, reasonable people recognise the need for (and perhaps expect there to be) mechanisms such as a 'scaled approach' to sentencing or intervention as being developed to accompany the Criminal Justice and Immigration Act 2008 (*Chapters 15 and 16*). In an era of cost consciousness, it becomes an everyday point that public funds are not endless (see *Chapter 5*). Not everyone sees each and every youth offender as a 'yob', 'thug', 'lager lout', 'Ratboy' or equally misleading stereotype.

It is also the case that most people 'know' (or at least think they understand) their own children which makes them doubt whether the situation is really as bad as it is sometimes portrayed, or, if there are problems, whether an escalation in terms of 'crack downs', punishments and a heavy-handed approach is a suitable answer.

Just one example to make people think

An interesting case which will no doubt attract debate for years arose in 2009. Two young people were tried for conspiracy to murder and cause explosions being treated the while like public enemies. It was alleged that they had 'planned' a Columbine-style massacre at their secondary school to coincide with the anniversary of that iconic event in the USA.[3] They were acquitted by a Crown Court jury (see generally *Chapter 13, Which Court?*) after the father of one of them, a police officer, gave evidence that his son regularly fantasised about something or other. In short, those closest to young people often have a more accurate take on their behaviour. After the case, the father, on the court steps in time-honoured fashion, informed the media:

> It's been purgatory, absolute agony. Neither of them has been in trouble [before, but they] have been in jail for the last six months ... I would like to make it clear that at no time was any person put at risk. This was just a fantasy.

It is perhaps a poor or inadequate community that does not want to get closer to young people generally; that looks to reject or exclude youngsters, rather than find

---

1. Or see on their TV screens: including a staple diet of police videos edited to 'pull in viewers'.
2. In support of this, see *Restorative Justice and the Clapham Omnibus* (2009), Cornwell D J, Waterside Press.
3. The Columbine Massacre (1995) has become a beacon for reformers of USA gun laws after 12 students and a teacher were shot dead by two disaffected youths who then turned their guns on themselves.

explanations or arguments in their support. As already indicated at the start of this chapter, modern-day youth justice is in part about 'getting to know them better'.

SOME FACTS AND FIGURES

There is still a widely held assumption that the blame for the majority of crime can be laid at the feet of the nation's youth.[4] The reality is that crimes committed by young people make up less than 20 per cent of the total not most of it.[5] Research conducted by YouGov (October, 2008) showed that the general public holds a negative view of children; with 49 per cent of people agreeing that children are increasingly a danger to each other and to adults. Nearly half (again 49 per cent) disagreed with the statement that children who get into trouble are often misunderstood and in need of professional help. Commenting on the research findings Martin Narey, chief executive of the children's charity Barnardos, said:

> It is appalling that words like 'animal', 'feral' and 'vermin' are used daily in reference to children. These are not references to a small minority of children but represent the public view of children. Despite the fact that most children are not troublesome there is still a perception that today's young people are a more unruly, criminal lot than ever before.

This mistrust or fear of young people is not new. The behaviour of young people and a 'breakdown in values' has been a matter of despair of adults for centuries

Since Victorian times several images of children have emerged – from the 'romantic child' to the 'factory child' and more latterly the 'delinquent child'. This later image has tended to become entrenched at least in media representations. It serves to perpetuate fear of crime or at the very least (possibly unwarranted) concern about behaviour which is often part of an ordinary process of maturation in which boundaries are tested and traces kicked over. The fact that children are growing up is largely ignored, as is the responsibility of communities to help them in this.

As can be seen from the following quotes from *The Times* archives, such concerns are not unique to the present era. The concept of 'adolescence' emerged in the 1800s, a term referring to young people in their teenage years. Nonetheless it tended to be applied to children of the 'working and lower classes'.[6]

Mid-Victorian society panicked about a form of violent robbery known as 'garrot-

---

4. Blame cast by adults of course. The 'blame culture' is an interesting area of study in itself.
5. Youth Crime Briefing, 'Some Facts About Children and Young People Who Offend' (2007), Nacro.
6. In his influential work, *Growing Out of Crime: The New Era* (2nd edn. 1992), Waterside Press, Andrew Rutherford points out that the upper-classes and middle-classes have always had their own ways of 'dealing with' their errant young. They range from the public school, rugby field, armed services and grand tour to dubious modern-day advances in the medicalisation of behaviour problems (including those concerning drugs or alcohol). Modern-day moves to fight social exclusion are a counter to this imbalance, but probably go nowhere near far enough.

ting' (choking a victim from behind usually in the furtherance of robbery). *The Times* described it as 'a modern peril of the streets [that has] created something like a reign of terror'. In November 1862 it declared 'Our streets are actually not as safe as they were in the days of our grandfathers…'. In 1856, that newspaper complained about the 'over-magnanimous spirit of British law, which always presumes a man innocent until he is proven guilty'. Flogging was abolished in 1861 but was brought back under the Garroter's Act 1863.

It is not hard to see the parallels between the above and modern-day concerns.

LABELLING, STEREOTYPING AND GATEKEEPING

The term 'hooligan' was used to described disorderly working-class youths on the August Bank Holiday of 1898.[7] The Times described hooliganism as 'something like organised terrorism in the streets' and reported that Europe and America 'have very little scruple about calling out troops and shooting down organized disturbances of the peace'.

Prominent concerns of the 21st century are about gangs, guns and knives. But even the 1920s and 1930s saw largely city-based 'razor gangs'. In July 1921, *The Times* ran a campaign to publicise the threat posed by razor gangs to law and order. Reports stated that 'These gangs are nothing but the scum of the earth'.

The 1950s saw the tragic case of Derek Bentley who, in 1953, was wrongly (as it ultimately transpired) executed for the actions of his juvenile police killer gunman accomplice Christopher Craig. Hardly typical, the case sent messages far removed from its peculiar facts about disaffected youth. That era also shows, with hindsight, media panics urging other crackdowns. When it was not fear of young thugs, it was of Teddy Boys and 'rock and roll' riots. One judge declared: 'What an invention of the Devil is the "flick" knife, which so often features in crimes of violence … committed by young people.' Yet what relatively small percentage of young people did or do carry a flick knife, or any other kind of knife?[8]

Labels and stereotypes can be convenient but highly misleading in the context of youth justice. Mods and rockers, hippies, skinheads, chavs, football hooligans, punks, goths and hoodies have all emerged over the years, as people set 'apart' by their dress codes, hairstyles and music, leading to notions that they must be deviant in a criminal sense. There is a preoccupation with outsiders of whatever kind. They are easy targets to 'bad mouth', demonise and spread rumour about. But what perverse community would want to marginalise its own future adult citizens in this way? Maybe society itself needs to 'grow up' a little. A community that seeks

---

7. The term hooligan has a rich and fascinating history: see the *Glossary*.
8. Reliable evidence is emerging showing an increase in knife-carrying, but the true risks as opposed to the use of knives as 'fashion items' remain unclear. Naturally, it can be argued that carrying any weapon increases the chances of its use, but even then punitive responses could be escalating the problem.

to depict its own children as criminals rather than look to its own responsibilities might be thought to belong not to real life but some ingenious work of fiction.[9]

Even the fictional creation Vicky Pollard, who began life as a figure of fun in a television series,[10] entered the penal lexicon after judges and lawyers used her name as shorthand for 'angry young woman from a deprived background'. By 2005 a *Guardian* newspaper editorial was able to assert that Ms Pollard was:

> an out-of-control . . . [and] inarticulate, abusive and feckless teenage single mother ... In [treating the character as more than a parody and] attempting to hijack that image for its own ends, media Britain ... is creating something more dangerous: a stereotype that dissolves the difference between fiction and reality.[11]

This 'dissolving of the difference between fiction and reality' may be particularly worrying in an age of popular culture in which democratic ideas are driven by media images and sound-bites.[12] It is also of course about how youths perceive themselves. Portrayed as bad people they may act the part.

Tough on crime

A common angle taken by the popular press, and many politicians, has involved focussing on the need for stronger law enforcement and tougher measures against young people involved in certain activities.[13] On 15 July 2008, e.g. a statement from the Home Office claimed that while youth crime remained stable, 'challenges remain particularly around alcohol-related crime, delinquent peer groups and gangs and young people carrying knives.' The then Home Secretary, Jacqui Smith, said:

> We know that the vast majority of young people recognise right from wrong and make a positive contribution to our society. There are a minority however who persist in anti-social behaviour and some in more serious criminal activity ... Youth crime can have a devastating effect on victims and communities and must be tackled head-on. Today I want to send the message to perpetrators that their actions are unacceptable. They must understand the consequences their behaviour has not only on victims and communities but on their families and their futures ... Increasingly we are able to identify these young people early and intervene to address the root causes of their behaviour, including supporting and challenging their parents in meeting their responsibilities ... But I want to call on parents to play their part. Tough enforcement and policing is only one part of the solution. The new action we are launching today gives equal weight to the triple-track approach of intensive prevention, tough enforcement and support for parents.

9. As per perhaps William Golding's *Lord of the Flies* in which schoolchildren descend into chaos.
10. 'Little Britain', BBC TV, 2002 onwards.
11. 12 May 2005.
12. Whether it is more misleading than Victorian novelist Charles Dicken's naming a pickpocket 'the Artful Dodger' is open to debate. There are many other examples of influential fictional stereotypes.
13. This can be traced to the pre-1997 Tory Government; then the 1997 Labour Party manifesto ('Tough on crime, tough on the causes of crime'). Youths, in particular, may have suffered from this kind of politicking.

Jacqui Smith was correct to emphasise the various sides of the equation. Nonetheless, the balance she strikes between intervention (and what should, seemingly, be a natural response of concern) and the urge to punish raises questions. This book shows how the ideas which she expounded when Home Secretary have been built upon by Government and others. But real progress still needs something of the order of a cultural shift as to how youngsters are perceived.

Later chapters of this book describe two kinds of approach. Punishment standing alongside rehabilitation (or welfare). But as Chris Stanley writes in his *Foreword*, the emphasis is still perhaps too strongly on the criminalisation of significant numbers of young people who will carry that label and experience for many years.

Diversionary tactics

There have in fact long been initiatives to mitigate this tendency to criminalise young people. Youth justice practitioners (and later) multi-agency youth justice teams[14] developed a practice of 'gatekeeping' to prevent those cases which did not really warrant criminal proceedings from reaching the courts; or, deeper into the YJS, custodial institutions (see *Chapters 11* and *17*). Although we live in different times, this can with hindsight, be seen as a watershed: the precursor to the more sophisticated arrangements that exist today as described in later chapters. It is also interesting that the Crown Prosecution Service (CPS) now uses the term 'gatekeeping' to describe its role in deciding which behaviours justify a prosecution and which do not.

The courts still have a central role, but many cases will be diverted and dealt with elsewhere. The custodial institutions still need to exist for the purposes of public safety and protection, but more forward-looking methods and approaches have emerged. The YJS must distinguish between and work with those whose lives it *can* turn around and those who *whatever it does* are bound for the deeper recesses criminal justice. The new law and practice described in the chapters which follow are central to all of this.

PUBLIC PERCEPTIONS AND THE FACTS

Despite falls in crime since 1995 and more people having confidence in the police and the criminal justice system, public concern about crime remains high. During 2006/07, almost two thirds of those sampled by the *British Crime Survey*[15] considered that crime had risen during the previous two years, with 33 per cent believing that it had 'risen a lot'. As indicated at the start of this chapter, public perceptions of youth crime are not necessarily reliable indicators of the true facts. Measuring the

---

14. The forerunners of the modern-day youth offending teams (YOTs): *Chapter 3*.
15. The *British Crime Survey* (BSC) is a large scale research project which asks people aged 16 years and above who are living in private households about their experiences of crime.

extent of youth crime is complex for a number of reasons. Only a small proportion of those who admit offending come into the YJS proper. During 2005, whilst 26 per cent of young people admitted offending within the previous 12 months, only five per cent reported being arrested, with two per cent going to court.[16]

In part, the reason for this discrepancy is the fact that most crimes are not reported to the police. For instance, during 2006/07 only 41 per cent of offences were brought to attention of the police, including those where victim's perception was that the incident was too trivial, where there was no loss, or a belief that the police would not, or could not, do much about the incident in any event.

From the early 1990s until 2003, the official *Criminal Statistics* showed a 27 per cent decline in detected youth crime. Since 2003 there has been a 20 per cent increase, although the 2006 'Offending, Crime and Justice Survey' shows no statistically significant differences between 2003 and 2006 in the proportion of 10-17 year old people admitting any offence or self-reporting serious or frequent offending.[17]

How confident are people in the system?

The same investigations as are mentioned above disclose that:

- the proportion of people who think their local police do a good or excellent job was higher in 2007/08 (53%) than in 2006/07 (51%)
- there are higher levels of confidence in the police treating people fairly (64%) and with respect (83%), but less confidence that they are effective in dealing with crime and related issues, for example, only 43% of people thought their local police could be relied on to deal with minor crimes
- there has been an increase in the proportion of people who have confidence in the criminal justice system (CJS) being effective in bringing people to justice; 44% of people said they were very or fairly confident in 2007/08 compared with 41% in 2006/07
- thirty-seven per cent of people were confident that the CJS as a whole was effective and 56% thought that it was fair; and
- if asked what they think are the main causes of crime in Britain today, drugs and lack of parental discipline are the two most common causes given.

Statistics

The *British Crime Survey* (BCS) and police recorded crime figures differ in their coverage of crime, but both show that overall crime fell in 2007/08.[18] All BCS crime has fallen by ten per cent and recorded crime by nine per cent compared with

---

16. *Offending, Crime and Justice Survey* (2005), Home Office Statistical Bulletin No.17/2006.
17. Youth Crime Briefing, 'Some Facts About Children and Young People Who Offend' (2007), Nacro.
18. The last year for which figures are available.

2006/07; and most crime types have shown decreases.

Long-term trends show that crime (as recorded by the BCS) rose steadily from 1981 through to the early 1990s, peaking in 1995. Crime then fell, making 1995 a significant turning point. The fall was substantial until 2004/05, when crime levels stabilised until the further decline in 2007/08. Crime is now at the lowest ever level since the first results in 1981. Trends in violence, vehicle related theft and burglary broadly reflect the trend of all crime. The 2007/08 BCS also shows a statistically significant decrease in the risk of becoming a victim of a crime, which has fallen from 24 per cent to 22 per cent, representing just under a million fewer victims. The chance of being a victim is now at its lowest level since BCS surveys began in 1981.

Offence types

The majority of offences committed by young people are directed against property. In 2007 theft, handling stolen goods, burglary, fraud and criminal damage accounted for over 62 per cent of indictable offences committed by young people. Theft and handling represented 46 per cent of the total and accounted for the largest rise in detected youth crime over the previous 12 months.

Violent offending is less common and accounts for less than 17 per cent of indictable offences (i.e. generally meaning more serious offences) committed by children and young people. Thus, despite certain media images to the contrary, violent offences saw the largest fall of any offence type between 2006 and 2007.[19]

Age

Two thirds of young people coming into contact with the YJS fall within the 15–17 year age group. Around 31 per cent of these are aged 12–14 years and just three per cent are below the age of 12.

Gender

Although historically girls have been less likely to offend than boys, there has been a growth in detected offending by girls. According to data from the Youth Justice Board (YJB) (2008), offences by girls aged between eleven and 17 had risen by 25 per cent since 2005 to 59,000 per year. The majority of offences that resulted in a police warning or court sanction involved theft, then criminal damage and public order crimes. Violent offences increased too and now represent about 40 per cent of convictions for which girls are under supervision. It is over 50 per cent for boys.

Race

The Criminal Justice System (CJS) as a whole (of which the YJS is part) has regularly seen an over-representation of suspects or defendants from black and minority ethnic (BME) backgrounds. The YJS reflects this. Children and young people classi-

---

19. Youth Crime Briefing, 'Some Facts About Children and Young People Who Offend' (2007), Nacro.

fied as black, or black British are more likely to be remanded in custody or to secure accommodation, and are disproportionately represented among those receiving custodial sentences. During 2007/08, while black young people made up three per cent of the general 10-17 year old (inclusive) population (the age range dealt with by the youth court as a whole), they accounted for seven per cent of those coming to the attention of the YJS and 14 per cent of those receiving a custodial sentence.

Causes of youth crime and risk factors

What causes some children and young people to offend, and the reasons for others not offending, has perplexed societies for a long time and there remains a tension between popular opinion, often influenced by the media, and research findings.

The 2007/08 *British Crime Survey* showed that drugs and lack of discipline from parents were the two factors most commonly selected by respondents to that survey as one of the major causes of crime in Britain (71 per cent and 69 per cent of respondents respectively). When people were asked which single factor they believed was the main cause of crime in Britain today, 30 per cent said drugs, while a further 30 per cent thought lack of discipline from parents was the main cause.

The most reliable research information comes from longitudinal studies that follow same-age cohorts of children from birth, or an early age, into adolescence and adulthood. Evidence consists of correlations and distinguishing features in the lives and backgrounds of offenders and non-offenders.

Factors which are considered to be the causes of offending behaviour are commonly referred to as 'risk factors', whereas elements of a person's life that are considered to increase resilience and help prevent the likelihood of offending are referred to as 'protective factors'.

Although there is no single factor that can be identified as the cause of anti-social behaviour (ASB) or criminal offending, it is now better understood how multiple risk factors cluster together and interact in the lives of children. Research from the YJB[20] classifies factors into four domains:

- family
- school
- community
- personal or individual.

Family

Family conflict, family involvement in offending, poor levels of parental supervision, inconsistent, harsh or neglectful parenting are all correlated with a higher risk

---

20. Youth Justice Board (2005), *Risk and Protective Factors Associated with Youth Crime and Effective Interventions to Prevent It*, Youth Justice Board.

of involvement in youth crime. Other factors such as poor housing and low income or poverty are also predictors of delinquency.[21]

Education

Eighty four per cent of children and young people referred to youth offending teams (YOTs) have been excluded from school on at least one occasion, and 50% report truanting on a frequent basis.[22] Truants are three times as likely to offend as those attending school regularly. Inadequate teaching, inconsistent discipline and poor relations between staff and pupils are associated with higher rates of offending.[23]

Community

Children growing up in disadvantaged neighbourhoods are at increased risk of involvement in crime.[24] The prevalence of gangs in a neighbourhood and gang membership is correlated with an increased risk of criminality. In one study the volume of self-reported delinquency among gang members aged 17 years, was 6.4 times as high as among those who did not consider themselves to hang around in a gang.[25]

Individual

At the individual level, it is well established that young people coming into contact with the YJS are more likely to be male and that boys are at a higher risk of being involved in more serious and persistent offending.[26]

Drug and alcohol use among young people who offend has consistently been found to be higher than in the general population. Poor health, and in particular, poor mental health, are also associated with increased criminality. Research suggests that the prevalence of mental health problems in young people in contact with the YJS is between two and seven times what would be expected for that age group.[27] More than half of young people who offend have also been victims of offences.

Implications of identifying risk and protective factors

By defining the risk or protective factors in this way, we can begin to identify those factors which can, to an extent, be modified by community-based interventions. Other features such as gender, or genetic and biological influences, are either not

21. Ibid.
22. Youth Justice Board (2003), *Speaking Out: The Views of Young People, Parents and Victims About the Youth Justice System*, Youth Justice Board.
23. Youth Justice Board (2005), *Risk and Protective Factors Associated with Youth Crime and Effective Interventions to Prevent It*, Youth Justice Board.
24. Wedlock E (2006), *Crime and Cohesive Communities*, Online report 19/06, Home Office
25. Smith, D and Bradshaw P (2005), *Gang Membership and Teenage Offending*, Report No. 8, Edinburgh Study of Youth Transitions and Crime, University of Edinburgh.
26. Smith, D and McCara L (2004), *Gender and Youth Offending*, Report No.2, Edinburgh Study of Youth Transitions and Crime, University of Edinburgh.
27. Hagell, A (2002), *The Mental Health of Young Offenders*, Mental Health Foundation.

capable of being influenced or less easily so, but are recognised as a starting point for YJS approaches, and in some instances the development of individuals. Taken into consideration alongside other pointers, they may help identify children who are at risk and may need preventive services, e.g. health, education or counselling.

CRIMINAL CAPACITY AND THE DOLI INCAPAX RULE

Doli incapax is a Latin tag meaning 'incapable in law of committing a criminal offence'. It is necessary to look at the history of this concept in England and Wales to see how some youths are now being more readily criminalised. Before the Crime and Disorder Act 1998, a three tier approach applied:

- children under ten years of age could not be held criminally responsible for their actions, but were doli incapax without further ado
- children aged 10-13 years inclusive were subject to a presumption of fact that they were *doli incapax*, unless there was satisfactory evidence brought by the prosecution to rebut this presumption, ultimately due to legal rulings, meaning evidence that the child 'knew that what he or she was doing was seriously wrong'; and
- young people of 14 years of age or over were considered to be developed sufficiently to he held fully accountable for their behaviour (subject to any relevant mitigation that might apply due to an individual young person's own personal traits).

Section 43 of the 1998 Act abolished the second of these criteria, the presumption for 10-13-year-olds. Since then, all children and young people over the age of ten are deemed to be responsible and accountable for their behaviour. Children under ten are still *doli incapax* and the age of criminal responsibility in England and Wales remains at ten (despite competing views that it should be lowered or raised).

Thus among other things the police do not have any powers of arrest or detention with regard to children below the age of ten years (although they can take them into their temporary care for their own safety, welfare and protection).

By comparison the age of criminal responsibility is 18 in Belgium and Luxembourg, 16 in Portugal and Spain, 15 in Denmark, 14 in Germany, 13 in France, 12 in Greece, and 10 in Northern Ireland. In 2009, Scotland announced an intention to increase its age of criminal responsibility from eight to 12.

Children below ten years of age
As fully explained in *Chapter 7*, a kind of inroad has occurred under the law relating to civil child safety orders under which a child committing what would be an offence in the case of someone aged ten years and over can be the subject of such an order.

OTHER AGE-RELATED FEATURES OF YOUTH JUSTICE

Readers are referred to three other places in this book in particular to better understand age-related powers, responsibilities and terminology:

- *Age and Terminology: A Note* which is essential reading (pages xiii-xiv)
- *Chapter 13, Which Court?*; and
- *Chapters 15-17* which deal with various aspects of sentencing.

Whilst all age-related terms are relevant, one paragraph is worthy of repetition from page xiv since it is central to much of what is discussed in this book:

> This book uses the term 'youth' (rather than the former term juvenile) to mean someone of an age to be dealt with in the youth court and associated purposes such as the work of youth offending teams (YOTs) and youth offender panels (YOPs), i.e. someone aged 10-17 years (inclusive). If further distinction needs to be made, he or she will be either a child (10-13, inclusive) or young person (14-17, inclusive).

SOME LEGISLATIVE RESPONSES TO YOUTH CRIME

The first legislative recognition of separate treatment for young offenders was the Parkhurst Act 1838 (when that establishment opened as a 'juvenile prison'). Until the 1980s, youth justice policy was, despite certain rigours, based on a predominantly welfare model of intervention. From the 1980s penal sanctions or 'corrections' have been more prominent, but latterly against a restorative backdrop (*Chapter 4*).[28]

From 1854 several Reformatory School Acts were passed. The Prevention of Crime Act 1908 also reflected a growing demand for the 'reformation' of young offenders. It provided for institutions throughout England and Wales for young offenders aged 16-21 years. In the same year, the Children Act 1908 established the first juvenile justice system. Juvenile courts sat in private with specific penalties and legislation stipulated that the courts must act in the best interests of the child.

As Chris Stanley, a long term observer of these events, has explained in his *Foreword*, the Children and Young Persons Act 1933 developed this approach and the Children and Young Persons Act 1969 significantly extended the welfare model. It phased out borstal institutions.[29] It required, wherever possible, consultation between the police and social services with the aim of dealing with as many aspects as possible of a youth court case prior to court, and it directed courts to deal with cases informally to avoid the stigma of court appearances and the spectre of 'mainly

---

28. See further the *Timeline* at the end of the book.
29. See the *Glossary*.

working-class juvenile offenders [being put under] the scrutiny of unsympathetic middle-class magistrates'.[30] The 1969 Act determined that social workers would prepare reports for courts and that sanctions would be fitted to a child's needs.

The Criminal Justice Act 1982 reflected a move towards a more justice-based model, introducing the sentence of youth custody.

The later Criminal Justice Act 1991 was rooted in the widely supported view of Home Secretary Douglas Hurd that imprisonment could be an 'expensive way of making bad people worse'. Lord Woolf, then Lord Chief Justice, also urged that the numbers of people in prison should be kept to a minimum. The majority of offenders convicted of property crime would get their 'just deserts' (the then in vogue term in sentencing) through punishment in the community. Whatever may have been said in relation to adults, then wherever welfare, rehabilitation or notions of restoring harmony was involved, it applied with yet greater force to youths.

The Crime and Disorder Act 1998 introduced significant youth justice reforms, requiring each local authority to co-ordinate the provision of multi-agency youth justice services through youth offending teams (YOTs); and the youth referral panel better known as the youth offender panel (YOP) which (under the auspices of the YOTs) was to devise interventions for most first-time offenders rather than their being sentenced by a youth court. The next major reforming statute was the Criminal Justice and Immigration Act 2008, which is the focus for much of this book.

CHILD PROTECTION

Many children and young people who offend are known to have experienced varying levels of abuse and neglect by adults. As a result, some will be the subject of a 'child protection plan', or be removed from their parents or carers and placed in public care becoming what are termed 'looked after' children, i.e. looked after by a local authority or through the authority foster parents.

Looked after children are likely to leave school without qualifications, become unemployed, or young parents or commit offences that eventually result in a prison sentence, disproportionately so.[31] It is likely that the reason for this is not the fact that they are looked after, but the intensity with which the risk factors (see earlier in this chapter) that led to them being looked after in the first place cluster together.

Addressing parenting

Poor parenting has been identified as one of the key factors in offending behaviour by young people. It is known that erratic or harsh discipline, poor supervision and conflict at home will almost certainly increase the likelihood of offending or anti-

---

30. Omaji, P (2003), *Responding to Youth Crime*, Federation Press: Sydney.
31. Social Exclusion Unit (2001).

social behaviour (ASB). Conversely, positive and consistent discipline and supervision, coupled with supportive parent-child relationships are known to reduce the risk of offending.

It is recognised that parents of young people who are involved in crime or ASB are often amongst the most needy and vulnerable parents, and likely to experience a multitude of problems. These could include poverty, alienation or isolation, lack of parenting skills or experience, ill-health, domestic abuse. Some of these factors have in modern times been categorised as social exclusion (SE) which the government and many other agencies now seek to confront by various means.

Since the creation of YOTs under the Crime and Disorder Act 1998 (above) there has been a focus on working directly with and supporting parents of young people who offend. For parents of children and young people who are subject to youth justice interventions, or for parents of young people who persistently truant from school, this can be achieved in a number of ways through:

- a *voluntary agreement* between parents and statutory or voluntary agencies, such as YOT, Children's Services or other providers of parenting programmes
- a *parenting contract* drawn up between parent and service provider, committing both sides to levels of contact; and/or
- application to a court for a parenting order.

Parenting orders were introduced in section 8 Crime and Disorder Act 1998. These and other measures affecting parents are discussed in appropriate chapters. They require parents to attend a programme for between three and 12 months to help them carry out their parenting responsibilities. Other powers include:

- section 34A Children and Young Persons Act 1933 which empowers, and in some cases obliges, a court to require the parent of a child or young person to attend court; and
- section 37 Powers of Criminal Courts (Sentencing) Act 2000,which imposes a duty on a court to order the payment of a fine, compensation or costs imposed on a child to be paid by the parent or guardian (with a discretion along similar lines where such financial orders are made against a young person).

PATTERNS ACROSS EUROPE

As will be seen in *Chapter 2*, the development and implementation of penal policies and practices in most countries are subject to both internal and external provisions, obligations and pressures.

Most international pressure comes from a number of United Nations (UN) agreements. The most significant of these is the UN Convention on the Rights of the Child,[32] which states that the best interests of the child must always be the primary consideration and that custody should only be used as a last resort. Other UN agreements have set standards for the process of youth justice, with a focus on:

- children's rights, including recommending that the age of criminal responsibility is not set too young
- early intervention in the cases of abused children; and
- rules governing the custody of young people.

European countries are also subject to the European Convention On Human Rights noted in *Chapter 2* now part of the law of the United Kingdom. One example of developments turning on European law are events in the wake of the Bulger case[33] as to the less formal way in which all cases involving children in the courtroom are now dealt with whether in the Crown Court or youth court.

The most established difference between justice systems internationally is the way in which they balance welfare against the interest of justice. The welfare approach emphasises paternalism and protection, and has resulted in treatment rather than formal justice and punishment. The justice approach emphasises ideas of judicial rights and accountability for crimes, favouring formal justice and proportionality in sentencing. Although acting in the best interests of the child is a dominant principle in youth justice systems around the world, a number of other principles have emerged. These include:

- the principle of 'preventing offending', which is influential in England and Wales (crime prevention is a stated objective of many CJS and YJS services)
- the principle of treating young offenders as 'children in trouble' who require welfare responses
- minimal intervention (as intervention may be counter-productive)
- public protection; and
- restorative justice (see in particular *Chapter 4*).

One study by the YJB highlights[34] some illustrations of different models and principles within youth justice systems relating to age within systems, decision-making and proceedings, and outcomes and disposals.

---

32. 1989.
33. See the *Glossary*.
34. 'Cross-national Comparisons of Youth Justice', Youth Justice Board, 2008.

Age thresholds within systems

Age is a defining characteristic that distinguishes youth justice systems in relation to the young people that they cater for. The ages of criminal responsibility found in 90 jurisdictions included countries with no stated age range and then an outer range from six-to-18 years of age inclusive. The threshold of ten years in England and Wales was young in comparison to most countries, The median average was 14 years. Most European countries set the age between 14 and 16 year. Criminal majority is the age at which the CJS processes offenders as adults. That age across 34 countries studied also varied greatly, but was typically set at 18 years – the same level as in England and Wales, as already outlined. Countries with higher ages of criminal responsibility also tended to have higher levels of criminal majority.

Decision-making and proceedings

The main divergence and debate concerning decision-making surrounds the extent to which young people should be dealt with through formal judicial channels (i.e. the courts), or be diverted away from these into less formal child-focused mechanisms and processes. Delays in proceedings vary considerably internationally. The estimated average time from investigation until prosecution ranges from three months to more than a year.

Alternatives to court proceedings are informal hearings, among the best-known being family group conferences (FGCs) and the Scottish children's hearing system. In the less formal hearings, decisions are not made by professionals, but by lay members of the community or sometimes the child's own family. The idea of community involvement in decision-making is perhaps strongest in those countries which have adopted a restorative justice approach (again see *Chapter 4*).

Outcomes and disposals

There are a number of distinctive community penalties being implemented around the world. These include:

- an emphasis on the accountability of parents, with a variety of sanctions
- public censure of children, despite international agreements to the contrary
- referrals to social welfare agencies
- the use of education, including individualised social programmes
- methods of intensive supervision and social control; and
- the use of community-based institutions as alternatives to full custody.

The rise in restorative justice is one of the strongest trends in youth justice, resulting in mediation and reparation to victims of crime or the community as case outcomes. Restorative justice processes can occur as an alternative to traditional disposals, or as outcomes reached before or after a conventional trial.

Mediation between victims and offender has become particularly prominent internationally since its early use in the 1970s. However, there are variations in the extent of its integration into law, and of its use in practice.

There is huge variation in the proportionate use of custody for young offenders, ranging from virtually zero in some jurisdictions to the incarceration of over 100,000 young people at any one time in the USA. England and Wales has a particularly high rate of custody compared to the vast majority of other western countries, despite a pronounced commitment by the YJB to reducing the use of custody through the use of community alternatives. This is one context in which the following chapters of this book will need to be understood.

CHAPTER TWO

Human Rights and International Obligations

Increasingly it is necessary to view UK domestic matters,[1] both criminal and civil, in the light of international instruments: agreements, treaties, conventions, etc. which the UK has entered into. These instruments will be mere acts of the Executive and not have any strict enforceable national and internal UK effect unless, until and to the extent that there is UK legislation or ratification by Parliament or its Ministers[2] to bring the particular instrument within the provisions of UK law.

That said, in some instances, as with the European Communities Act 1972, certain external instruments (e.g. concerning transport or consumer matters) can have direct effect as if made under domestic law. In other situations, notably in relation to human rights, dedicated legislation, primarily the Human Rights Act 1998, melds domestic law with international instruments.

Following the 1998 Act, the courts in the UK, including youth courts, magistrates' courts and the Crown Court must read relevant domestic legislation in accordance with the European Convention On Human Rights (see later in this chapter).

In some circumstances, national legislation and procedures will have been directly created or amended to give effect to the international instrument, although the completeness of such action may sometimes remain open to debate.

The above situations apart, domestic courts are not directly concerned with such international agreements, etc. and are not empowered to apply them in wider ways.

However, once an international agreement has been ratified by Parliament, there is a general assumption that any subsequent legislation relevant to matters covered by such an instrument will, in broad terms, have been intended to be consistent with it and should be so construed whenever reasonably possible.

Thus, the aims, values, etc. within all such international agreements may be called into play to help provide direction in interpreting and applying subsequent national law and also where that law provides areas of discretion to its courts. One example of this is the recurring ideal that custodial sentences on youths should incorporate plans for their reintegration into the community.

Extra safeguards until children become adults

As might be expected, this position is forcibly and extensively present in matters relating to youth justice due to special provisions contained in instruments to safeguard the interests of children until they become adults. The existence of the all-

---

1. Alternatively domestic matters are described as UK 'national' or sometimes UK 'local' ones.
2. The latter acting under delegated powers contained in primary legislation, i.e. Act of Parliament. There are other possible mechanisms for achieving the same end such as an Order in Council.

pervading European Convention On Human Rights (1950) also needs to be noted in addition to the following key youth justice-related measures:

- United Nations (UN) Declaration of the Rights of the Child 1959
- UN Standard Minimum Rules for the Administration of Juvenile Justice (also known as the 'Beijing Rules') (1985)
- UN Convention on the Rights of the Child (1989)
- UN Guidelines for the Prevention of Juvenile Delinquency (the 'Riyadh Guidelines') (1990); and
- UN Rules for the Protection of Juveniles Deprived of their Liberty (1990).

On occasion these provisions overlap or cover not dissimilar ground, albeit often in different terms. Whereas this might, at first sight, appear to be a possible source of confusion, it does, at least, provide the benefit of approaching matters from a range of viewpoints, which sometimes serves to amplify common themes and the underlying approach of the various separate measures.

Two specific and fundamental issues that may still have to be aired at a future date in England and Wales within the terms of these international agreements are the age of criminal responsibility (already noted in *Chapter 1*) and whether the 'welfare' model of youth justice (also touched upon there) should hold greater sway in preference to the 'criminal' or 'justice model' model.

THE EUROPEAN CONVENTION ON HUMAN RIGHTS

The European Convention On Human Rights and Fundamental Freedoms (to give it its full title) was drawn up in Rome in November 1950 by the Council of Europe as a direct response to the UN's Universal Declaration of Human Rights of December 1948. That declaration was itself a response to the atrocities of (and came in the immediate aftermath of) the events of the Second World War. They include events now familiar to many people as more and more files are opened to the public and discoveries made. Centrally, they concern events such as the Nazi Holocaust and politically-based purges. But to critics who consider human rights to be 'an inconvenience' or sometimes 'petty', it is important to note a lesson of history that State repression and other terrible events may begin in small ways.

Adherence to human rights is thus something in which nations should take positive pride; and they are in fact obliged by the European doctrine of 'positive obligation' to encourage reliance on human rights friendly legislation, procedures and other measure. Central to these is the right to a fair trial discussed below which permeates not just the hearing of criminal cases in court but the way in which suspects and offenders are dealt with at all stage of the youth justice process. Some other international measures of the kind already noted above are youth specific, thereby adding a further layer of protection over and above that applicable to adults. But that protection is not usually embedded in legislation.

The European Convention On Human Rights is universal in its terms and application, i.e. it applies to all human beings falling under its protection once their State has adopted it, whether they are adults, youths or children. It contains a range of rights, which for the immediate purposes of youth justice, can be abstracted and summarised as follows:

ARTICLE NUMBER	TERMS OF ARTICLE	NATURE OF THE RIGHT
3	Prohibition on subjecting people to torture or to inhuman or degrading treatment	Absolute
4	Prohibition of slavery or forced or compulsory labour	Part Absolute Part Limited
5	The right to liberty and security	Limited
6	The right to a fair trial (incorporating the giving of reasons and explanations)	Part Absolute Part Limited
7	No punishment without law	Absolute
8	The right to respect for family and private life	Qualified
10	The right to freedom of expression	Qualified
11	The right to freedom of assembly	Qualified
14	Prohibition of discrimination in the enjoyment of the other Convention rights	Absolute
First Protocol	Protection of property	Qualified

If a right is *absolute* there can be no limits or qualifications as to its application.

If a right is *limited* then there may be circumstances when that right will cease to apply, e.g. it is possible to require unpaid work (arguably 'forced or compulsory labour' in other circumstances), albeit only in accordance with clearly defined and reasonable statutory provisions. Similarly, lawful imprisonment or being held in custody is provided for specifically by law and also protected by *habeus corpus*.

If a right is *qualified* there may be a need, applying proper provisions, to interfere with it in order to balance it with another Convention aims or with the rights of others.

Although the Convention does not address youth justice as such, it confers, as already noted, rights on all 'human beings' in countries which have adopted it, irrespective of age or status. This universality is, perhaps, one reason why it is probably so widely known by the general population ahead of the other child specific international agreements noted later in the chapter. The Convention is nevertheless as capable of influencing matters relating only to youth justice as it is those relating solely to adult justice. Thus, the manner in which such generic rights are applied to youths in practical situations may have to be interpreted and determined in the light of the fact that the beneficiary of the rights is in fact a youth. For instance, both the European Court of Human Rights and UK national courts have said that where the rights of both adults and children are engaged but in conflict then the child's interests will generally take precedence.

THE HUMAN RIGHTS ACT 1998

In the UK the Convention is most commonly accessed via the widely known measures of the Human Rights Act 1998 which in 2000 effectively incorporated the Convention into UK law.

Since then, UK law requires all courts as far as possible to interpret and apply all legislation (whenever enacted and not just after a specific start date) so as to give effect to Convention rights.

All legislation now introduced into Parliament will usually have been accompanied by an express statement by the relevant Minister of State (in youth justice terms either the Justice Secretary and Lord Chancellor or the Home Secretary) that its terms are believed to be compliant with the Convention rights. This is not the end of the matter and the proof of the pudding lies in how the courts themselves (and ultimately the European Court of Human Rights) interpret matters.

Given that the Convention itself has to be interpreted in the light of ever changing circumstances (it is said to be a 'living instrument'), it will be necessary to continue to interpret and apply all legislation on a human rights basis from an up to date perspective.

Human rights legislation also has to be interpreted and applied on a 'purposive' rather than literal basis (and 'positively' as already mentioned). It is not the strict wording of the Article that is so important, rather the intent behind it and how that intent needs to be addressed at a given time and in particular circumstances.

One of the most important aspects of human rights considerations relates to the fairness of court hearings and the need to give a reasoned explanation as to how any decision has been arrived at. These are the fair trial provisions of Article 6 writ large. They apply from the moment that a youth falls under suspicion until the time when he or she, if convicted and sentenced, e.g. completes his or her programme of activities or serves out a custodial term and associated residual post-custody supervision. He or she must be treated fairly at all times and by all practitioners and public officials that he or she comes into contact with.

This same article also requires courts and officials to give reasons and explanations at appropriate points. This forms the basis for fairness: so that the person concerned can both understand and make informed representations.

Other Articles of particular interest for youth justice purposes are Article 8, the right to private and family life and given what has already been said in *Chapter 1* Article 14 which requires that all Convention rights be applied without discrimination. Article 14 does not confer any free-standing right 'not to be discriminated against', which exists due to other UK legislation and also under the Common Law, which contains long standing protections against bias in the courts or elsewhere if processes are abused. It is also inherent in Article 6 above, the right to a fair trial. But Article 14 is still a powerful provision in itself which reinforces the way in which other human rights ate safeguarded and applied.

KEY YOUTH-SPECIFIC INTERNATIONAL INSTRUMENTS

As has been explained above, there are at least five youth-specific United Nations agreements to which the UK is a party and which are relevant to present purposes.

It is possible here to give only the briefest of outlines and for convenience these have been set out in table form to which practical examples have been added concerning how such agreements have been put into effect in a UK youth justice context. The examples are enlarged upon within other chapters as and when appropriate.

In general terms these provisions are concerned with providing a higher point of reference than merely national or domestic law and practice. Governments and public services look to the rules when making legislation or implementing it respectively. What is important however is that there is a positive stance, a real feel for the importance of such provisions and the will to ensure that they are upheld. As with human rights law (above) it can be all too easy to pay lip-service to them but in fact provide policies or systems which in some way circumvent them. Knowing of their existence is a starting point; and day-to-day vigilance the next step.

UN Declaration of the Rights of the Child 1959		
Ten principles that have informed later UN conventions, guidelines and rules		
Principle	**Summary/extract of the contents**	**Example of UK application**
Principle 1	Children's rights as enshrined in the UN declaration are universal and without any kind of discrimination	UK's anti-discrimination laws, e.g. race, gender, etc
Principle 2	Children to enjoy special protection	Enshrined in UK legislation in a wide range of examples, e.g. by having a special Youth Justice System (YJS) with child-specific provisions
Principle 3	Right to name and nationality	Enshrined in UK legislation in a wide range of arrangements, e.g. formal birth records, official records and nationality and passport provisions as well as those concerning the changing of children's names
Principle 4	Security within society	State health, education, welfare, and social services

Principle 5	Special help if physically, mentally or socially handicapped	State health, education, welfare, and social services
Principle 6	Development via appropriate parenting where possible	State support for concept of 'the family' State support to parents and families Parenting provisions in relation to youth justice
Principle 7	Right to free, compulsory education in at least the elementary stages	State education system Prescribed age for compulsory education
Principle 8	First to receive protection and relief	Children Act 1989
Principle 9	Protection from neglect, cruelty and exploitation Restrictions on child labour	Children Act 1989 Local Authority Social Services Departments Minimum working age and control on hours
Principle 10	Protection from discrimination	Race, religious, gender and disability legislation

UN Convention On the Rights of the Child 1989		
Article	**Summary/Extract of Contents**	**Example of UK Application**
Article 3	All concerned with children should work towards what is best for the child	1933 CYPA 'welfare' statement still in force (*Chapter 1*) System's aim of preventing them offending is in child's interests
Article 5	Respect for rights and responsibilities of families to direct and guide their children	Attendance of parents at police station and court promoted Measures such as state-provided parenting orders to support parents
Article 12	Children have a right to say what they think when adults are making decisions about them	Youth courts now 'engage' directly with youth defendants even if parent or lawyer present
Article 40	Prison sentences for children should only be used for most serious offences	Statutory custody threshold based on 'seriousness' Sentencing Guidelines Council's new youth-specific sentencing guidelines (2009) with renewed focus on custody as a last resort The new youth rehabilitation order offers a wider range of community-based alternatives

UN Guidelines for the Prevention of Juvenile Delinquency 1990 (The 'Riyadh Guidelines')		
Paragraph	**Summary/extract of the contents**	**Example of UK application**
Paragraph 9	Comprehensive prevention plans should be instituted at every level of government	Creation of relevant ministerial departments Statutory principal aim of Youth Justice System Youth Justice Board Statutory obligations on local authorities Youth offending teams
Paragraph 55	Pursue legislation and enforcement aimed at restricting and controlling accessibility of youths to weapons	Initiatives such as those targeting the proliferation and use of knife and guns
Paragraph 60	Promotion of multidisciplinary and interdisciplinary interaction and coordination of youth justice services	Youth Justice Board Youth offending teams Long history of multi-agency working and partnership in relation to youth justice Common principal aim of the Youth Justice System

UN Rules for the Protection of Juveniles Deprived of their Liberty 1990		
Provision	**Summary/extract of the contents**	**Example of UK application**
Fundamental Perspective 1	Imprisonment is last resort	See note under Article 40 of the UN Convention above
Section III of Rules	Presumption of innocence and people treated as innocent unless and until found guilty of an offence Pre-trial detention	Longstanding principle in the UK whereby the prosecution must prove its case beyond reasonable doubt Special bail considerations for younger defendants Bail support packages including intensive supervision and support (*Chapters 10 and 15*)
Section IV	Management of juvenile facilities	Various relevant statutory rules Specific oversight of the youth secure estate

CHAPTER THREE

The Youth Justice System

'System' - a group of independent but interrelated parts comprising a unified whole working together towards a common purpose[1]

The above is one of many possible definitions of a system and it would probably be recognised in many spheres. Jack Straw, speaking as shadow Home Secretary in 1997 (shortly before New Labour came to power in that year), in furtherance of its 'Tough on crime, tough on the causes of crime' agenda,[2] described the then Youth Justice System (YJS) as 'In short … a system which needs radical overhaul.' Addressing the annual general meeting of Nacro,[3] he identified fundamental problems with the then YJS (paraphrased):

- delays in dealing with charges (the average time then being put at four and a half months, with delays of over a year reported as not uncommon)
- inconsistency of approach
- not enough being done to 'nip offending in the bud'[4]
- cumbersome youth court procedures
- insufficient attention being paid to changing offending behaviour
- geographical unevenness[5] re intensive community supervision in place of custody
- a fragmented, costly and inadequate range of custodial facilities whose regimes had a poor track record in preventing offending on release; and
- wastage: much of the estimated £1 billion then spent annually by public services responding to youth crime being on processes rather than on changing behaviour.

It can be argued that there was not really a 'system' at all at that time, more a loose collection of services. Practitioners, committed in themselves, might not share or agree on objectives. Each became involved with offending youths as a matter of routine, often reactively, when the baton was passed his or her way.

It had been estimated that, at the time, around 70 per cent of everyday crimes (as opposed to 'one-off' or out of the ordinary ones) were committed by a relatively

---

1. As created by the authors from a selection of definitions.
2. See the note in *Chapter 1* for the origins of this phrase.
3. See the *Glossary*.
4. This is one of many recurring motifs of youth justice and indeed of criminal justice generally. Opinions vary concerning the extent to which too ready intervention can prove to be counter-productive.
5. Inconsistencies of this kind may be dubbed 'justice by geography'. For one seminal work, see *Alternative Strategies for Coping with Crime* (1973), Tutt N (ed.), Blackwell.

small number of young (mainly male) offenders, virtually all of whom had started offending in their early teens.

General widespread public concern over what became known generically as 'anti-social behaviour'[6] was also identified as adversely affecting the ability of people to use streets and public areas with confidence and in conditions of safety. The first duty of a government was recognised by Jack Straw as being 'to guarantee the safety and security of its citizens'.

May 1997 saw New Labour in power and its 'follow through' on the above in terms of the Crime and Disorder Act 1998 (CDA 1998). This encompassed three overarching measures:

- identification (or, arguably, the creation) of a clear 'Youth Justice System'
- giving each part of that system a common goal; and
- the start of a process of creating new powers and orders.

A true Youth Justice System

The 1998 Act addressed the question of creating a true system of youth justice through a number of provisions, i.e. by:

- establishing a national Youth Justice Board (YJB) to give the system national focus, direction and consistency
- placing direct requirements on local authorities to create and support the system at local level
- requiring local authorities, after consultation with relevant people, to create and implement annual 'youth justice plans'
- requiring local authorities to set up local youth offending teams (YOTs); and
- placing a requirement on other public bodies (police, probation and health services) at local authority level to cooperate with YOTs, including the provision of staff to work within the YOT structure.

A common goal: a principal aim for the the YJS and its various parts

The 1998 Act provided that:[7]

- 'It shall be the principal aim of the youth justice system to prevent offending by children and young persons'; and

---

6. Whether constituting a specific provable crime or possibly falling short of that but, in either case, especially as indulged in by the young.

7. This was effectively, if somewhat obliquely, amended by section 9 Criminal Justice and Immigration Act 2008 which, in creating a new section 142A Criminal Justice Act 2003, encapsulated the statutory aim. In summary terms, this read 'to prevent offending (including reoffending) by persons aged under 18'

- 'In addition to any other duty to which they are subject, it shall be the duty of all persons and bodies carrying out functions in relation to the youth justice system to have regard to that aim'.

Clear and direct though this new statutory aim might be it must also, at times, be set against a number of other provisions (some new and emerging) which might, at first sight, appear to be competing if not actually contradictory:

- sentences on youths, as for adults, must still generally be commensurate with the 'seriousness of the offence' (or combination of offences associated with it): a concept often referred to as 'proportionality'
- section 44 Children and Young Persons Act 1933 (which, as mentioned in *Chapter 1,* following on from the Children Act 1908, established the special ethos of the original juvenile court) still requires that:

Every court in dealing with a child or young person who is brought before it, either as an offender or otherwise, shall have regard to the welfare of the child or young person, and shall in a proper case take steps for removing him from undesirable surroundings, and for securing that proper provision is made for his education and training.

- as from 30 November 2009, there are, for the first time, 'statutory purposes of sentencing' for those aged under 18 years
- the fact that the YJB is adopting a 'scaled approach' based on 'risk' to its activities, especially re how it proposes and operates sentencing disposals (see *Chapters 15 to 17*)
- the Sentencing Guidelines Council's (SGC's) *Overarching Principles: Sentencing Youths,*[8] which mirror this to accompany implementation of the youth provisions of the Criminal Justice and Immigration Act 2008 (CJIA 2008); and
- the Criminal Procedure Rules 2005 (which deal with procedural and case management issues), including by providing that their 'overriding objective' is 'that criminal cases be dealt with justly', a potentially wider concept, which implies addressing and balancing the rights of all participants.

On first encountering these considerations it might appear difficult to reconcile them in a consistent and cohesive fashion. As will be seen later, the SGC's *Overarching Principles* addresses this issue and effectively integrates sentencing law and wider youth justice practice. They also locate them within a convenient, workable structure for both sentencers and practitioners.

---

8. (2009) Sentencing Guidelines Council. In the remainder of this book these principles (which are frequently referred to) are referred to as 'the SGC's *Overarching Principles*'. Other SGC 'overarching principles' exist re adults and, e.g. 'seriousness' and are mentioned by reference to their full title.

SOME KEY CHANGES INTRODUCED BY THE 1998 ACT

Among other things, the 1998 Act:

- created the YJB and associated developments: below
- replaced the statutory framework of reprimands and warnings for those aged 10-17 years, inclusive, thereby doing away with the former, essentially non-statutory, arrangements for cautioning youths:[9] see *Chapter 11*
- made changes concerning how and where certain youths are remanded to await their trial or sentence: *Chapter 10*; and
- introduced the first laws to deal with anti-social behaviour (ASB): *Chapter 6*.

These aspects are examined in the chapters referred to above, along with considerable subsequent legislative and other changes in each of these areas.

The Youth Justice Board for England and Wales

The creation of the YJB stands at the centre of the overhaul (or creation) of the YJS. It was established a an independent body corporate wholly independent from the Crown, State or other influences although its main official reference point is the Ministry of Justice (MOJ). However, it should be noted that whilst its chair and 12 members are appointed by the Justice Secretary,[10] many other functions of youth justice now fall in practical day-to-day terms to the Department of Children, Schools and Families (DCFS) which since 2007 has played a leading role. Crime prevention, public safety and criminal policy are the remit of the Home Office, although the first of these is an aim now widely shared within the Criminal Justice System (CJS) and YJS. Members of the YJB are appointed from amongst people who appear to the Justice Secretary to have 'extensive recent experience of the YJS'.

The YJB has a number of statutory functions. These (paraphrased) include to:

- monitor the operation of the YJS and the provision of youth justice services
- advise the Justice Secretary on the operation and provision of youth justice
- advise him or her on how the principal aim of youth justice ('to prevent offending': above) might most effectively be pursued
- advise him or her on national standards in respect of the provisions of such services and in respect of the accommodation of children and young persons kept in

---

9. Conditional cautioning of youths being introduced in 2009: see *Chapter 11*.
10. Full title 'Secretary of State for Justice and Lord Chancellor'. One chair disagreed with the Government's approach to YJB responsibilities, sufficiently so to resign his position: Rod Morgan a former HM Chief Inspector of Probation and respected academic, of considerable standing in criminal justice circles. The key Minister at the time (2007) was the Home Secretary, under the pre-MOJ arrangements.

custody that is safe and secure

- advise him or her on preventing offending by children and young persons and addressing their offending behaviour
- monitor the degree of achievement of the principal aim and the observance of national standards
- for the above purposes, to obtain and publish relevant information
- identify, make known and promote good practice
- make grants (with the approval of the Justice Secretary or other Minister as appropriate) to local authorities or others to develop or research good practice
- enter into agreements in respect of secure accommodation or custodial facilities; and
- offer assistance to local authorities to help the latter to carry out their statutory obligations in relation to youth justice.

Through these functions the YJB also seeks to provide nationwide youth justice benefits such as:

- leadership
- direction
- common and raised standards
- quality and consistency of service; and
- checks of youth justice measures against international obligations (see *Chapter 2*).

The priorities of the YJB have developed from its overall aims of reducing offending and the use of custody to a more pro-active and prominent role in the prevention of youth crime. It has secured funding to enable YOTs to develop crime prevention services, including the provision of parenting support and what are termed Youth Inclusion and Support Panel (YISP) arrangements.

At the other end of the scale, the YJB spends around 75 per cent of its annual budget on placements within the secure estate (i.e. custodial placements of one kind or another) and funds YOTs to provide robust community sentence options in the form of Intensive Supervision and Surveillance (ISS) programmes (*Chapter 15*).

Local provision of youth justice services

The duty to ensure locally appropriate provision of youth justice services is placed by the 1998 Act on local authorities, who must act in cooperation with the following local bodies or officials (each with a reciprocal statutory obligation to cooperate), i.e. the:

- chief officer of police
- police authority
- local probation board

- strategic health authority
- health authority; and
- primary care trust.

The statutory definition of 'youth justice services' is lengthy and technical (and open to amendment by the Secretary of State) but its main components can be summarised as follows:

- the provision of appropriate adults to safeguard the interests of children and young persons under 17 years of age (see *Chapter 10*) detained or questioned by the police during an investigation
- assessment for reprimands, warnings and related rehabilitation programmes
- bail support measures
- remand placements in local authority accommodation
- pre-sentence reports (PSRs) (*Chapter 15*) and the provision of other information in criminal proceedings
- operation of parenting contracts or parenting orders where children or young persons have engaged (or are likely to engage) in criminal conduct or anti-social behaviour
- provision of 'responsible officers' in relation to parenting orders, child safety orders, reparation orders and action plan orders (all covered in later chapters)
- supervision of relevant community-based orders
- supervision of any community licence part of a custodial sentence; and
- the operation of referral orders (again covered later).

In addition youth justice services are now also involved in helping to engage victims in the restorative justice process as discussed in *Chapter 4*.

Linked to these matters are other non-youth specific statutory obligations placed on local authorities and others, to formulate strategies in relation to items such as a general reduction in crime, combating the misuse of drugs, making arrangements with regard to vulnerable people and so on.

Statutory arrangements are in place to provide for either direct financial contribution by the above bodies for youth justice services or for them to pool funds for related purposes.

PLANNING YOUTH JUSTICE SERVICES

At national level, the YJB's Youth Justice Planning Framework incorporates key features of an Effective Practice Quality Assurance (EPQA) process involving self-assessment. It is also underpinned by the priorities contained within the national Criminal Justice Strategic Plan for the relevant public spending review period. Key elements of effective practice are intended to underpin the work of the YJB and its responsibilities in relation to a range of youth justice services, allow delivery to be shaped by need, local context and to support consistency of delivery. Local authorities and YOTs, e.g. are able to use this mechanism as a tool in their internal planning processes and for 'benchmarking'[11] their services.

Local authorities annual Youth Justice Plans

The CDA 1998 requires each local authority to create an annual Youth Justice Plan (YJP) having first consulted at least the following (or more widely), i.e. the:

- chief office of police
- police authority
- local probation board
- strategic health authority
- health authority
- primary care trust; and
- district council (where the local authority is a county council).

This annual youth plan must address matters such as:

- how youth justice services in the area are to be provided and funded
- how the local YOTs are to be composed and funded, how they are to operate, and what functions they will carry out. This will, in particular, cover how the local authority will, via the local YOT, address its statutory obligation under Schedule 2 the Children Act 1989 to, for instance, take steps to encourage children (all those under 18 years old for these purposes) within their area not to commit criminal offences (or what would be criminal offences re someone aged ten or over).

The plan is submitted to the YJB and published as the Secretary of State directs. In 2008 the YJB revised targets for YOTs. YJPs must now say how YOTs plan to:

- reduce the use of custody for sentences
- reduce re-offending by young people
- reduce the number of first time entrants to the youth justice system

11. The term 'benchmarking' as used by the YJB appears to connote that EPQA can be used as a yardstick to test whether local arrangements will be appropriate. For further information about the planning process as it operates at the national and local level, see yjb.gov.uk/en-gb/practitioners/ImprovingPractice

- facilitate young people's access to full-time education, training and employment
- reduce any disproportionate representation of minority groups in the YJS
- manage risks presented to the public by young offenders
- safeguard young offenders; and
- promote public confidence in the youth justice system.

YOUTH OFFENDING TEAMS

The practical local delivery of youth justice services falls in the main to local youth offending teams (YOTs), which as already noted each local authority is required to establish (be it one or more for the area concerned) in consultation with what might be termed its feeder bodies as noted below. These bodies or officials have a statutory duty to cooperate in the creation and operation of YOTs and provide staff resources, i.e. the:

- chief officer of police
- local probation board
- strategic health authority
- health authority; and
- primary care trust.

The staff membership of a YOT will thus by law involve a range of specialists and experts (in addition to other staff employed directly by the YOT, including, e.g. a team manger or ad hoc contractors such as medical personnel, counsellors, criminal psychologists and so on: see further below). At the YOT's core, at least one of each the following will be seconded by their employer, i.e. a:

- probation officer
- social worker from local authority social services department
- police officer
- individual nominated by a health authority; and
- individual nominated by chief education officer.

It is also quite common for YOTs to have within their office structure (or alternatively to have access to) the services of other people such as:

- drug, alcohol or substance misuse workers
- housing or accommodation officers
- psychiatrists
- psychologists.

Duties of the YOT

The duties placed on YOTs can be simply stated (although they are extensive, varied and detailed in their day-to-day execution). Whether as a matter of statutory duty or of everyday practice they extend to such matters as:

- coordinating youth justice services (as set out above) for all those in the area who are in need of them
- carrying out any additional functions assigned at any time by the annual local Youth Justice Plan noted above
- involvement in the placement of those remanded to local authority accommodation
- providing 'appropriate adults': see later chapters and particularly *Chapter 10*
- delivering programmes to accompany formal warnings: *Chapter 11*
- bail support: *Chapter 10*
- reports to courts: see mainly *Chapter 15*
- providing 'responsible officers' for parenting orders, child safety orders and reparation orders
- supervising and enforcing community-based orders: *Chapter 16*
- supervising the community licence part of custodial sentences: *Chapter 17*
- enabling community reparation and other restorative justice processes: *Chapter 4*
- engaging with victims in restorative processes; and
- recruiting and training volunteer youth offender panel (YOP) members below.

As a multi-agency service, YOTs are able to provide a range of services such as those referable to mental health, substance misuse, parenting support, education and housing support in order to meet the identified needs of young people subject to their supervision or involvement.

Services are allocated according to need, identified through an assessment process known as ASSET. There is also an ONSET framework for use in preventive work where youths are at-risk of offending, rather than with offenders as such. The assessment identifies factors in a youth's life that have led to his or her offending behaviour and seeks to address these to reduce the likelihood of further offending. The 'scaled approach' implemented nationally in 2009 (see in particular *Chapters 15* to *17* seeks to match available resources to the level of risks of re-offending and harm to others as identified by the YOT using professional risk-assessment tools.

National standards and inspection

As already indicated, YOT and other locally-based work takes place against the background of a national Youth Justice Planning Framework. All activities undertaken by a YOT in relation to young people are also governed by National Standards.

These dictate levels and timescales for contact with young people and also set out the responsibilities of the YOT manager and chief officers in terms of their account-ability for the management elements of the YJS.

YOTs are subject to inspection by multi-agency inspectorate teams co-ordinated by Her Majesty's Inspectorate of Probation (HMIP), which focus on such matters as the case management of young offenders over a three-year cycle. There is particular emphasis on inspecting the quality of the management of risk and the safeguarding of children and young people. Inspection reports are submitted to the Ministry of Justice. In mid-2009, Government Ministers somewhat controversially said that they would seeking to create legislation to enable them to put in their own teams to any YOT deemed to be failing to meet minimum standards.[12]

THE VOLUNTARY AND COMMUNITY SECTOR

It is now recognised, more than ever, that the prevention of youth offending and general support for all youths is not just a matter for the government or its official arms within the 'system' but something for society as a whole to embrace. Many voluntary organisations have long been involved in youth justice activities and a sample list would include:

- Nacro
- Catch 22
- Barnardos
- Children's Society
- National Youth Association.

The remit and contact details of these and a selection of other non-statutory sector organizations is briefly noted in the *Glossary* at the end of the book. Among other things, they lobby on behalf of disadvantaged young people including youth offenders. They work with some local authorities who commission organizations such as these to provide direct services to children and families. Voluntary organiza-tions offering services are often more likely to engage with young people and fami-lies due to not obviously being part of official, formal or local government systems.

Bodies such as the Howard League for Penal Reform (howardleague.org) and the Prison Reform Trust (prison-reform-trust.org.uk) have a general role in challenging government and others in relation to custodial punishments in particular as well as a general interest in matters of criminal justice.

---

12. There have been a number of high profile reports of a minority of failing YOTs when the Ministry of Justice (MOJ) also indicated it would look to default powers. For further discussion, see *Chapter 18*.

The community in general

There are also many opportunities for individual members of the community to become involved and play a part in the YJS. They include acting as:

- mentors to youth offenders including within YOT arrangements
- members of a youth offender panels (YOPs): see the separate heading below
- appropriate adults: *Chapter 10*
- monitoring the secure estate
- employers who allow supported placements within their organizations
- helpers to people who lack literacy and numeracy skills

YOUTH OFFENDER PANELS

Youth offender panels (YOPs) are one of the most innovative changes of modern times, focusing final decision-making attention away from the youth court (or even the Crown Court) and onto the YOP.[13] It is now by a YOP that most first time youth offenders (and since 27 April 2009 some second time offenders) must normally (or on occasions may at the youth court's discretion) be dealt with. These arrangements and powers are fully discussed in *Chapter 15*. For present purposes, it is the make up, training and contribution to the YJS by lay members of YOPs that is of immediate interest.

Once a young person aged 14-17 is given a referral order (*Chapter 15*) he or she is referred to the YOP which will consider the most appropriate course of action. It must meet for the first time no later than 20 working days from the referral order being made. It will normally be chaired by a lay member.

Nature and role of the panel

A YOP consists of two volunteer lay members recruited from the local community plus a member of the YOT. They meet with the young person, and his or her parents or guardians, to talk about the reasons for the offending and agree a tailor-made contract[14] aimed at putting matters right. The victim is given an opportunity to attend the YOP meeting to let the young person know how it affected him or her.

The contract can include a range of requirements or expectations such as a letter of apology to the victim and reparation to him or her or to the community in general. It may also include activities to prevent further offending such as a commitment to take part in programmes to tackle substance misuse, motoring offences or to comply with education plans. The contract is supervised by the YOT and reviewed

---

13. YOPs may also be referred to as 'referral order panels' or 'community panels' and members simply as 'panel members'. There is a national Association of Panel Members (AOPM): see the *Glossary*.
14. See the *Glossary*.

by it at regular intervals, usually of three months. One incentive is that the conviction is treated as 'spent'[15] when the order is successfully completed. If the youth fails to comply, the case is sent back to court and a different sentence may be given.

Recruitment and training of YOT members[16]
Volunteer YOP members must be

- 18 years-of-age or over 'from all ethnic and social backgrounds who can represent their local community'
- ideally live in the community local to the YOT
- pass an enhanced Criminal Records Bureau (CRB) check; and
- undertake a training course run by the YOT.

The last of these involves around seven days training initially. This will also provide the YOT with an insight into the suitability of the volunteer. Other ways of assessing new members can be observation and attendance at support meetings where issues about young people, crime and the YJS are discussed. Annual meetings with a YOT practitioner or manager to undertake a review and appraisal of the panel member give opportunity for discussion about performance. Throughout the year any concerns brought to the attention of the YOT manager responsible for the recruitment and training of panel members will be taken up directly with the person concerned.

Panel members can undertake any number of panel meetings each month, but ideally should expect to attend at least three a month in order to maintain their experience and develop their skills in what is a demanding and sensitive role.

Length of service and a need for more YOP members
The legislative changes of 2009 are likely to result in an increase in YOP hearings and increased demand for trained panel volunteers. The YJB has estimated that, on average, YOPs will need to increase their current volunteer capacity by 17 per cent across the country to cover the expected additional panel hearings, bearing in mind the statutory requirement for at least two volunteers to be on every panel.

Following a review of YOP volunteer service, Ministers have decided that:

- the tenure of current members can be extended for a maximum of two years
- recruitment in the coming 12 months will be for a maximum of six years; and
- the plan is to review the situation in 2010.

---

15. For a short note on the Rehabilitation of Offenders Act 1974, see *Chapter 15*.
16. For anyone wishing to join a YOP as a volunteer, further information and sample case studies are available at yjb.gov.uk/en-gb/yjs/GetInvolved

CHAPTER FOUR

A Restorative Approach

In July 2003 the government published its strategy on restorative justice.[1] This sought to build on the progress made in this arena within the Youth Justice System (YJS). It emphasised the need to recognise the needs of victims of crime and to involve them in processes that would address the harm caused to them. It also recognised that restorative justice can help to reduce the likelihood of repeat offending.

WHAT ARE RESTORATIVE PROCESSES?

The formal Criminal Justice System (CJS) is adversarial in nature, meaning that its processes involve a contest between opposing sides, prosecution and defence, to 'win' their case.[2] It is thus fundamentally 'conflict intensive'. At one level, the YJS reflects this, but practitioners have long since tried to temper that conflict in youth cases, not simply for the detrimental way in which it can affect the attitudes of young people but also because a rigorous trial, which may involve aggressive cross-examination of witnesses and pursuit of technicalities, can be a daunting experience for adults never mind young people.

Restorative processes are a structured, non-adversarial way of trying to resolve problems. They are of general application and have been applied in a range of situations not just in the criminal justice arena. They are associated with the idea of 'repairing harm' and 'restoring harmony', in the case of youth justice as between victims, offenders and their communities. They are also generally seen as empowering people who are affected by the behaviour of others.

In the criminal justice context, restorative processes are usually referred to as 'restorative justice' (also widely known as RJ). A quite considerable body of materials and research has built up in this sphere in the past 20 years or so. Restorative justice focuses not only on repairing the harm done by an offence - including through physical (or failing that symbolic) 'reparation' - but also on mending or building more positive relationships by those who have committed offences. A key aim of restorative justice is to balance the concerns of the victim with the need to mark the offence in an appropriate way but also reintegrate the offender into his or

---

1. (2003). See homeoffice.gov..
2. For the origins, history and intrinsic values of English law to arise from this, see *Fighting For Justice: The Origins and History of Adversary Trial* (2006), Hostettler J, Waterside Press. Restorative justice apart, the adversarial method can be contrasted with the inquisitorial one of continental jurisdictions (and Scotland) where an independent official, investigating magistrate, or procurator fiscal looks into a case from its outset to see whether evidence is emerging of an offence and to guide the investigation.

her community, whether that is a local community, school or his or her home environment. The technique can be used with regard to all aspects of the youth justice process in relation to offending behaviour or anti-social behaviour (ASB) (see generally *Chapter 6* for the latter). They have also been applied in situations involving bullying, neighbourhood disputes and other situations which can benefit from the resolution of conflict rather than escalating it.

Origins of RJ

Restorative justice is not new. The principles of RJ can be traced back hundreds of years and found in various parts of the world. It seems to carry a universal message that resolution is better than division as evidenced by its acceptance within diverse cultures, faiths and beliefs.[3] In the 1970s there was a resurgence of interest in mediation between victims and offenders.[4] In the 1990s this broadened to include other settings and restorative processes were recognised as having the potential for enhancing social cohesion and reducing social exclusion, seen as a cause of crime.

Maintaining social discipline raises many questions and challenges for those in society who have an authority role. This includes parents, teachers, employers or justice professionals. Historically, Western societies have relied heavily on punishment to discipline those who misbehave or commit crime, with many considering it to be the only effective way to deal with such behaviour. This punitive approach is also referred to as 'retributive' and is acknowledged as stigmatising and applying negative labels to those subjected to its methods.

Whilst a more 'permissive' approach tends to protect wrongdoers from experiencing the consequences of their actions, the restorative approach confronts and disapproves of the wrongdoing while affirming the intrinsic worth of the offender. In some contexts the marking of unacceptable behaviour, criminal or otherwise, is dubbed 'naming and shaming'. Whilst restorative processes vary, the idea of public acceptance of responsibility and showing remorse is an integral part of the purposes of most models of restorative justice.

Some key features of the restorative approach

Other key features of restorative processes involve communication between the victim and offender. This can be either direct communication, face-to-face (when appropriate), or facilitated through a third party negotiator or mediator enabling communication without direct contact.

It is important, motivation and effectiveness-wise, that such processes are entered into on a voluntary basis by all parties, and the offender must have admitted responsibility for the offence. As already indicated, this acceptance is key to progress.

---

3. For an expert analysis see the trilogy of works on this topic by David J Cornwell at WatersidePress.co.uk
4. Again for a seminal work, see *Justice For Victims and Offenders* (2nd. edn. 1996), Waterside Press.

Restorative justice cannot work, e.g. where the offender remains in denial or is (still) seeking to blame someone else. It also demands analogous bona fides on the part of a victim and a wish, in those cases where there is direct or indirect mediation, to wish to convey his or her feelings to the offender in a constructive way (although being able to 'let of steam' can be seen as beneficial).

One of the outcomes of communication between victim and offender (which are always carefully managed) is that the victim can influence how the offender makes amends for the harm caused by the offence. This can be in the form of financial or practical reparation, but will more often be in the form of an apology (written or oral), accompanied by reassurance that the offence will not be repeated. When a court is sentencing a youth, reparation made in any of these ways will be a key considera- tion, a mitigating factor which can lead to a more constructive final outcome.

Other benefits of restorative methods

Victims can be assisted in recovering from the harm done by having their views and feelings listened to in a sensitive way and having the harm done to them recognised by the offender. In turn, offenders are helped to recognise the harm caused by their behaviour and the impact which it has had on the victim or wider community.

For many victims a key question is 'Why' or 'Why me'. Victims can have their questions answered about why and how the offence happened and why they were the victim. This also helps to deal with fear of crime which if left unaddressed may persist for years. Despite often coming from different backgrounds or communities, the information available shows that many victims and offender *can* communicate and empathise with one another and begin to understand each other's perspective.

For victims there are further reported benefits in achieving 'closure' and general satisfaction with the processes involved. Too often, the experiences of those who come up against formal aspects of the CJS in general have a negative tinge. Thus, e.g. an evaluation of the Northern Ireland Youth Conference Service revealed that 81 per cent of victims preferred a restorative conference to court proceedings and 88 per cent said they would recommend a conference to a person in a similar situation.[5]

The 1998 *British Crime Survey* noted that 41 per cent of victims said they would like to meet their offenders. Later evidence from studies worldwide show that more than 75 per cent of the victims who take part in restorative justice processes are glad they did so (see 'Restorative Justice: the Government's Strategy').[6]

---

5. Evaluation of the Northern Ireland Youth Conference Service N/O Research and Statistical Series; Report No.12.
6. (2003), HMSO.

RESTORATIVE APPROACHES AND YOUNG PEOPLE

The use of restorative processes within the YJS is explained below, but there are a number of other settings where these processes have been used effectively with young people and the 'victims' of their behaviour. These have included in schools to deal with bullying or other forms of unacceptable behaviour, neighbourhood disputes, youth clubs or other institutions when there is conflict.

Restorative justice in the YJS

The formal and systematic application of restorative justice processes within the youth justice system has gained momentum since the implementation of the Crime and Disorder Act 1998. Prior to that, restorative justice was a recognised practice, but not routinely applied.

The process of facilitating the engagement of victims, offenders, or both in some form of restorative process is now applied to all those who are the subject of a referral order and increasingly to those who are subject to a police reprimand or final warning. Restorative justice is now also being used as a formal 'restorative disposal"' by many police areas as an alternative to a police reprimand.

YOTs are required to contact victims of youth crime to offer them an opportunity to enter into a restorative justice process. This could be in the form of:

- **a written apology**: the victim receiving a written apology from the offender.
- **direct reparation**: the offender making a form of practical reparation to the offender e.g. mending a garden fence or cleaning-up mess
- **indirect reparation**: the offender undertaking a form of reparation directed by the victim, e.g. undertaking a piece of work for a chosen charity
- **mediation**: a structured communication between victim and offender facilitated by a third party
- **indirect mediation**: contact whereby an offender and victim communicate through a mediator. This may or may not lead to a meeting of victim and offender if both parties want this and the situation is otherwise appropriate
- **a restorative conference**: a facilitated and structured meeting between victim, offender, family, friends or supporters. Both parties share their perspective of the offence. A desired outcome is an apology by the offender and acceptance of the impact of their behaviour on the victim as observed by members of the conference.

This last type of restorative process is in fact how restorative justice began, through what is called a 'family group conference' or community 'sentencing circle'. The view of many proponents of restorative justice is that primitive methods have a lot to tell us about how to resolve conflict. The theory also suggests that they are yet more effective with young people at an impressionable age or when they are still capable of grasping the opportunities on offer.

THE YOUTH RESTORATIVE DISPOSAL

A youth restorative disposal (YRD), although still at its pilot stage and in its infancy, is now playing a practical part in developments in this field. The YJB notes that:

> in Greater Manchester, one of seven areas nationwide in which the pilot has been running, around a hundred YRD's have been issued in Wigan alone since October 2008. Recent figures for the town show an 8.1 per cent reduction in young people entering the ... system for the first time, and a 28.3 per cent reduction in re-offending rates.[7]

The YRD works by using the principles of restorative justice, which means that the young person is encouraged to address the consequences of his or her actions, offer an apology, examine why the offence took place and improve his or her behaviour. By the end of 2009, nearly 4,000 police officers and police community support officers (PCSOs) had been trained in its use across eight of the pilot areas.

RESTORATIVE JUSTICE CONSORTIUM

Many practitioners of youth justice belong to organizations which are part of a key independent umbrella and networking body, the Restorative Justice Consortium (RJC). The RJC was established to support people and organizations in the field of restorative justice 'to meet the needs of victims and reduce offending'.

The RJC works with Government bodies to bring about 'the best use of restorative justice' in a wide range of settings. It's vision (paraphrased) is that anyone suffering harm from crime or conflict should have the opportunity to resolve this through restorative processes.

The RJC's aims encompass promoting restorative justice 'for the public benefit' including the use of restorative approaches in the Criminal Justice System (CJS) (which for present purposes includes the YJS, where the RJC is particularly prominent). It develops and promotes standards, principles and guidance, as well as conducting research in this field and publishing useful data.

The contact details of the RJC, which represents a gateway to a wide range of materials and details of RJ-based organizations, can be found in the *Glossary*.

---

7.   *YJ* magazine, September 2009, Youth Justice Board

CHAPTER FIVE

Targeting Attention and Resources

It is difficult to give an accurate picture of the total costs of the Youth Justice System as a whole. Many of those costs are met by different agencies or bodies, some of which such as the police, courts (through HM Court Service) and Crown Prosecution Service (CPS) have broader remits within which all or part of their YJS-related costs are subsumed. The 'Annual Report and Accounts 2008/9' of the Youth Justice Board (YJB) itself shows that it received funding of £495.287 million, including £431.697 million from the Ministry of Justice (MOJ), £29.379 million from the Home Office and £33.961 million from the Department for Children, Schools and Families (DCFS). Among other things it spent:

- £470.620 million on frontline youth justice programmes
- £297.952 million (63%) on the youth secure estate (*Chapter 17*)
- £53.761 million on direct funding to youth offending teams (YOTs) conditional on the achievement of, or progress towards, performance targets
- £33.166 million on grants to YOTs for the intensive supervision and surveillance (ISS) programme (*Chapter 16*)
- £36.479 million on preventative programmes (see generally *Chapter 6*); and
- £17.652 million on a 'Wiring Up Youth Justice' programme to support various technological advances.[1]

All of this is in addition to the direct and indirect costs incurred by local authorities, schools, health services, certain referral services and others (to which might easily be added the work of the charitable or voluntary sector, substantial parts of which involve no public funding by grants or otherwise: *Chapter 3* and see the *Glossary*). Best use of resources is thus a priority as it is in any modern-day undertaking.

EXPEDITION AND PERSISTENT YOUNG OFFENDERS

Following hard on the heels of the post-1998 YJS described in *Chapter 3* and picking up on official assertions that a disproportionate amount of crime is committed by a small group of mainly young offenders, the New Labour Government set the YJS

---

1. This included, e.g. development of an eASSET, an electronic version of the ASSET assessment tool: *Chapter 15*. The full 2008/9 report (the last available at the time of going to press) and full details of all YJB expenditure and other management data can be accessed at official-documents.gov.uk.

an immediate task. This was to identify and address that small group of offenders and their disproportionate offending behaviour. This was to be achieved through the non-statutory concept of the 'persistent young offender' (PYO).[2]

It was felt, with some justification, that, if this PYO group could be identified and their criminal behaviour addressed and processed expeditiously then, not only would the public (and the public purse) ultimately benefit, but the principal aim of the system would be served. The youths themselves would also benefit.

The concept of a PYO was somewhat complex and involved subtle changes after its initial inception, but latterly signified, roughly speaking, an offender aged from 10-17 years (inclusive) who had three or more separate prior sentences for record-able offences[3] on their criminal record.

Where such offenders offended again the entire investigation, prosecution and court processes were to be expedited with the aim of reaching the final outcome (acquittal or disposal on conviction as appropriate) within an average of 71 days from the date when the youth was first arrested.

The figure of 71 days may appear to have been a little arbitrary and not neces-sarily the result of a detailed analysis of the time taken for each step in the process and, to some extent, this view would be correct. It was arrived at by a halving of the 142 days identified as the average time taken to bring cases to court immediately before the new YJS came into being. Subsequent monitoring showed that this was an achievable average (especially once the Criminal Procedure Rules 2005 were in place: *Chapter 3*) and that the following sub-targets could often be achieved within that average for the more straightforward cases:

- seven days from arrest to first court appearance
- 28 days from entry of not guilty plea to trial; and
- 14 days from guilty plea or finding of guilt to sentence.

This 49-day period, if achieved in a fair number of cases, then gave some latitude in reaching an overall average of 71 days when the demands of more complex or involved PYO cases were taken into account.

Not only were the bodies contributing to YOT membership involved in meeting this target but so were the Crown Prosecution Service (CPS) and the courts (at both the magistrates' court and Crown Court level).

Defending lawyers, had they initially felt uneasy about being requested to help to meet Government PYO targets (even if, arguably, in the interests of their youth

---

2. Care must be taken to distinguish this non-statutory term from the statutory concept of the 'persistent offender' as applied to certain youths when considering the additional threshold custody criteria for a detention and training order: see *Chapter 17.*
3. i.e. those recordable by the police, as required by the Home Office.

clients), came to have a specific duty under the Criminal Procedure Rules 2005 to help to expedite criminal hearings so they may well, in practice, have met the 71-day PYO target albeit by a different route.

However, there were at least two aspects of the PYO arrangements which required particular care and attention:

- the interests of justice had always to take precedence and occasionally this may have driven different timescales (although appropriate expedition is usually said to be in the interests of justice in any event); and
- there had to be no direct or inadvertent disclosure[4] to any court determining guilt or innocence that the defendant was a PYO as this, of itself, showed that the youth had previous convictions and adversely affected the fairness of the trial (although, it may, on occasions, have been permissible for the prosecution to seek to admit previous convictions by other routes for evidential purposes).

The benefits of (appropriate) expedition, sometimes called 'fast-tracking', with regard to the processing of young offenders (as now encapsulated by the Criminal Procedure Rules 2005) is readily apparent in the arrangements for processing of PYOs (above). It has more general benefits which can be summarised as follows:

- any response to unacceptable behaviour is usually best if it follows as soon as possible after the event and relates as directly to it as possible
- youths may need immediate help and guidance to learn from their mistakes; and
- the circumstances of young people's lives can change very quickly and they may soon have moved on from the factors that prompted earlier behaviour.

FROM PYO TO DETERRING YOUNG OFFENDERS

In late 2008, Jack Straw (by then Justice Secretary and Lord Chancellor) announced discontinuation of the PYO system from 31 December 2008. This was to be in favour of one which now addressed 'the most high risk offenders'. The former PYO approach was noted by him as having been successful on a number of fronts:

- a halving of the 142 day period had been achieved as an average across the country (and had even been bettered in 2007, at 65 days)
- it had been the first real cross-criminal justice system target and, as such, had not only achieved its basic aim but had also served to bring the various criminal justice

---

4. e.g. by leaving the file lying open on the prosecutor's desk in court.

agencies closer together (as originally envisaged when the YJS was created under the Crime and Disorder Act 1998 (*Chapter 3*); and

- this coming together of the various criminal justice agencies was also seeing consequential benefits in wider initiatives such as the Prolific and Other Priority Offender (POPO) programme in which those agencies, usually through the Local Criminal Justice Board (LCJB)5 or dedicated POPO liaison arrangements, address a wide range of specific offenders of all ages

However, the PYO approach also had suggested drawbacks, such as:

- it was more quantitative than qualitative
- it was perhaps more reactive than proactive
- prevention of (re)offending was more a by-product than a prime objective
- the scheme was unduly complex
- local PYO monitoring groups had often been chaired by a magistrates' court legal adviser which, whilst effective, raised certain issues of judicial impartiality; and
- defence lawyers had not been directly involved in the monitoring groups but had subsequently, via the Criminal Procedure Rules 2005, become more involved with case management obligations within the court proceedings themselves.

The new approach introduced on 1 January 2009 therefore requires the various partner agencies in the LCJB, as part of their POPO programme, to concentrate on those youths who are at greatest risk of offending, whether based on past criminal behaviour or otherwise.

Premium service and 'levels of ambition'
Local YOTs identify youths who are at risk as part of the 'deter' (as well as the 'catch and convict') strand of the LCJB's POPO programme. Hence the emergence of the 'Deter Young Offenders' (DYO) of the title.

Should such youths, despite the ensuing deter and support measures, come to be prosecuted, the relevant agencies apply a 'premium service' in respect of matters such as expedition of the proceedings, bail support packages, report-writing, sentencing options and sentence management.

No national targets have been set, but performance in respect of timeliness of processing cases and of reoffending by such youths is measured and LCJBs supported and challenged to create 'local levels of ambition'.

Courts managers continue to be involved at LCJB level but legal advisers are not

---

5.   Both a National Criminal Justice Board (NCJB) and local, i.e. area-based Local Criminal Justice Boards (LCJBs) exist whereby practitioners from across the CJS meet to discuss matters of common interest. POPO is sometimes referred to as PPO.

involved in the operational aspects of the DYO initiative, although they continue to be closely involved in case management generally and the progression of cases in accordance with the Criminal Procedure Rules 2005.

A SCALED APPROACH

It has already been noted that local YOTs now play a large part in identifying and interacting with DYOs and therefore equally in addressing the risk factors relating to such youths. The idea of a 'scaled approach' is also a theme of other chapters.[6]

In providing their part of the 'premium service' described above, YOTs, from late 2009, adopted their own scaled approach'[7] in deciding how to assess and address risk factors. This extends to matters such as:

- how risk is addressed in pre-sentence reports (PSRs) on youths
- this will include aspects of the ASSET and ONSET assessment tools as used to examine the risk of reoffending (see *Chapters 15* to *17* in particular). These are the current assessment frameworks used by YOTs for all young people in the YJS to identify concerns about a youth and to identify the factors that may have led to his or her offending. Factors such as health, education, use of drugs, peer and family relationships, lifestyle and attitudes are examined in this analysis and in the planning of appropriate interventions.
- it will also extend to the risk of serious harm (ROSH) assessment
- some questions in the core ASSET assessment will be indicators of the risk of serious harm to others. If answered 'yes' this will lead to a further, specific assessment to analyse the potential risk of serious harm
- what factors are identified for consideration once a referral order has been made: see generally *Chapter 4*
- which of the potential 15 basic requirements of the new youth rehabilitation order (YRO) are to be proposed: see *Chapters 15* and *16*
- how any YRO is to be managed and enforced; and
- how any community element of a detention and training order (DTO) in respect of a youth is to be managed and enforced: see generally *Chapter 17.*

Three broad categories of youth offender and corresponding levels of intervention are suggested by this 'scaled approach':

---

6. e.g. it applies to the work of YOTs (*Chapter 5*), pre-sentence reports (PSRs), referral orders, youth rehabilitation orders and the community element of a custodial sentence: see generally *Chapters 15* to *17.*

7. See further yjb.gov.uk/scaledapproach

OFFENDER RISK PROFILE	INTERVENTION LEVEL	EXAMPLE OF INTER-VENTION MEASURES
Low to medium likelihood of reoffending *and* **Low** risk of causing serious harm to other people	**Standard**	Standard level of contact for a referral order (*Chapter 15*) or youth rehabilitation order (YRO) with a supervision requirement (*Chapter 16*). Voluntary parenting support.
Medium to high likelihood of reoffending *or* **Medium to high** risk of causing serious harm to other people	**Enhanced**	YRO with supervision, education and drug testing requirements (*Chapter 16*) Parenting contract or parenting order.
High likelihood of reoffending *or* **Very high** risk of causing serious harm to other people	**Intensive**	This could include the new intensive supervision and surveillance and fostering form of YRO as an alternative to a custodial sentence (*Chapter 16*).

Note: The third category above could also help to identify those youths to be considered within the new deter young offender (DYO) initiative outlined earlier in the chapter

The scaled approach was promoted by the YJB following extensive trials and consultation. It is covered by revised National Standards for Youth Justice Services. Matching intervention to the assessed risk of (re)offending can be viewed as a 'what works' approach (see the *Glossary*). But the approach must also take into account the seriousness of the offence and other proportionality aspects of sentencing practice as addressed by the SGC's *Overarching Principles*: see mainly *Chapter 15*.

The YJB's chart opposite shows the approach in greater detail.

THE YOUTH JUSTICE BOARD'S SCALED APPROACH

	Function	Typical case management approach	Possible sentence requirement/component (not exhaustive)
STANDARD	Enabling compliance and repairing harm	• Organising interventions to meet basic requirement of order • Engaging parents in interventions and/or to support young person • Monitoring compliance • Enforcement	• Reparation • Stand alone unpaid work • Supervision • Stand alone attendance centre
ENHANCED	Enabling compliance and repairing harm Enabling help/change	• Brokering access to external interventions • Co-ordinating interventions with specialists in YOT • Providing supervision • Engaging parents in interventions and/or supporting young person • Providing motivation to encourage compliance • Proactively addressing reasons for non-compliance • Enforcement	• Supervision • Reparation • Requirement/component to help young person to change behaviour, e.g. drug treatment, offending behaviour programme, education programme • Combination of the above

| INTENSIVE | Enabling compliance and repairing harm

Enabling help/change

Ensuring control | • Extensive
• Help/change management function plus additional controls, restrictions and monitoring | • Supervision
• Reparation
• PLUS
• Requirement/component to help young person to change behaviour
• Requirement/component to monitor or restrict movement (e.g. prohibited activity, curfew, exclusion or electronic monitoring)
• Combination of the above |

Intervention level	Minimum no. of contacts in the first 3 months of the order	Minimum no. of contacts for the remainder of the order
Standard	2	1
Enhanced	4	2
Intensive	12	4

CHAPTER SIX

Crime Prevention and Youth Support

The prevention of offending by youths has enjoyed a statutory basis for many years. The Children Act 1989 placed a duty on local authorities to take reasonable steps to reduce the need for criminal proceedings against children of all ages and to encourage those in their area not to commit criminal offences.

PREVENTIVE JUSTICE

Preventive justice is a term used to cover a range of orders or interventions which take place at the 'front end' of the criminal justice process generally, in the expectation that it will avoid further or more serious offending or anti-social behaviour. It has an historic pedigree going back to the origins of the modern-day court system and has been applied to youth justice, where the expectation is that it can have a particularly beneficial effect.[1]

The Crime and Disorder Act 1998 introduced a greater focus on crime prevention and early intervention. It also made preventing offending the primary aim of the YJS. It imposed obligations on local authorities to carry out crime and disorder audits and produce crime and disorder reduction strategies. This also involved the creation of crime and disorder reduction partnerships (CDRPs) as between local authorities and police.

Other relevant crime prevention-related measures (but not directly 'criminal') measures) contained in the 1998 Act included anti-social behaviour orders (ASBOs), child safety orders, local child curfew schemes, parenting orders and truancy powers (see below for further details).

The Anti-Social Behaviour Act 2003 built on these measures and clarified, streamlined and reinforced the powers available to tackle ASB.

The measures contained in the above legislation tend to be reactive and some people would say, somewhat punitive, holding young people and parents to account without requiring local services to provide support or intervention to help to avoid the need for such measures.

The Children Act 2004 reflected the government's drive to create a wider preventative agenda for a range of children's services. It gives them a duty to work together

---

1. To use a common but somewhat imprecise motif, by 'nipping offending in the bud'. Apart from the selection of preventive orders in this chapter, such orders also include binding-over to keep the peace (now largely superseded by ASBOs), civil behaviour orders (CBOs) such as football banning orders (FBOs) and the so-called criminal anti-social behaviour order (CRASBO) (see the *Glossary*). For a more substantial treatment, see *The Magistrates Court: An Introduction* (2009), Gibson B, Waterside Press.

to ensure that every child, of whatever background or circumstances, has the support he or she needs to achieve their full potential. It provides for earlier support for parents with difficulties and for children and young people who may be at risk.

Policy on preventing offending

Preventive justice and crime prevention are clearly inter-related notions. Broader prevention aims have become a strong policy theme in modern times across all government departments dealing with children and families. This ranges from safeguarding children, parenting, health and social exclusion to offending and anti-social behaviour. The prevention of offending and anti-social behaviour rightly sits in this broader context, with responsibility for addressing the risk factors associated with youth crime being as much concerned with mainstream services for children as with youth offending teams (YOTs) and the police.

In 2004, the Audit Commission review of the reformed youth justice stated:

> Many young people who end up in custody have a history of professionals failing to listen, assessments not being followed by action and nobody being in charge. If effective early intervention had been provided for just one in ten of these young offenders, average [annual] savings in excess of £100 million could have been made. We found that, although investment in early intervention has increased substantially in the last five years, it is often undermined by pressures to deliver improved outcomes in the short term. But we also found that targeted and well-managed early intervention programmes can be effective if they are properly co-ordinated both nationally and locally, such as those managed by youth offending teams. Better still, mainstream agencies, such as schools and health services, should take responsibility for preventing offending by young people.

EARLY INTERVENTION

Key policy developments reflecting the emphasis on prevention given by the government were set out in the *Every Child Matters* Green Paper (2003), *Youth Matters* Green Paper (2005) and the *Youth Crime Action Plan* (2008).

Every Child Matters: Change for Children

The 2003 Green Paper, *Every Child Matters*,[2] outlined a programme of reform setting out a framework of services that cover children and young people from birth to the age of 19. It included policies to reduce the number of children who experience educational failure, suffer ill-health, become pregnant as teenagers, are the victims of abuse or neglect, or become involved in offending and anti-social behaviour (ASB). Through emphasising prevention rather than responding to crises it identified five outcomes to be achieved for all children and young people:

---

2. (2003). See dcsf.gov.uk/everychildmatters

- **being healthy:** enjoying good physical and mental health and living a healthy lifestyle.
- **staying safe:** being protected from harm and neglect and growing up able to look after themselves.
- **enjoying and achieving:** accessing opportunities to develop broad skills for adulthood.
- **making a positive contribution:** to the community and to society and not engaging in anti-social or offending behaviour.
- **achieving economic well-being:** overcoming socio-economic disadvantage to achieve their full potential.

The Children Act 2004 provided the statutory framework to carry forward the agenda set out in *Every Child Matters* and emphasised the joint responsibilities in achieving the five outcomes above.[3] It placed duties on agencies to work together to safeguard and promote the welfare of children, to share information and develop common assessment frameworks.

To support these aims the government introduced several initiatives to address the broader social problems that increase the chances of youth crime. These included:

- **Sure Start:** targeted services for the up to four year olds and their families in areas of high deprivation
- **ConneXions**: a school-based programme providing support and advice to young people to improve behaviour, reduce truancy and assist in gaining access to education, training and employment
- **Neighbourhood Renewal**: a programme aiming to improve community services in areas that struggle economically
- **Extended Schools Service:** which places greater responsibility on schools and local partners to provide services before and after traditional school hours and holidays
- **Positive Activities for Young People**: diversionary and developmental activities for young people; and
- **Youth Inclusion and Support Panels** (YISPs): provision targeted to support 8-13 year olds identified as being at risk of offending or anti-social behaviour.

Youth Matters
The *Youth Matters* Green Paper of 2005[4] applied the same principles of *Every Child*

---

3. See also *Every Child Matters: Change for Children in the Criminal Justice System* (2004), Department for Children, Schools and Families (DCSF). Both also at dcsf.gov.uk/everychildmatters.
4. (2005). Followed by *Youth Matters: Next Steps* (2006). See dcsf.gov.uk/everychildmatters

Matters, to services for teenagers, recognising the need for co-ordinated targeted services for 13-19 year olds thought to be most at risk. This has been supported by the development of the Youth Offer, setting out a commitment by the Government, through local authorities, to offer every young person 'somewhere to go, something to do and someone to listen'. In order to support this aim local authorities have developed in 2009 Integrated Youth Support Services (IYSS), encouraging collaboration between a range of services including youth services, ConneXions, youth offending teams, education welfare services, sexual health and teenage pregnancy services, other health agencies and organizations working with young people.

MEASURES TO TACKLE YOUTH CRIME AND ASB

What should or should not be classed as anti-social behaviour is a controversial topic and there is a fine dividing line between some anti-social acts and criminal offences. At the lower end there are issues about whether some targeted behaviour is anti-social at all or merely a convenient way of demonstrating that something, at least, is being done about local concerns. However, stemming anti-social behaviour is now seen by politicians in particular as an aim in itself and there are legal definitions to assist courts even if sometimes criticised as relatively vague. The central tenet is that by tackling certain behaviour displayed by young people this should help to reduce the likelihood of progression to more worrying, or criminal, behaviour.

The government's 'anti-anti-social behaviour' strategy the 'Together' campaign was launched in 2003,[5] backed by new powers in the Anti-Social Behaviour Act 2003. The provisions relating particularly to young people included:

- widening the use of anti-social behaviour orders (ASBOs) to allow local authorities, registered 'social landlords' and British Transport Police to apply for them
- allowing police to issue dispersal orders to any group of two or more people, within a designated area, whose behaviour they believe to be likely to cause harassment, alarm or distress to members of the public
- granting police the power to order young people under the age of 16 years to return home after 9pm; and
- on-the-spot fines for noise, graffiti and truancy.

The Respect Action Plan in 2005[6] built on the drive to reduce ASB and focused on its causes as well as law enforcement. Issues identified in the plan were parenting, school, community factors and individual factors. Specific measures that emerged

5. A nationwide campaign run locally, see, e.g. westminster.gov.uk/services/communityandliving
6. See homeoffice.gov.uk/documents/respect-action-plan

around the same time included the use of acceptable behaviour contracts (ABCs) and individual support orders (ISOs). Some further information about ASBOs, acceptable behaviour contracts (ABCs) and the child safety order appears below.

The Youth Crime Action Plan (YCAP or Y-CAP)

The Youth Crime Action Plan published in 2008[7] is jointly funded by Department for Children, Schools and Families, Ministry of Justice and Home Office. The measures set out in the plan aim to prevent youth crime by providing positive activities, greater police enforcement, targeted intervention and greater support for parents. Through tackling broad issues such as poor or inconsistent parenting, domestic abuse, anti-social behaviour, and education the clear aim of the YCAP is to prevent youth crime and anti-social behaviour. YCAPS are also replicated locally.

The anti-social behaviour order (ASBO)

ASBOs were introduced in April 1999 as part of the Crime and Disorder Act 1998. This is a community-based order which can be applied for by the police and local authority in consultation with each other (and in appropriate cases 'social landlords') against an individual whose behaviour is anti-social. The scope of ASB is broad, but for the purposes of a court application it must 'cause alarm, distress or harassment to one or more people not in the same household as the offender'.[8]

Application is made in a civil capacity to the magistrates' court.[9] Such applications are initially civil in nature, but attract the criminal standard of proof even at this initial stage due to the possible later consequences if there is a breach of the order as described below (and as confirmed by human rights rulings).

When the order is made the court can impose prohibitions or restrictions, e.g. not to enter a particular place or associate with a given individual.

Critically, breach of an ASBO without reasonable excuse is a criminal offence. In the case of a youth this carries a maximum penalty of a two year detention and training order (DTO) (subject to the standard criteria for the use of that sentence: see *Chapters 15* and *17.*)[10] This potentially criminalising aspect of the ASBO causes

---

7. For details of YCAPs see justice.gov.uk or any of the other participating government websites.
8. Section 1 Crime and Disorder Act 1998
9. For the argument that such applications might be heard by a youth court, see *Chapter 13, Which Court?*, under *Civil applications: a note*. What *is* clear is that such applications in the magistrates' court have been legitimated by a side wind: *The Magistrates' Courts (Anti-social Behaviour Orders) Composition of Benches Practice Direction 2006* provides that any adult court hearing an application for the making or variation of an ASBO against a youth should generally comprise youth court magistrates (save where this is impracticable or in respect of an interim application): see hmcourts-service.gov.uk/cms/481 Note also the dichotomy that occurs due to the fact that breach of an ASBO is a matter for the youth court since it is a criminal offence (see the text); and that an ASBO made following conviction for some other matter (the so-called CRASBO) (see *Chapter 15* and the *Glossary*) can only be made in the youth court (to which a youth may even need to be remitted by an adult court simply for that purpose (*Chapter 13*)).
10. The maximum for an adult is five years in the Crown Court; six months in the magistrates' court.

some critics to point out that, e.g. many young people do not truly comprehend (or in some cases are not capable of comprehending) the full implications of being made subject to an ASBO. Also, the order itself can last for up to five years, which is 'a lifetime' in the mind of a child or young person; and rather than progressing into the YJS subject to safeguards and diversion schemes noted in other chapters, he or she enters it already, at least theoretically, at risk of custody. Initial behaviour which could never have led to such an outcome suddenly places the youth in real jeopardy. However, the proportionality of the courts response to any given set of circumstances will be highly important; whilst the Criminal Justice and Immigration Act 2008 introduced a requirement for all youth ASBOs to be reviewed by the police and local authority (possibly in conjunction with others) every 12 months which will also serve to ensure that the youth does not lose sight of his or her obligations.

An unavoidable concern regarding the use of ASBOs for young people stems from the fact that, since 1998, there is in effect, a presumption in favour of publicising the fact that the youth has received an ASBO (this by way of an exception to the ordinary rule concerning reporting restrictions on youths: see *Chapter 14*).

Some of these wider issues affecting ASBOs have been addressed by the campaigning group ASBO Concern (see further in the *Glossary*). However, others take a tougher stance, pointing to events such as the tragic case of a mother who burnt herself and her daughter to death in the mother's car having, so it is said, been subjected routinely to ASB by youths with an allegedly inadequate police response. Indeed, despite some signs that enthusiasm for ASBOs beginning to ebb away in the face of suggestions that any crime prevention effect was beginning to be overtaken by ASBOs being seen as a 'badge of honour', Gordon Brown, Prime Minister, speaking at the annual Labour Party Conference of 2009, once again made them a main flagship of Government policy in what is the run-in to a General Election.

Acceptable behaviour contracts (ABCs)

ABCs are not provided for in legislation but are essentially an informal 'agreement' or 'contract'. An ABC comprises a written agreement made between any person who has been involved in anti-social behaviour and their local police, youth inclusion and support panel, local authority and/or landlord and would not normally last beyond six months. They are used with adults as well as young people, and when applied to a young person the YOT or those acting on its behalf, e.g. a Youth Inclusion and Support Panel (YISP), will be notified and thereafter become involved in supporting the youth and his or her family.

An ABC is flexible and can be adapted for use by a range of agencies. It can include conditions that the parties agree to keep and it may also contain the agreed consequences of a breach of the agreement. Where an ABC has been unsuccessful it may lead to the application for an ASBO.

Individual support orders (ISOs)

These were created under the Criminal Justice Act 2003 and have been available since May 2004. They are civil orders and can be attached for up to six months to an ASBO made against young people aged 10-17 years inclusive. An ISO cannot last longer than the ASBO it is attached to.

ISOs impose positive conditions on the youth and are designed to tackle the underlying causes of his or her behaviour, such as requiring the provision of counselling to tackle substance misuse. It can require a person subject to the order to attend a maximum of two sessions a week and can specify the times and places where attendance is required. The YOT is asked to advise on whether such an order is necessary and if so, what the content of the order should be. The YOT must identify a 'responsible officer'[11] who will be then have a duty to arrange the fulfilment (aka 'delivery') of the requirements of the order and monitoring compliance.

Child safety orders

Child safety orders were introduced by the Crime and Disorder Act 1998 (as amended by section 60 Children Act 2004). They only apply to children below the age of criminal responsibility (i.e. nine or under) and can last for up to 12 months.

The order can be applied to a child who has committed an act which, had he or she been ten or over, would have constituted a criminal offence; or where they have behaved anti-socially (in a manner that caused or was likely to cause harassment, distress or alarm to others); or where an order is necessary to prevent such an act.

Designed to help the child improve his or her behaviour they are used alongside other work with the family to address underlying problems. The order places the child under the supervision of a 'responsible officer' from a YOT or childrens' services team. It requires compliance with requirements that the court considers will assist in changing the child's behaviour and is designed to ensure that:

- the child receives appropriate care, protection and support
- the child is subject to proper control
- that repetition of the kind of behaviour that led to the order is prevented.

The order is made in the magistrates' court (family proceedings court) and there is provision to make a parenting order alongside the child safety order.

---

11. For the general meaning of this term, see the *Glossary*.

PARENTING ORDERS

Introduced in 2001 by the Crime and Disorder Act 1998 these can be obtained by:

- an education authority (or others in governing roles in education)
- a youth offending team
- a local authority; or
- a registered social landlord.

Parenting orders can be made in respect of children and young people up to the age of 17 years by a youth court, magistrates' court or Crown Court or a family court or a county court. They can be given when parenting is considered to be a factor in a child's behaviour in the following circumstances:

- a child has been excluded from school for serious bad behaviour, either permanently or for the second time in 12 months
- persistent truanting by a child or young person
- a child or young person displaying anti-social behaviour
- a child has committed a crime.

Parenting orders last up to a maximum of a year and any course or programme specified in the order can last up to three months. They consist of two elements:

- a parenting programme designed to meet parents' needs to help them address their child's misbehaviour.; and
- requirements to exercise control over their children's behaviour to address particular factors such as escorting a child to and from school to ensure their attendance.

LOCAL CHILD CURFEW SCHEMES

A local child curfew scheme is designed to tackle the anti-social behaviour of groups of children and young people. It does not involve the youth justice court system.

A local authority can apply to the Home Secretary[12] for a local child curfew to be imposed in an area where children are causing alarm or distress to others living in a particular area. It can last up to 90 days and applies to children and young people up to the age of 16 years. Under the curfew, all children under 16 years must be in their homes by a certain time in the evening. The power allows police to disperse groups

---

12. Note that this is an executive rather than a judicial act; albeit one subject to the supervisory jurisdiction of the High Court in terms of its reasonableness, etc. Reportedly, such powers have been barely used.

of children or remove those under 16 years to their homes. There is no penalty for breach of a curfew as it designed to protect children. However, children aged ten years and under out after curfew, can be the subject of a child safety order (above).

DISPERSAL ORDERS

The Anti-social Behaviour Act 2003 gives the police power to designate an area as a dispersal area (or 'dispersal zone') where there is persistent ASB and a problem with groups causing intimidation. The local authority must agree to the designation and the decision must be published in a local newspaper or by notices in the local area. The designation can be for up to six months. Police and designated police community support officers (PCSOs) can then:

- disperse groups where their presence or behaviour has resulted, or is likely to result, in a member of the public being harassed, intimidated, alarmed or distressed; and
- after 9pm return those under 16 years to their homes if at risk from crime or ASB or causing, or at risk of causing, such behaviour, and who are not under the control of an adult.

TRUANCY POWERS

Non-school attendance is frequently quoted as a cause of youth crime although the exact connection is less-well documented. Unavoidably, however, the already underhand or 'subversive' nature of staying out of school may itself become a risk factor. The Crime and Disorder Act 1998 gives the police powers to 'pick up', but not arrest, children who are registered at a school and who are absent without permission. They can be taken to a designated area or back to school. This power has been relied upon in occasional 'truancy sweeps' where police and education welfare services work together for a day, concentrating on specific areas, such as shopping centres.

Despite these powers and the fact that in practice schools and the police have been taking a tougher line, figures released late in 2009 showed truancy rates to be rising by a small margin. However, the number of 'persistent absentees' (which the Department for Children, Schools and Families (DCFS) defines as those missing at least one day of the school week) fell dramatically and, according to Ministers at the DCFS, the overall trend was a 'positive one', with some 70,000 more pupils in school on a regular basis than just over a decade ago.[13]

---

13. The figures for current and earlier years can be accessed at dcfs.gov.uk. They require careful study and interpretation and are difficult to summarise by way of simple percentages. This is partly due to differences in levels of absence as between primary and secondary schools and partly the use of the variety of terms, measurements or calculations. Whatever, truancy does appear to be diminishing.

CHAPTER SEVEN

Children Below Ten Years of Age

Debates about raising (or lowering) the age of criminal responsibility (also known as the age of 'criminal capacity') in England and Wales are often clouded by the existence of a relatively small but disproportionately active number of younger children who are sometimes portrayed in the media as being 'out of control', 'feral' and indulging in overtly criminal or seriously forms of ASB. The tabloids like to convey the impression that they are 'street rats' who know 'the law can't touch them'.

Even allowing for the media hype, it is known that they can cause considerable concern to communities (*Chapter 1*). Unchecked, they may well continue to do so well into later life, which is hardly in their own interests, nor those of society.

Welfare versus sanctions
The underlying debate may well be about whether society should, taking extremes, adopt a wholly welfare-oriented approach or one based completely on criminal justice methods. Or if a line is to be drawn, where it should lie in terms of the balance between welfare and sanctions, or the age at which reliance (or greater reliance) on sanctions rather than welfare should depend. The point of underlying importance, it seems, is that there has to be in place *some* effective system to address offending behaviour (or what would be offending behaviour) on the part of all young people below the age of 18, even those who are very young.

As noted in *Chapter 1*, the age of criminal responsibility in England and Wales is set at ten years. This presupposes that, by that age, children can be or assumed to have at least a broad understanding of the difference between what is 'wrong' (i.e. what society deems to be 'criminal') and what is merely 'naughty' behaviour. It also suggest that at ten years of age children are capable of understanding the notion of being held to account for their behaviour by someone other than their parents.

The Crime and Disorder Act 1998, in setting up the current Youth Justice System (YJS) at the same time abolished the earlier *doli incapax* rule which provided that youths aged 10-13 years inclusive, although over the age of criminal responsibility, had, nevertheless, to be shown by the prosecutor to have been able to appreciate the wrongful nature of their behaviour (see further *Chapter 1*).

This was followed by the abolition, by the Sexual Offences Act 1993, of a rule under which it had, until that time, been a presumption of law (incapable of rebuttal by even plain evidence) that boys aged below the age of 14 years lacked the physical capacity to commit rape (and whatever the actual facts).

The void concerning children below the age of ten goes further. Not only can they not be prosecuted for what would otherwise be a criminal offence, but they cannot be made subject to an anti-social behaviour order (ASBO) (see generally *Chapter 6*). So that if it is correct that there is a (hopefully) small, but nevertheless significant, number of under-tens whose behaviour truly harms society, this presents a problem: for society itself and for the children, who are themselves at risk.

INFORMAL AND NON-COERCIVE INTERVENTIONS

Factors which put children and young people at risk of entering the Youth Justice System when they do reach the age of criminal capacity have become more widely understood. Tackling those such as poverty, inconsistent parenting, poor school attendance and social exclusion are increasingly the responsibility of a wide range of services in both the statutory sector and the voluntary sector.

The *Every Child Matters* Green Paper[1] sets out the aims of the Government and the expectation that all agencies working with children and families have a part to play in helping all children meet the five ECM positive outcomes

- be healthy
- stay safe
- enjoy and achieve
- make a positive contribution; and
- achieve economic well-being.

Services offered to children and families which are designed to meet their needs and avoid more formal interventions (such as civil, criminal or family court proceedings) are vast and varied. They can be divided into the categories 'universal' and 'targeted' both of which can also be distinguished from 'acute' statutory services such as child protection. Readers should also note the often voluntary nature of the relationship between the service and the user, except where lawful intervention is allowed whatever their wishes. They can be summarised as follows:

- **universal services** include those *on offer* to all children and such as education and health. There is an expectation that all parents will use these services to promote the welfare of their child; whilst
- **targeted services** are designed to be *on offer* to groups identified as being at a higher level of risk than others. Identification of such risks can be on a geographical basis, a 'unit' basis (e.g. in relation to a particular school), or an individual basis.

---

1.   (2003). See dcsf.gov.uk/everychildmatters

On a *geographical basis* need can be assessed broadly through analysis of aggregated data such as national indices of poverty, crime rates, unemployment rates, health records and so on. Where particular need is identified, services can be targeted at those groups and taken up if those in the 'targeted area' choose to take advantage of the services offered. An example of such services is SureStart which focuses on support for young families in areas of particular deprivation.

On a *unit* basis, need can be identified by analysing data relating to a specific school or group of houses: factors such as truancy or other school absence, ASB, or burglaries. Here, prevention services such as holiday play schemes, youth clubs or, Safer Schools Partnerships, will be targeted to reduce levels of specific behaviour such as ASB and to divert children from the risk of such behaviour.

On an *individual* basis need is identified through schools, health workers, communities, police, housing agencies or other forms of intelligence showing that people are concerned about the behaviour of individuals. Agencies such as youth services, family centres, parenting support groups and so on will be on offer to support parents and children on a voluntary basis.

When services offered on a voluntary basis are not taken up, or when ASB persists, youth agencies have certain other options to explore with families and children before taking more formal proceedings. These include the use of parenting contracts and acceptable behaviour contracts (ABCs) (*Chapter 6*) which, although entered into on a voluntary basis, can be used as a means of evidence-gathering in case there are formal proceedings if the agreements are not kept. ABCs are not legally binding in the sense that a true legal contract is;[2] and although they can be used at any age, in reality the younger the subject, the more responsibility needs to be placed on the parent to ensure the child's cooperation. Any expectation of ABCs has to be 'age-appropriate'.

PUBLIC CHILD LAW APPROACHES

The Children Act 1989 provides for local authorities to apply to the magistrates' family proceedings court for the making of a supervision order or care order in respect of all children under 17 years of age (thereby encompassing, for present purposes, those under ten years of age). Such an approach might be appropriate if the behaviour of the child is such that a two-part test is met, i.e. that:

- the child is suffering or likely to suffer significant harm (for present purposes possibly, but not necessarily exclusively, arising from their own behaviour, e.g. the child is being lured into such behaviour rather than independently embracing it or

---

2. i.e. one backed by consideration or value passing between both of the parties under the law of contract.

that the child may suffer as a consequence of their own behaviour); and
- the fact that such harm is attributable to the standard of care being given to the child or the child being beyond parental control.

At first sight, this use of child welfare protection measures where the individual might initially appear more as a perpetrator than as a victim may seem strange, but is well within the parameters of the Beijing Rules (see *Chapter 2*), e.g. rule 5 ('aim of juvenile justice to emphasise well-being of juveniles') and rule 11 ('diversion from formal criminal proceedings').

Applications for public law orders might be preceded by an application for a child assessment order where the local authority needs additional leverage for its initial investigations.

Should there prove to be urgent protection issues in respect of the child then application can be made for an emergency protection order (EPO) which can then be used to remove the child from its parents and surroundings.

However, as noted in the following below, more direct statutory measures exist, certainly earlier on in the process, so that the use of public law measures to intervene is usually reserved for very particular sets of circumstances, or as a last resort.

Private law cases

Private law cases involving the welfare and upbringing of children are those involving disputes between parents (or in some instances grandparents). They are dealt with under an entirely separate regime within the Family Courts hierarchy.

LOCAL CHILD CURFEW SCHEMES

The Crime and Disorder Act 1998, in its push to reform youth justice, introduced the power for local authorities or chief officers of police, after certain consultations, to make a local child curfew scheme as already mentioned in *Chapter 6*.

Such a scheme effectively bans children under ten years (later extended to under 16 years) for up to 90 days from being in specified public places during specified hours unless under the effective control of a parent or responsible adult.

Failure by a child to comply enables a police officer to remove the child and take him or her home; and then the non-compliance might be used as evidence in other types of proceedings involving an individual child whose behaviour is causing concern.

Such schemes appear not to have found any real favour in practice, but the power does remain to deal (if only temporarily) with specific geographical problem 'hot spots'. One shortcoming is that the curfew does little, of itself, to address the underlying issues in respect of particular individuals. They are also said to be cumbersome in operation such that these schemes appear to have been used sparingly. But sometimes the threat of mounting one may have been used as a preventive measure.

CHILD SAFETY ORDER

As already noted in *Chapter 6*, anti-social behaviour orders (ASBOs) cannot be used for the under tens:. The ultimate sanction for non-compliance with an ASBO is a criminal conviction and those under ten years of age lack all criminal capacity.

The Crime and Disorder Act 1998 therefore introduced the child safety order in respect of under tens where one or more of the following conditions apply:

- the child has committed an act which would constitute an offence had he been aged ten years or over
- it is necessary to prevent such an act
- the child has not complied with a local child curfew scheme (above); or
- he or she has caused, or is likely to cause, harassment, alarm or distress to a person or persons outside his or her household (similar to the test for an ASBO).

There have to be formal arrangements in place locally. Assuming that there are, application can then be made by the local authority to the magistrates' family proceedings court for such an order.

Any child safety order will last for up to 12 months and place the child under the supervision of a 'responsible officer' (in practice a local authority social worker or youth offending team (YOT) member).

The child can also be required to comply with any specified requirements aimed at care, protection and support and also at prevention of further behaviour similar to that which formed the basis for the original application.

Failure on the part of the child to comply with the order carries no direct sanctions (other than the power of the family proceedings court to cancel or add requirements); but non-compliance may help found other types of approach such as supervision or (possibly more likely) public law care proceedings (see above). It may also lead to an application for a parenting order (see next section).

ADDRESSING PARENTING OR GUARDIANSHIP

A lack of appropriate parenting may often be at the root of many problems concerning the improper public behaviour of youths, be it from 'bad parenting', a direct omission of parenting or a parental lack of awareness or understanding of the situation or of the skills required to deal with certain kinds of behaviour.

The Crime and Disorder Act 1998 therefore introduced the concept of the parenting order to address relevant aspects of parenting commitment and/or skills.

The making of a parenting order is not a totally freestanding matter but comes 'on the back of' other court-ordered interventions in respect of youths which are covered as they arise elsewhere in this book. For present purposes such an order can be made either:

- at the same that a child safety order (above) is made in respect of a child aged under ten years (see above); or
- when a child has failed to comply with a child safety order made when he or she was aged under ten years.

Any parenting order (arising here inevitably only via the family proceedings court making or enforcing the child safety order) will be aimed at preventing a repetition of the relevant original actions of the child. It can last overall for no more than 12 months. It has two main elements:

- an obligation which is placed on the parent or guardian to comply with specified requirements for up to 12 months: in practice such requirements are drafted by the court, depending on the individual circumstances, and are aimed again at preventing the original behaviour of the child; and
- a concurrent obligation on the parent or guardian to attend a specified counselling or guidance programme (including possibly a residential one) over a three-month period.

A parenting order will be supervised by a 'responsible officer' provided via the local YOT.

Failure without reasonable excuse by a parent or guardian to comply with a parenting order is a summary criminal offence carrying a fine of up to £1,000.[3]

Should the behaviour of the child continue to give significant cause for concern during the parenting order (whether or not the parent or guardian is complying with such order) this may well give rise to consideration of supervision or care proceedings if the criteria for these are likely to be satisfied.

---

3. October 2009.

CHAPTER EIGHT

Crisis or Watershed?

With its more definite structure, common goal and coordinated approach, the new Youth Justice System (YJS) described in *Chapter 3*, should provide a vastly improved service.[1] Taking the system as it stands, it is possible to identify certain improvements which occurred soon after implementation of the Crime and Disorder Act 1998:

- YOTs were successfully set up and operating as planned
- all the youth justice agencies became 'attuned' to the new arrangements and values
- persistent young offender (PYO) targets were being widely met
- bail support packages were in place
- preventive measures were in place and appeared to be working well
- communities were becoming more engaged in youth justice matters; and
- improvements had been made in the way youths were held in custody.

So, why as early as October 2006 were there media headlines such as the following:

Britain's Youth Justice System in Meltdown *Yorkshire Post*

And why, in June 2008 did *The Guardian* report that:

A shakeup of the youth justice system is being planned by Ministers …

And why did the Government feel the need to create the substantial youth justice changes contained in the Criminal Justice and Immigration Act 2008 which are examined in later chapters. Why, in 2009, did the incoming Home Secretary, Alan Johnson, Home Secretary in succession to Jacqui Smith, working with Jack Straw, the Justice Secretary and Lord Chancellor, announce in his first major speech on youth crime issues, significant action on ASBO procedures (*Chapter 6*) such as:

- cutting delays
- limiting the number of adjournments
- introducing local ASBO 'action squads'; and
- making it easier for the victims of anti-social behaviour to register their experiences with the authorities and to receive support.

---

1. The existing arrangements do of course beg the question posed by Chris Stanley in his *Foreword* as to whether they are the best or an appropriate way of dealing with children (of whatever age) at all.

At around the same time, the Children's Secretary, Ed Balls, said that he hoped to live in 'the kind of society that puts ASBOs behind us'.

A range of views

The answer appears to be based around the fact that, for whatever reason, the earlier measures had resulted in little difference in youth reoffending rates since 1997 and 'record high' numbers of youths being held in custody (3,350 when the *Yorkshire Post* reported, with the average cost of a place being put at £45,000 when the *Guardian* reported).

Various criminal justice related non-statutory bodies made comment such as:

- 'Locking vulnerable young offenders in institutions would only create more problems, not solve them' (The Prison Reform Trust)
- 'With reconviction rates running at over 80 per cent, it's just not smart to create a revolving door of prison and youth crime when there are effective solutions out there in the community' (Smart Justice)
- '[The increasing toughness of the courts] … increases reoffending because overstretched institutions find it harder to rehabilitate young offenders' (Nacro); and
- '… there will be a swing back to a model with the local authority as the prime agency with responsibility for young people in trouble' (Napo).[2]

The increase in the youth custody population appeared not to have arisen from any particular increase in youth crime or more serious youth crime (save possibly for knife crime) but perhaps from the following factors:

- the various statutory considerations when dealing with youth offenders (as discussed in outline in *Chapter 2*) may not have resolved themselves strongly enough in favour of the 'welfare' approach to youth justice
- addressing the PYO issue (*Chapter 6*) may have brought numbers of serious youth offenders before youth courts where a custodial sentence was a distinct likelihood
- measures for dealing with anti-social behaviour might not have been effective enough in preventing youths from moving on to committing crimes – indeed it had been reported anecdotally (and publicly recognised by the Government) that being the subject an ASBO had become a 'badge of honour' in some youth circles
- failure to comply with an ASBO was (rightly but with inevitable consequences) seen as a serious matter and appeared to expedite the 'criminalisation' and incarceration of youths – indeed, in 2006, breach rates in respect of ASBOs on teenagers were officially reported as running at 61 per cent

---

2. See the *Glossary*.

- the range and nature of community-based options for offenders was perhaps not enough for them to operate as credible or effective alternatives to custody; and
- once custodial institutions experience increased numbers, their ability to work with individual offenders was reduced and the likelihood of re-offending on release increased accordingly.

As for knife crime amongst youths, the House of Commons' own Home Affairs Committee on knife crime in May 2009 noted factors such as:

- knife-carrying and use is increasingly affecting children and younger teenagers
- between April and August 2008 in the Metropolitan Police Area 31 per cent of knife-enabled offenders and 27 per cent of knife possessors were aged under 18 years; and
- anecdotal reports of children as young as 7-9 years of age carrying knives.

WILL THE NEW LAW PROVIDE ANSWERS?

The possibility of a further major structural reform of the YJS remains to be seen, although there will inevitably be calls for further discussions about matters such as raising the age of criminal responsibility (with Scotland already planning to increase this to 12 years of age in line with many parts of Europe).

There may also be calls to pay greater attention to the various international agreements relating to children (as considered in *Chapter 2*).

The Children Act 2004 had required local authorities to appoint a director of childrens' services, bringing together the local education authority and social services. Working in partnership under the auspices of a Children's Trust, agencies such as the police, health and childrens' services have clear responsibilities to prevent offending by young people. They have responsibility for the work of YOTs, supporting their targets to reduce offending and reducing the need for custody. Debate began in 2009 about a proposal for that part of the budget of the Youth Justice Board (YJB) used to commission placements in the secure estate being transferred to local authorities who would then pay the full cost of custodial sentences passed in their area. This is a fraught debate, illustrating some of the tensions within the YJS.

For the present, the significant legislative and other changes scheduled to take effect in 2009 (as considered in *Chapters 16* and *17* in particular) will hopefully address some of the perceived problems of the present system, including through:

- the introduction of national youth sentencing guidelines by the Sentencing Guidelines Council (SGC) which should help to reinforce and rebalance the welfare approach to youth offending

- reinforcing the idea that custody is a measure of last resort for youths; and
- introducing a single generic 'youth rehabilitation order' for youths which should provide a much more comprehensive and responsive option for community-based disposals.

On a more novel tack, the 'carrot and stick' approach adopted a new guise with the practice of the police at Torbay, Devon of issuing what they term 'fixed reward notices'. This involves giving out shopping or cinema vouchers to youths who are well-behaved as demonstrated, e.g. by picking up litter or handing in lost property rather than stealing it.

This may be a somewhat more subtle approach to the outright 'tough on crime' agenda of politicians and contrasts with that in some other geographical areas where a zero-tolerance approach is adopted towards crime and anti-social behaviour.[3] But Torbay-style methods, however 'quaint' or traditional they may seem,[4] also have something intuitive about them. They represent lateral thinking and whatever their apparent novelty do demonstrate a constructive, pragmatic and optimistic approach. They are both preventive and 'scaled', which are aspects of youth justice discussed in other chapters. Above all they seem to exhibit simplicity. The issue of where youth justice is heading is something to which we return in *Chapter 18* along with a critique concerning its rapidly growing complexity more generally.

---

3. Leading also to a revival of 'broken windows' theories as applied to youth justice. The idea, that poorly maintained areas gradually sink further and begin to attract offending by people who, e.g. lack normal forms of esteem (including for their locality and self-esteem) is usually attributed to the American criminologists James Q Wilson and George L Kelling: see 'Broken Windows', *Atlantic Monthly*, March 1982
4. One can almost see the ubiquitous Sergeant George Dixon reaching for a top pocket which is bursting with vouchers. But one also imagines that there is far more to the scheme than its newsworthy aspects.

CHAPTER NINE

Summary of the Changes of 2008 and 2009

Chapter 8 looked at some of the factors which suggest that the youth justice system, whilst undoubtedly more 'together' than it had been prior to the Crime and Disorder Act 1998, still needed changes to make it fully 'fit for purpose'.

MAJOR INITIATIVES

A number of modern-day approaches have already been noted in earlier chapters with the sentencing regime as it will exist from 2009 onwards to follow in *Chapters 15-17*. Two other major initiatives now need to be considered before looking in detail at the prosecution, court hearing and sentencing aspects of the YJS. These are:

- **The Criminal Justice and Immigration Act 2008 (CJIA 2008)** This is an extensive piece of legislation which, as its name suggests, covers far more than just youth justice issues. It contains a range of criminal justice measures which affect both youths and adults alike, but also some that are youth-specific; and
- **The Sentencing Guidelines Council's 'Overarching Principles: Sentencing Youths'** This is a youth-specific document but which also reflects the general backdrop of work of the SGC covering a wide range of other sentencing issues.

The measures mentioned in the two points above come together in their application with the commencement of the CJIA 2008. However, some particular aspects of the 2008 Act which are relevant to youths (whether specifically, or as an offshoot of sentencing law in general) came into effect before the general commencement date.[1] An overview of the main youth-relevant provisions and their respective commencement dates is contained in the following chart.

Both the CIJA 2008 changes and the SGC's *Overarching Principles* are considered in greater detail as they arise and apply in relation to the content of later chapters.

Important notice
See also the *Important notice* about commencement and implementation at the start of this book on page xx. The chart opposite should now be read with that in mind.

---

1. General commencement date 30 November 2009 (but see other dates in the chart)

MAIN REFERENCES IN CJIA 2008	SUMMARY OF PROVISION	COMMENCEMENT DATE	NOTES
Section 10	Just because the threshold has been met for the imposition of a community sentence (and just because certain restrictions on liberty therein may be justified) a court is *not* required to impose such an order or restrictions.	14 July 2008	The seriousness of an offence sets a sentencing ceiling but does not thereby fix a sentencing goal.

Lesser interventions than are indicated by the seriousness of an offence may be justified in appropriate circumstances. |
| Section 12 | Although pre-sentence reports (PSRs) can usually be received orally in court, any PSR in respect of an offender aged under 18 years with a view to considering whether the custody threshold is met must be in writing | 14 July 2008 | The oral instead of written presentation of PSRs can be effective in expediting matters but, given the very special considerations around custodial sentences for youths, the need for PSRs at that level to be in writing is retained. |
| Sections 21-23 and Schedule 6 to the 2008 Act | Credit must be given against a custodial sentence for prior time on bail with an electronically monitored curfew (*Chapter 10*) | 3 November 2008 | This is now relevant for youths aged 17 years and above as well as those who are younger than this. |

Section 49 and Schedule 10 to the 2008 Act	Cautions (whether simple or conditional), reprimands and warnings (*Chapter 11*) all now come within the ambit of the Rehabilitation of Offenders Act 1974	19 December 2008	Further assists youths in leaving their past offending behaviour behind.
Section 48 and Schedule 9 to the 2008 Act	Creates the youth conditional caution to mirror some of the adult conditional cautioning provisions.	1 February 2009 but only for purposes of consultation and piloting for 16-year-olds and 17-year-olds	Cautioning as such for those aged under 18 years was replaced by the statutory reprimand and warning provisions of the Crime and Disorder Act 1998 (*Chapter 11*) but has now returned, albeit only in the form of the youth conditional caution.
Section 123	There is an annual review of anti-social behaviour orders (ASBOs) made in respect of those aged under 17 years.	1 February 2009	To check compliance and support available to help compliance. Can lead to application to vary or discharge the ASBO.

Sections 35-37	Referral orders (*Chapter 15*) can now also be made: • following a prior bind over or discharge • on a second conviction (if not made previously) • for a second time in exceptional circumstances.	27 April 2009	Power also now to apply to revoke a referral order: see *Chapter 15* for more information.
Section 9	Statutory purposes of sentencing now exist for those those aged under 18 years: see *Chapter 15*.	30 November 2009	Links with the other factors noted in *Chapter 3* as well as with the SGC's *Overarching Principles*.
Sections 1-8 and Schedules 1-4 of the 2008 Act	Creation of youth rehabilitation order (YRO) as a single, generic form of community order for youths with a choice of 18 specific requirements.	30 November 2009	Replaces the former individual youth community orders: see *Chapter 15* for more information.

Section 39	Creation of the youth default order (YDO) in respect of fine defaulters aged under 18 years: *Chapter 15.*	30 November 2009	Where a court could have issued a warrant of commitment had the youth fine defaulter been an adult, it may, instead of proceeding against the defaulter's parents, make the youth defaulter subject to: • an unpaid work requirement (if aged 16 or 17 years) • an attendance centre requirement • a curfew requirement
Section 1(3) and (4)	Where a YRO is to include intensive supervision and surveillance (ISS) or fostering, this can only be ordered where the offence has first met the custody threshold, i.e. it must pass the 'so serious' test and, thus but for ISS or fostering, custody would actually have been appropriate.		A statutory form of an 'alternative to custody'. Such a form of YRO must be considered before custody is actually imposed. See *Chapter 16* for more information

CHAPTER TEN

Arrest, Detention and Charge

Even before the the UK 'signed up' to the various international instruments noted in *Chapter 2*, long-established good practice and safeguards ensured that youths under arrest for a suspected offence were treated in special ways. The practice of giving a 'clip around the ear' has long disappeared in any physical sense, but the term remains as a metaphor for informal police advice, warnings, reprimands and conditional cautions of the kind described in *Chapter 11*. The decision for the police at the outset of a case now involves a discretionary choice, centrally whether to:

- to speak to the youth informally
- possibly to issue a fixed penalty notice (FPN)
- to question him or her as a potential witness
- to arrest and charge him or her with an offence (possibly giving street bail on the spot to diffuse the situation)
- detain him or her under arrest for questioning which will normally take place at a police station (when he or she may be later charged with an offence); or
- to proceed against him or her by other means (see *Chapter 12*).

Central to to these considerations is the penultimate option above, since this involves the youth in temporary deprivation of his or her liberty at the behest of the police, without charge or the intervention of judicial processes initially, and in circumstances where his or her rights are safeguarded by law but he or she is 'in the hands of the police' and behind closed doors.

The present arrangements are, to a large extent, provided for by the Children and Young Persons Act 1933, Police and Criminal Evidence Act 1984 (PACE) and codes made under the 1984 Act. In particular, PACE Code C sets out the procedures for 'The Detention, Treatment and Questioning of Persons by Police Officers'.

Extra safeguards for 10-16 year olds
The relevant provisions contain extra protections for people *who appear to be 16 years of age or under.* By an anomaly in English law, those appearing to be 17 years of age are, largely speaking, treated as adults and can, e.g. be held within an adult custodial institution (albeit usually in separate facilities: see later in the chapter).[1] The extra PACE Code C safeguards for 10-16-year-olds, inclusive (who for this

---

1. It is assumed in a book of this kind that the full adult provisions need not be set out. They can be found elsewhere in works on criminal justice and procedure or accessed at opsi.gov.uk/acts.

purpose are described in the code as 'juveniles'[2]) state that:

- they are not to be interviewed at their place of education save in exceptional circumstances and then only if the principal of the establishment (or his or her nominee) agrees
- if such an interview is to take place, then every effort should be made to notify a parent, guardian or other appropriate adult' (if neither of the former are contactible or 'looking after' the child) and, unless the delay would be unreasonable, time should be allowed for such people to attend before commencing the interview
- if such an interview has to take place before their arrival, the education principal (or his or her nominee) can act as the 'appropriate adult' unless the suspected offence is against the educational establishment
- they should not be arrested at their place of education unless this is unavoidable, whereupon the principal (or nominee) must be informed
- a duty is placed on the police as soon as practicable after arrest to try to identify a person responsible for the welfare of the child or young person and to inform that person of the arrest, the reasons for that arrest and where the detention is taking place[3]
- the local authority must be informed if the detained child or young person was, at the time of arrest, being provided with accommodation by or on behalf of a local authority
- if, on arrest, a juvenile is subject to a criminal or civil supervision order, the person responsible for the supervision must also be informed
- equally, any 'responsible officer' exercising any form of statutory responsibility for the juvenile must also be informed
- a duty is also placed on the police to prevent detained children and young persons from associating with any adult detainees (subject to certain exceptions)
- there is a requirement that any detained juvenile is not kept in a police cell save in specified circumstances
- any female detainees who are children or young persons must be kept under the care of a woman
- no youth should not be interviewed, asked to make or sign a statement under caution, or a record of interview, in the absence of an 'appropriate adult'; and
- additional provisions exist for juveniles in respect of searches, strip searches and the taking of intimate samples.

---

2. See generally the note on *Age-related Terms and Terminology* at page xiii..
3. Note that this applies even if the detention is in respect of a terrorism-related offence.

It will be seen that, from the outset, juveniles are to receive comprehensive and focused attention. *Chapters 11, 12* and *13* cover the diversionary and prosecution processes and describe fully how criminal proceedings are commenced against a youth by various mean other than arrest, detention and charge.

Extra provisions exist if a juvenile is to be detained in custody post-charge in readiness for production before the court (e.g. where the juvenile is charged on a Saturday afternoon and the next court is not due to sit until the following Monday morning). The police should then, unless impracticable, transfer the juvenile to local authority accommodation except where such accommodation needs to be 'secure' and no such secure local authority accommodation is available.

APPROPRIATE ADULTS

Reference has already been made above to an 'appropriate adult'. This person the PACE Code defines as being (in the following order):

- a parent or guardian (or a social worker if the juvenile is in care) unless the parent or guardian appears in some way to be connected to the matter under investigation, be it as joint suspect, victim or witness
- a social worker
- any other person who has, for the time being, assumed responsibility for the juvenile's welfare; or
- otherwise, another responsible adult aged 18 years or over who is neither a police officer nor anybody employed by the police.

The need for an appropriate adult arises even if the juvenile is legally represented at the time, given that the roles of the appropriate adult and legal representative, whilst complementary in some respects, are essentially different.

The fundamental role of the appropriate adult is to 'safeguard the interests of children and young persons detained or questioned by police officers' (see section 38(4)(a) Crime and Disorder Act 1998).

To some extent, of course, the 'custody officer' required under PACE 1984 will be there to safeguard the interests of children and young persons by ensuring the application of the relevant parts of the PACE Codes. In addition, he or she is under a specific duty to advise the detained juvenile about why the appropriate adult is there and of the juvenile's right to consult with the appropriate adult in private.

That said, the role of the appropriate adult is wider and totally independent and the duties are not that of a totally benign or 'unreactive' observer. He or she must not interfere with or obstruct the course of justice but has certain more proactive functions and responsibilities. These include to:

- be present at relevant key events at the police station such as when juveniles are informed of their rights, searched, interviewed, participate in an identification parade and are charged
- ensure that the juvenile understands his or her rights and that those rights are protected
- advise (other than, of course, on matters of law), support and assist the juvenile
- make sure that any interview is conducted properly and fairly and to inform the police of any concerns in this respect
- facilitate communication between the police and the juvenile
- take legal advice himself or herself in an attempt to assist an unrepresented juvenile, albeit without the right to force any form of legal representation on a juvenile who does not want it.

The role of the appropriate adult is, therefore, an important and responsible one and the Home Office has published its own 'Guidance for Appropriate Adults'.[4]

However, many researchers, practitioners and commentators have made reference to some drawbacks in the existing appropriate adult provisions. Whereas a juvenile under detention would usually welcome the presence of a parent or adult friend or at least of some other adult who is there just for them, it has to be questioned how many appropriate adults, save those specially trained for the role, would possess the necessary knowledge and skills to perform the role fully.

Local authorities and YOTs have a joint responsibility to secure the provision of people to act as appropriate adults but it might be suggested that PACE should be amended to provide that a parent, guardian and a *trained* appropriate adult should be present, unless the parent or guardian is the victim or a witness to the offence.

LENGTH OF DETENTION WITHOUT CHARGE

The usual provisions under PACE 1984 as to the length of detention before charge apply equally to youths as they do to adults and no extra safeguards are provided in terms of timescales just because of the age of the detainee.[5]

Such provisions are already quite tightly drawn in any event and the investigation and questioning processes to which they relate will be much the same regardless of the age of the detainee.

That said, the special provisions under PACE noted above in respect of children and young persons may, ironically, serve to prolong the overall time for which the police may wish to hold a young detainee, e.g. due to having to await the arrival of

---

4.   See police.homeoffice.gov.uk/publications/operational-policing/guidanceappadultscustody.pdf
5.   There are special provisions in relation to terrorism.

an 'appropriate adult'.

However, the general provisions (for both adults and youths) can briefly be summarised as follows:

- detainees usually have to be charged within 24 hours of the 'relevant time' (which will usually be the time an arrested person arrives at the police station although variations may apply) or released on police bail pending further enquiries (such bail can, in appropriate circumstances, be subject to police-imposed conditions)
- a police officer of the rank of superintendent or above may authorise the increase of that period up to 36 hours from the 'relevant time' if the offence is an indictable offence (i.e. indictable only or triable either way such as, respectively, murder or burglary) and such extended detention is necessary to secure or preserve evidence in the case (including obtaining evidence by questioning the detainee) and the investigation is being conducted diligently and expeditiously
- application can be made to a magistrates' court (i.e. the adult court, even in the case of youths) for a 'warrant of further detention' to provide up to 36 hours from the time of the issue of the warrant
- the application will usually have to be made within 36 hours of the 'relevant time' and the criteria to be applied are essentially the same, but to be applied by a superintendent
- the detainee has to be present and has the right to legal representation
- the application will be made on oath by a police officer and the hearing will take place in a closed court (i.e. *in camera*); and
- such warrants of further detention can be extended on application but the overall period of any or all warrants of further detention may not bring the overall court-granted period to more than 72 hours from first grant and cannot, in any event, go past 96 hours from the 'relevant time'.

CHAPTER ELEVEN

Diversion or Prosecution?

For many years a range of measures has been in place which can be categorised as alternatives to prosecution.[1] They include cautions,[2] conditional cautions, reprimands and warnings, fixed penalties notices (FPNs), e.g. for traffic offences or low-level crimes and measures to deal with anti-social behaviour (ASB) (*Chapter 6*). In addition, such alternatives include the involvement of the perpetrator in schemes aimed at 'offending awareness', anger management, drug or alcohol misuse, reparation and rectification.[3] Such measures are prompted by motives ranging from providing 'simple, speedy, summary justice'[4] (including 'simple speedy youth justice' as it has been dubbed: see *Chapter 18*) and other less formal but arguably effective ways of 'delivering justice', to crime prevention, encouraging future compliance and the interests of communities in targeting attention and resources (see *Chapter 5*).

Diverting young people away from the Youth Justice System
The special benefits of diverting young offenders in particular away from the full rigor of the criminal process was identified as early as 1980,[5] when a Government White Paper suggested that many offenders dealt with in the above ways were *less likely* to re-offend if not made to undergo court-based processes.[6]

It has often been said that (just as with too ready use of ASBOs: *Chapter 6*) youths can easily become 'criminalised' simply by being subjected to formal youth justice mechanisms; and that, in any event, they often move on in life very quickly from the circumstances which led to their offending. A feature of some formal proceedings is that there is a disconnection between the events which brought about 'the offence' and the experiences the young person is going through in the courtroom. As it is sometimes put, time can make for greater distance the younger someone is.

The possession of a criminal record (even allowing for specially reduced rehabilitation periods for young offenders under the Rehabilitation of Offenders Act 1974) can have a disproportionate effect on youths as they, hopefully, try to put aside their offending behaviour and move on into mature and responsible adulthood. Despite

---

1. Diversion from prosecution at the outset should be distinguished from diversion from custody and other intrusive forms of intervention at later stages in the youth justice process.
2. Cautions nowadays are for adults only, but 'conditional cautions' are used for youths: see later in the text.
3. Some mainly re adults: see *The Magistrates' Court: An Introduction* (2009), Gibson B, Waterside Press. But reparation is a strongly youth justice-related concept (*Chapter 4*), which is also relevant to referral orders (*Chapter 15*), the youth rehabilitation order (YRO) (*Chapter 16*) and the broader work of YOTS.
4. The correct overall banner is 'Criminal Justice, Simple, Speedy, Summary' (CJSSS).
5. If not before that time. This was an era of often local initiatives.
6. It may often be the case that cause and effect in criminal justice is 'counter-intuitive'.

the stance taken by the 1974 Act (*Chapter 15*) the mere existence of a criminal record may have a disproportionately adverse effect on a youth, especially in his or her attempts to find training or employment. The following options are the now central and regular ways of diverting young offenders from prosecution:

- an informal 'telling-off'
- a reprimand
- a warning (often called a 'final warning')
- a conditional caution (when fully in force for youths); or
- a fixed penalty notice (FPN) (for a limited range of offences).[7]

The Crime and Disorder Act 1998 replaced the non-statutory system of juvenile cautions with the statutory reprimand and warning scheme; whilst the Criminal Justice and Immigration Act 2008 introduces conditional cautions.

Informal 'telling-off'

Just because the police consider that they have secured the evidence to prove that a youth has committed a criminal offence, this does not require them to report that youth for formal prosecution or alternative measures.[8] In certain cases, perhaps where the offending is of a very low level and the likelihood of re-offending small, all that may be required is some form of quick, informal and metaphorical version of the proverbial 'clip around the ear' mentioned in *Chapter 10*.

The term 'telling off' has been used here in the text for want of any other appropriate term (although it is sometimes described using the grander term 'admonishment', particularly historically). It usually involves the police officer concerned in:

- reminding the youth of what he or she has allegedly done
- pointing to prosecution or other action that might have been relied upon instead
- informing the youth that no such action is to be taken (probably with reasons to be given at the time)
- offering the youth concerned, 'words of advice' as to his or her future behaviour; and
- involving parents, guardians, or where the child has been in police detention an appropriate adult (*Chapter 10*) in all of this as and when appropriate.

Any such 'telling off' will not be recorded other than by way of a note in the case file. It cannot be cited in court later on, or for any other formal purpose.

---

7. Sometimes just 'penalty notice'. Note also the term fixed penalty notice for disorder (FPND): see text.
8. This is a well-established Common Law principle: see works on policing and criminal justice.

Reprimands and (final) warnings

A police non-statutory practice of cautioning appropriate young offenders as a way of diverting them from the mainstream prosecution process was established long ago. However, as already noted, cautioning (as such) of youths disappeared under the Crime and Disorder Act 1998 in favour of a statutory system of reprimands and warnings often supported by input from a youth offending team (YOT).

Reprimands

The police can give a reprimand only if all the following criteria are satisfied:

- there is evidence of guilt
- there is a realistic prospect of a finding of guilt
- the youth admits the offence
- he or she has not been previously reprimanded or warned
- he or she has not previously been convicted by a court of an offence
- it is not in the public interest for the offender to be prosecuted; and
- the offence is not so serious as to warrant a (more serious) 'warning'.

Warnings

A warning is often referred to as a 'final warning' as it can be given only once. It can be used if:

- there is evidence of guilt
- there is a realistic prospect of conviction
- the youth admits the offence
- he or she has not been previously warned (a previous warning given more than two years before the present offence can be disregarded if the present offence is not so serious as to warrant criminal proceedings)
- he or she has not been previously been convicted before a court of an offence
- it is not in the public interest for the offender to be prosecuted; and
- the offence is not so serious as to warrant prosecution.

The local YOT will have to assess anyone given a warning and a programme of rehabilitation will be built around it unless this is inappropriate.

Informal support from a YOT may also be offered in the case of a reprimand.

In the case of both reprimands and warnings, the practical effect is to divert the juvenile away from criminal proceedings or any future criminal proceedings for the offence for which the reprimand or warning was given. Such proceedings will be precluded in relation to the existing offence regardless of future conduct.

Effect of reprimands and warnings on a youth's record

It must be noted that unlike the situation in relation to a 'telling-off' above:

- reprimands are recorded on the Police National Computer (PNC) and will remain on it for five years or until the youth reaches 18 years of age, whichever is later
- previous reprimands and warnings (and failure to participate in any support programme arranged) can be cited in court-based proceedings for any later offending by the youth; and
- if convicted of a further offence committed within two years of a *warning* the court cannot make a conditional discharge[9] save in 'exceptional circumstances'.

A dilemma caused by these particular measures for those youths who consider themselves to be 'not guilty' but wish to take advantage of diversion from prosecution is that they must nonetheless 'admit' the offence to the police. By maintaining their innocence they unavoidably risk prosecution. No truly satisfactory solution has ever been found to the possibility of a 'pragmatic choice', other than that a court can question a youth when it comes to sentencing about any reprimand or warning that appears on his record and deal with his or her response as it sees fit.[10]

Reprimands and warnings are usually administered in a police station or YOT office and by a police officer in uniform. If that officer is not a member of the local YOT then a YOT representative will usually be in attendance.

Youth conditional cautions

Although, as noted, the 1998 Act did away with 'cautions' for youth offenders, the practice of cautioning continued for adult offenders and extended into a statutory form of 'conditional cautioning'.

With a conditional caution the adult is not prosecuted but is required, as an adjunct to the caution, to comply with certain conditions stipulated by the authorised person administering the caution.

Such conditions are aimed at rehabilitation and reparation, although a punitive element can also be included.

Failure to comply with the conditions without reasonable excuse could result in prosecution for the original offence.

The CJIA 2008 thus reintroduces cautioning for youths, albeit *only in this novel conditional form*. Consultation and geographical piloting of the scheme for 16 and 17-year-olds began in 2009 but universal availability for youths will, even assuming nationwide adoption, not arrive for some time. Indeed. initially, youth conditional

---

9. See *Chapter 15*.
10. Police officers will explain that they are meticulous in such matters, but there could be many reasons why a conviction would might not result in circumstances where a reprimand or warning was given.

cautions are only being introduced for 16 and 17 year olds and in limited police areas under a 'Code of Practice for Youth Conditional Cautions for 16 & 17-year-olds' prepared by the Secretary of State under section 66G of the Crime and Disorder Act 1998 and the CJIA 2008 (Commencement No. 12) Order.

One conditions which may be attached to such a caution is a financial penalty. The Crime and Disorder Act 1998 (Youth Conditional Cautions: Financial Penalties) Order 2009 Order prescribes the offences and description of offences in relation to which a financial penalty condition may be so attached. The offences and description of offences listed in Schedule 1 of the Table in Schedule 1 of the order include theft, handling stolen property, going equipped for theft, certain offences of fraud and forgery and related attempts to commit those offences. The maximum amount are for those offences, etc. is £75.

The sums which are specified in Schedule 2 are:

- causing harassment, alarm or distress £50
- any summary offence, except an excluded offence, for which a person is liable on conviction to a maximum fine of level 5 on the standard scale £75
- any summary offence, except an excluded offence, for which a person is liable on conviction to a maximum fine of level 4 on the standard scale £50
- any summary offence for which a person is liable on conviction to a maximum fine of level 1, 2 or 3 on the standard scale, other than an excluded offence or causing harassment, alarm or distress £30.[11]

Fixed penalty notices

The Criminal Justice and Police Act 2001 set up what are known as fixed penalty notices for disorder (FPNDs)[12] which relate to specified types of offending such as low level forms of public disorder, theft from shops and criminal damage. The revised (July 2009) levels are: in relation to retail theft items under £100; and re criminal damage that under £300 (both previously being set at higher values).

As far as youths are concerned, FPNDs became available through the Anti-Social Behaviour Act 2003 in respect of those aged 10-17 years inclusive, although universally initially only for those aged 16 or 17 years. There were seven pilot areas relating to those aged 10-15 years. Any universal extension across the country is still under consideration pending evaluation of these schemes.

The obligation to pay a FPND rests with the parent and not the youth.

Other legislation covers the possibility of 'ordinary' fixed penalty notices (FPNs), for those aged 10-17 years, for a wide range of routine matters not involving disorder

11. SI 2009 No. 2781. See the order for the exact details of scheduled offences and the provisions under which those in Schedule 1 exist. All figures given are as at the commencement date, 16 November 2009.
12. As per an earlier footnote, these are also known simply as 'penalty notices for disorder'.

as such, e.g. for dropping litter or daubing graffiti.

In respect of both FPNDs and FPNs the arrangements are complex and there are different sets of guidance for 16-17-years-olds and those aged 10-15 years.

ROLE OF POLICE AND CROWN PROSECUTORS

Since the formation of the Crown Prosecution Service (CPS) in 1985, the underlying decision concerning whether there should be a prosecution lies with the CPS rather than the police (*Chapter 12*). The status of the CPS in this regard was enhanced by the Criminal Justice Act 2003,[13] so that in effect the entire decision about prosecution now rests with the CPS (albeit that the police may charge someone pending that CPS decision which may in any event not be needed for some lesser offences).[14] This is equally, it seems, the case in relation to a warning, reprimand or conditional caution since an 'alternative to prosecution' should only occur where there might actually have been a prosecution (above).

So on the face of things, it is arguable that the police can only really proceed to a warning, etc. where the CPS has, in effect, 'cleared the way' by deciding that, even if other prosecution criteria are satisfied, prosecution would not be in the public interest (*Chapter 12*). However, it appears in practice that police officers generally proceed directly to a reprimand or warning in many less serious cases and only refer to the CPS beforehand in respect of more serious ones.[15]

13. See Part 4 Criminal Justice act 2003 in conjunction with Schedule 2 to that Act.
14. The CPS may apply a lesser 'threshold test' based on reasonable suspicion of an offence for the purposes of police detention: see further *Chapter 12*.
15. There is then the bizarre prospect of a youth admitting to something he or she has not done (see earlier in the text) to the police who, technically, should not be making the decision to warn or reprimand.

CHAPTER TWELVE

The Prosecution Process

Once the police have decided that it is likely a youth would and should be prosecuted they will liaise with the Crown Prosecution Service (CPS) as to the appropriateness of prosecution and concerning the charge or charges upon which any prosecution should proceed.

Following the decision to prosecute

As soon as the decision to prosecute has been confirmed, notice must be given by the police to the local authority and the local probation service (in practice, usually via the local YOT). Each will then, depending on the age of the defendant and other factors, start to make enquiries into his or her home and school circumstances, health and general character, which can then be passed to the court in relation to, e.g. any consideration of bail or, later and more formally in the event of a finding of guilt, through the medium of a pre-sentence report (PSR) (*Chapter 15*).

In theory it is possible for any other public body or individual to start a prosecution against a youth although:

- the CPS can take over, review and conduct (or even discontinue) such proceedings
- in doing so, the CPS will (as it will have done for any police initiated proceedings) apply its own Code of Practice and, in particular, will consider the two-part prosecution test – the *evidential test* (is there enough evidence for a 'realistic prospect' of conviction) and the *public interest test* (i.e. whether prosecution is in the public interest: as to which the Code contains factors to be considered)[1]
- the CPS will also apply the youth-specific consideration in its code; and
- any attempt by an individual to prosecute a youth where the police have already administered say a reprimand or warning (*Chapter 11*) would usually be considered an 'abuse of process' (although prosecution after such a reprimand or warning is not totally impossible in principle if subsequent information shows that the offence appears to be significantly more serious than first thought).

It should be noted that, not only does the CPS Code of Practice have certain youth-specific aspects, but there are also dedicated and specially trained Crown pros-

---

1. Where a suspect is being considered for interview, arrest or detention and the CPS is advising the police (*Chapter 10*) it uses a lesser 'threshold test', i.e. 'Is there at least a reasonable suspicion that the suspect has committed an offence?' For details of this and also the evidential and public interest test, see the Code for Crown Prosecutors which can be accessed at cps.gov.uk.

ecutors in relation to youths. There may also be a youth justice unit (YJU) within the CPS or police administration comprising both police and Crown prosecutors. The Code for Crown Prosecutors states:

> 8.8 Crown Prosecutors must consider the interests of a youth when deciding whether it is in the public interest to prosecute. However Crown Prosecutors should not avoid prosecuting simply because of the defendant's age. The seriousness of the offence or the youth's past behaviour is very important.

> 8.9 Cases involving youths are usually only referred to the Crown Prosecution Service for prosecution if the youth has already received a reprimand and final warning [for a previous offence: *Chapter 11*], unless the offence is so serious that neither of these were appropriate or the youth does not admit committing the offence. Reprimands and final warnings are intended to prevent re-offending and the fact that a further offence has occurred indicates that attempts to divert the youth from the court system have not been effective. So the public interest will usually require a prosecution in such cases, unless there are clear public interest factors against prosecution.

Starting a prosecution

There are several different ways in which a prosecution against a youth (or adult for that matter) can be commenced or the individual brought to court.

Information and summons

Here the youth will remain at liberty and await service by the police on him or her (and on at least one of his parents or guardians) of a summons requiring that he or she and at least one parent or guardian attend the local youth court (or adult court if jointly charged with an adult)[2] at a date, time and venue notified in the summons.

The police will have obtained the summons usually by submitting to the court a written 'information' (essentially an application for the issue by the court of a written summons). This will have been received and considered by a magistrate, justices' clerk or court legal adviser designated by the justices' clerk. It will be checked for matters such as a clear statement of offence, statutory authority, time limits, the next appropriate youth court listing slot and so on.

This process has the benefits of an extra level of (independent judicial) consideration, of involving the parent directly and of the matter being entered directly onto the courts' computerised system. But it can, even where local practices have been streamlined, take a certain amount of time. Against this, there is now a general momentum in favour of 'Simple, Speedy Youth Justice'.[3] Failure to attend court can result in application to the court for a warrant of arrest.

---

2. See further *Chapter 13*.
3. Under the wider 'Criminal Justice: Simple, Speedy, Summary' Justice' (CJSSS) banner: see the *Glossary*.

Written charge and requisition

This is an alternative to the information and summons route that is being phased in across the country in place of the information and summons procedure.

It essentially involves the police serving on the defendant both a 'written charge' detailing the offence or offences to be prosecuted and a 'requisition' requiring the defendant to attend court at a specified date, time and venue.

This covers the same sort of ground as an information and summons would but is considerably quicker as there is no intermediate consideration by the court.[4]

Charge and bail

In many cases it is possible (especially now that Crown prosecutors are regularly based in police stations or on call) for the decision whether or not to prosecute a youth, and on what charges, to be made whilst the youth is still at a police station. This will be subject to the Police and Criminal Evidence Act 1984 (PACE) considerations outlined in the previous chapter; and also the possibility of 'street bail'. As noted in *Chapter 10*, the bail provisions now extend to the granting of bail at the time when a suspect is arrested by a police officer, usually soon after the offence.

In either case, he or she will be released on bail ('bailed') to attend the youth court (or the adult court if jointly charged with an adult: *Chapter 13*) at a time, date and venue fixed by the custody sergeant or arresting police officer. The details are contained in a bail notice which is given to the defendant.

There is a general right to bail under the Bail Act 1976 unless certain grounds and reasons exist (see further below). Police bail may contain conditions addressing matters to ensure attendance, the prevention of further offending, interference with witnesses and so on. Conditions can also be added for the youth's own welfare.

Failure to attend court or to leaving court before a case is called on in the courtroom (generally known as failing to surrender to bail and absconding, respectively) usually results in an application to the court for a warrant of arrest.

Although charge and bail may not be the least intrusive method of commencing a prosecution of a youth (as opposed to an information and summons above) it does have the benefits of initial certainty and speed and it appears to be becoming the method of choice of the police whenever possible.

Charge and production in custody

This is essentially the same charging process as that outlined above at the police station but the youth is detained in police custody pending his or her 'production' before the court. However, note that the PACE provisions require removal to local authority accommodation after charge if feasible and otherwise appropriate and unless the youth is to be produced in court fairly expeditiously: see *Chapter 10*.

---

4. These procedures could be phased in and overtake general use of the information and summons at any time; although certain applications will continue under the existing processes. This is a specialist area.

This procedure, convenient and quick though it may be, should not be used routinely but must be justified on the merits of each individual case.

Warrant backed for bail

If the decision to prosecute has been confirmed but the youth is not in police custody and, say, his whereabouts are not known, then the police may lay an 'information' before a magistrate and ask that, instead of a summons (above), a warrant of arrest be issued.[5]

The warrant can 'backed for bail', i.e. on arrest the police will bail the youth to attend the relevant court in accordance with instructions of the court as contained in the 'backing'. This type of bail cannot have any conditions placed on it.

This process is quite intrusive and should, therefore, only be applied in wholly appropriate circumstances.

Warrant not backed for bail

Failure to attend in answer to bail can result in an application to the court for a warrant of arrest without bail. Similarly, where a warrant is issued at the outset, provided that this is appropriate. On arrest under such a warrant, the defendant will be detained by the police and produced before the court in custody (albeit possibly after transfer to local authority secure accommodation in the meantime).

CRIMINAL DEFENCE SERVICE

As with adults who are suspected of or arrested for a criminal offence the existence of the Criminal Defence Service (CDS) guarantees that people under police investigation or facing criminal charges can get legal advice and representation. It is run by the Legal Services Commission in partnership with criminal defence lawyers and representatives. For further information see legalservices.gov.uk

---

5. This is also known as 'a warrant in the first instance'.

CHAPTER THIRTEEN

Which Court?

The underlying three-part classification of criminal offences applies as equally to youths as it does to adults:

indictable offences (also known as 'indictable only' or 'purely indictable)
either way offences (also know as 'indictable either way'; and
summary offences (also known as 'summary only' or 'purely summary').

However, the mode of trial considerations, i.e. those to determine which court will hear a case are different for youths. The vast majority of cases are dealt with to their conclusion in the youth court (*Chapter 14*) except as described in this chapter.

Which court will initially receive the case?
This depends on a range of situational factors so that:

- if the youth is jointly charged with an adult, then he or she will initially usually appear alongside the adult in the adult court
- if the adult then pleads guilty and the youth pleads not guilty then the youth can be remitted to the youth court for the hearing of his or her case (and he or she has no right to elect trial on indictment in the Crown Court as an adult has)
- equally, if on a joint charge for an either way offence the adult is committed or (or discharged in committal proceedings) and the youth is to be dealt with summarily (see next bullet point), then the youth can again be remitted to the youth court for the hearing of his or her case (again with no right of trial by jury)
- if a jointly charged adult does go to the Crown Court for trial then the youth may also be sent to the Crown Court but only if this is necessary 'in the interests of justice' (e.g. where there is likely to be some common defence)[1]
- a youth may be tried in the adult court if an adult is charged at the same time with aiding, abetting, causing, procuring, allowing or permitting the youth's offence or vice-versa
- furthermore, a youth may again be tried in the adult court if charged with an offence arising out of circumstances which are the same as, or connected with, those in respect of an adult offender who is charged at the same time; and

---

1. Since different outcomes could otherwise arise and problems about which case should be heard first. Also, particularly where older youths and younger adults are involved there may be less incentive for courts to separate them out and with only potential problems for the management of cases.

- production by the police of a youth in custody after charge (see *Chapters 10* and *12*) for a remand hearing can be before an adult court (especially if a youth court is not then sitting), but here the matter would then usually be referred to the youth court as a matter of course with regard to any subsequent hearings.

Variations and permutations on the above can and do arise in practice and great care must always be taken by a court to analyse each situation and arrive at the correct procedural and jurisdictional considerations.[2] In particular, once a youth is convicted he or she can in any event be remitted to the youth court for sentence and must be remitted to it in certain circumstances: see later in the chapter.

Civil applications: a note
Civil applications against youths (e.g. applications for bind-overs or anti-social behaviour orders (ASBOs) (*Chapter 6*)) are, by a legal quirk, not specifically assigned to the youth court and as a result opinions differ about whether the youth court or the adult court is the correct venue for such matters.[3]

SUMMARY TRIAL OR TRIAL ON INDICTMENT?

Save for the circumstances already noted above, the basic position (subject to the four further exceptions noted later in this section) is that:

- all charges against youths must be heard summarily (even if otherwise by definition indictable only or either way, with the youth having no right to require trial on indictment in the Crown Court); and
- all charges against youths so heard will be heard by a youth court rather than the magistrates' court.

Thus even quite serious offences as well as run-of-the mill cases are dealt with by the youth court. This basic position recognises factors such as the greater formality and public exposure in the Crown Court and international obligations to deal with youths in the more appropriate environment of a specialist youth court whenever possible (*Chapter 2*). The level of specialist knowledge and skills required of magistrates or district judges who sit in the youth court is considerable: see further Chapter 14. and the comments in Chapter 18. The four exceptions to the basic rule concerning hearings by the youth court apply to:

---

2. The provisions are positively labyrinthine but court legal advisers are specialists in this area.
3. It is astounding that something so basic remains a matter of debate. Some people argue that a youth court is, technically speaking, a magistrates' court for this purpose, others that only the adult court may act. See also *Chapter 6* in relation to ASBOs and the *Practice Direction* referred to in a footnote there.

- cases of homicide
- cases of the possession or distribution of certain prohibited weapons or imitation weapons where a mandatory minimum sentence of three years applies in respect of youth offenders aged 16 or 17 years
- dangerous offenders; and
- grave crimes.

The question whether the youth court must or may commit to the Crown Court for trial in these situations varies as noted under the sub-headings below.

Homicide *(section 24 Magistrates' Courts Act 1980)*

Charges against youths involving 'homicide', although starting in the magistrates' court or youth court, must always ultimately be heard by the Crown Court.

'Homicide' is not defined by statute but would presumably include murder, manslaughter, infanticide, child destruction and possibly some other less common situations involving the death of a human being.[4] However, it is now generally accepted that, for present purposes, homicide does not include the situation where a youth is charged with one of various offences of causing death in relation to the driving of a motor vehicle, such as causing death by dangerous driving. However, some of the more serious of these offences may well find their way to the Crown Court under the 'dangerous offender' or 'grave crime' routes below.[5]

Weapons *(section 24 Magistrates' Courts Act 1980; section 51A Firearms Act 1968)*

Essentially, these provisions provide that, on conviction for one of the various offences relating to prohibited weapons, a youth aged 16 or 17 years at the time of the offence must be committed to a minimum of three years detention[6] unless there are 'exceptional circumstances'.

Such cases, although again starting at magistrates' or youth court level, are, by statute, ultimately reserved to the Crown Court.

Dangerous offenders *(as set out in Chapter 5 of the Criminal Justice Act 2003)*

Taken in outline, the somewhat complex dangerous offender provisions of the 2003 Act apply where an offender (of any age) is convicted of:

- a 'specified' violent or sexual offence as listed in Schedule 15 to the 2003 Act; or
- a 'serious specified offence' i.e. a specified violent or sexual offence which carries, in respect of an adult, life imprisonment or imprisonment for ten years or more.

---

4. Scotland has a more general offence of unlawful homicide, but not England and Wales.
5. Attempting or soliciting murder is not homicide (as no-one will have died), but the case may still qualify to be sent to the Crown Court as a grave crime or under the dangerous offender provisions.
6. As opposed to five years in the case of an adult.

For present purposes, where a youth (here someone aged 10-17 years, inclusive) is convicted of either of the above types of offence then, subject to detailed statutory considerations, detention for life, for an extended period or for an indeterminate period must be imposed by a Crown Court if it is of the opinion that the offender poses a 'significant risk ... of harm' to the public by the commission of further specified offences.

Youth courts (and possibly also magistrates' courts) may have to take an initial view on the effect of the 'dangerous offender' in relation to the facts of the case before embarking on the summary trial of a youth, although a residual power exists to commit him or her to the Crown Court for sentence if later, following conviction, an assessment of 'dangerousness' is arrived at by the youth court.[7]

The issue of whether or not an offender can be classed as 'dangerous' is relevant both in relation to choosing the venue for trial at the start of the proceedings and also for possible for committal for sentence towards the end of the proceedings after a finding of guilt. The CJIA 2008 added a further criterion that, before imposing a sentence for public protection on a 'dangerous offender', the court must be satisfied that it is appropriate that *at least two years* in actual custody be served.

Furthermore, the application of any potential credit for a guilty plea (*Chapter 15*) against a possible custodial sentence, if indicated (as opposed to actually entered by the accused) at the outset, would also be an initial consideration in determining the venue. For this reason, and also because of Parliament's clear intention that youths be generally dealt with in the youth court, the SGC now advises that the decision on 'dangerousness' be made in most cases *after a finding of guilt*.

Grave crimes *(section 91 Powers of Criminal Courts (Sentencing) Act 2000)*
These provisions apply to youths aged 10-17 years inclusive in respect of any of the following offences:

- one punishable with 14 years imprisonment or more in the case of an adult (e.g. burglary, arson, handing stolen goods, robbery, causing death by dangerous driving and causing death by careless driving whilst over the permitted alcohol limit)
- sexual assault
- child sex offences committed by children or young persons
- sexual activity with a child family member;
- inciting a child family member to engage in sexual activity.

On being convicted of such an offence it is possible for a Crown Court, subject to certain criteria, to impose extended detention for any period up to the maximum permitted period of imprisonment.

---

7. Is this sentence or 'to be dealt with'?' (as it was) and is it affected by dormant committal for sentence provisions?

Youth courts (and possibly also magistrates' courts when applicable: see the start of this chapter) must also bear in mind that:

- they have no power at all to order the detention of ten and eleven-year-olds
- youth courts can only impose detention on those aged 12-14 years, inclusive, if they are a 'persistent offender': see *Chapter 6*.
- there is no general power to commit a youth to the Crown Court for sentence (the only such power being in respect of 'dangerous offenders' as above); and
- the youth court's maximum power to impose a detention and training order (DTO) for those aged 12-17 years, inclusive extends only to 24 months: *Chapter 17*.

Thus, where a youth appears before the youth court (or possibly a magistrates' court) in respect of a 'grave crime', that court must undertake an initial mode of trial consideration and decide whether to decline jurisdiction and commit to the Crown Court or whether to retain jurisdiction to itself. This will require weighing up factors such as:

- the alleged facts of the case (usually taking a 'worst case scenario', i.e. it must be assumed, for present purpose, that the prosecution will be able to prove all aspects of its case as outlined by the prosecutor)
- the likely sentence (inducing, as appropriate, reference to 'persistence' and any previous convictions in general)
- prosecution and defence representations
- any significant 'advance mitigation' not disputed by the prosecution
- the likelihood of a guilty plea (and any possible resulting sentence credit)
- guidance from the Sentencing Guidelines Council (SGC) (see *Chapter 15*) or the higher courts in guideline and other sentencing judgements
- Parliament's intention that nobody aged 14 years or under would normally serve any form of custodial sentence and that any detention order in respect of such individuals should be rare and tightly restricted; and
- the criteria to be applied to determine whether detention in excess of two years would be available; whether there is a real prospect of such a sentence being ordered; and whether there are any particularly exceptional features to the case.

If the court considers that the grave crime test is satisfied then it will proceed to commit the youth to the Crown Court for trial. Otherwise it will proceed to summary trial in the youth court.

SGC guidance on grave crimes

The new SGC guidance restricts the practical application of these provisions by:

- reflecting Parliament's intention that youths should generally be dealt with in the youth court
- advising that only the most serious allegations against youths should be heard in the Crown Court (this recognises the greater formality in that court and also some of the human rights considerations around trial before that court)
- advising that those aged ten or eleven years (where a detention and training order (DTO) is not available: *Chapter 17*) should only be sent to the Crown Court under the grave crimes provisions if the offence is 'of such exceptional gravity that, despite the normal prohibition on a custodial sentence for a person of that age, a sentence exceeding two years is a realistic possibility'; and
- advising that for those aged 12-17 years inclusive (where a DTO would otherwise be available in principle: *Chapter 17*) the test is changed to 'where the shortest term commensurate with the seriousness of the offence(s) is substantially beyond the two year maximum for a detention and training order'.

This has then also effectively tightened the threshold for 'grave crimes'.

REACHING CERTAIN AGES DURING THE PROCEEDINGS

Jurisdiction is also affected if a youth turns 18 years of age during the currency of the proceedings, Similarly, where the court discovers that it made a mistake concerning his or her age at the outset. The following general considerations apply:

- section 48 Children and Young Persons Act (CYPA) 1933 allows a youth court to continue to hear a case in respect of somebody it initially considered to be under 18 years-of-age where it transpires that he or she was in fact older
- section 29 CYPA 1963 enables the youth court to see out the case if the defendant turns 18 years of age during the proceedings, so that it can continue to deal with the defendant as if a youth if it sees fit
- however, if, in such circumstances, any new charges emerge, then those new charges must go before an adult court (which may in turn affect the youth court's decision concerning offences committed when the offender *was* under 18); and
- once a youth court has (where relevant) made a mode of trial decision in respect of a youth or has taken a formal plea (be it 'guilty' or 'not guilty') from him or her then summary trial has been commenced and it is not possible for that aspect, i.e. the venue for trial, to be reviewed if the youth subsequently turns 18 years-of-age.

Special considerations also arise where a youth, during the proceedings, reaches an age relevant for sentencing (*Chapter 15*) (e.g. all other criteria being met, a 14 year old is only liable to detention if a 'persistent offender' whereas there is no such restriction in respect of a 15 year-old).

Other key aspects of the relationship of age to sentencing powers

Case law has determined that the usual date for determination of sentencing powers will not be the date of the commission of the offence or sentencing, but of 'conviction' (i.e. when a guilty plea is entered, or the date when a case is found proved after a trial).

However, the starting point when looking at the most appropriate sentence in practice will usually still be the date of commission of the offence, i.e. youths should generally not receive higher sentences just because they have subsequently passed some age threshold in the meantime.[8]

Remitting youths to the youth court

Section 8 Powers of Criminal Courts (Sentencing) Act 2000 further supports the practice and goal of having youths dealt with in an appropriate environment. In summary, section 8 contains the following features:

- a youth court that has convicted a youth of any offence may, if appropriate, remit the youth to his or her 'home' youth court[9] if different (which is potentially relevant if the youth has offences pending at his or her home court or if the offence might involve the use of local sentencing programmes which need to be considered in detail by youth court magistrates who would be familiar with them); and
- an adult court on convicting a youth must remit him or her to a youth court (its own or the youth's home youth court) unless it can properly deal with the case by way of a compulsory referral order,[10] absolute or conditional discharge, fine or parental recognizance to take proper care and exercise proper control of the youth (see generally *Chapter 15*).

---

8. The usual position is for the statute giving the court power to make a certain youth sentencing order to make direct provision by referring to age on conviction. Thus, e.g. the CJIA 2008 in respect of YROs (*Chapter 16*) provides 'Where a person aged under 18 years is convicted ....'. Similar provisions exist for DTOs (*Chapter 17*). The sentencing powers are then usually fixed as the time of conviction - this has been clarified regularly by case law as the date on which a formal unequivocal plea of guilty was entered and accepted or on which the court formally convicted the youth following a contested hearing. This is now also echoed by the new SGC definitive guidance. However, that guidance (echoing but now technically superseding earlier case law) now makes it clear that, within those powers, the usual sentencing starting point in practice for youths is the sentence that would have been likely to have been imposed on the date the offence was actually committed. Thus, youths should generally not be dealt with more severely just because they have reached a particular age threshold after they committed the offence.
9. i.e. the one for the area where he or she normally resides.
10. Only a youth court can make a discretionary referral order: *Chapter 15*.

Given that many adult court members may have little or no experience in even this limited range of youth sentencing, youths convicted in the adult court are often remitted to a youth court as a matter of routine and especially if there is any doubt as to the appropriateness of the adult court's limited range of options.

Remitting older youths to the adult magistrates' court

Section 9 Powers of Criminal Courts (Sentencing) Act 2000 is also worthy of mention as it empowers a youth court to remit to the adult court a youth who was before it and has just turned 18 years old. This is particularly useful in enabling any outstanding youth matters to be tied up with any subsequent adult charges.

The position in the Crown Court

A Crown Court convicting a youth (other than of homicide: above) must remit the youth to a youth court (the original committing youth court or the youth's home youth court depending on the circumstances) unless satisfied that it would be 'undesirable' to do so. This might be considered undesirable if, e.g. the Crown Court's higher powers need to be considered, parity of sentence across a range of co-offenders who are being sentenced at the Crown Court, or if key facts are likely to be better understood by the Crown Court judge. This then leaves the Crown Court with all its exclusive higher sentencing powers if required, plus those which fall within the lesser range of the youth court if these are more appropriate.

However, by virtue of the Courts Act 2003, Crown Court judges now have the same powers as a district judge (magistrates' court) so could, in theory, presumably sentence as a youth court following an 'instant remittal', effectively to the judge himself or herself. This might have the potential advantage that any appeal against sentence could go to another Crown Court judge (and youth panel magistrates) at the Crown Court instead of involving the expense and delay of an appeal to the Court of Appeal.

YOUTH COURT OR CROWN COURT?
Defendants aged 10-17 years inclusive

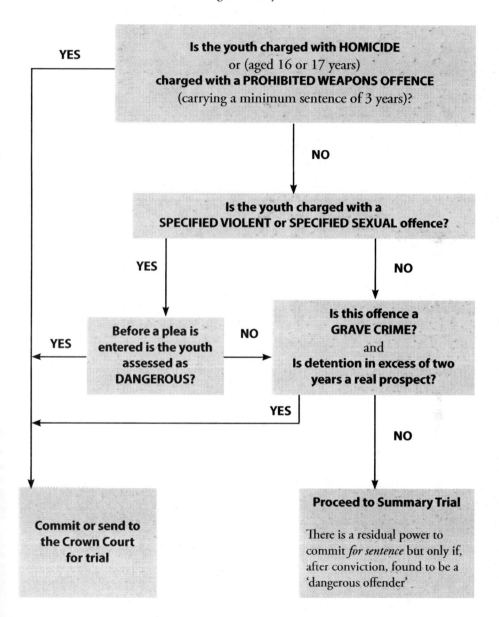

Note: Irrespective of the considerations above (and possibly in the light of them), youths jointly charged with an adult who is to go for trial before the Crown Court may also be committed for trial there if 'necessary in the interests of justice: see earlier in the text.

CHAPTER FOURTEEN

The Youth Court and Some Everyday Procedures

As explained in *Chapter 1*, the youth court has its roots in the Children Act 1908 and the Children and Young Persons Act 1933, but in its modern guise dates from the reforms of the Children and Young Persons Act 1969. It subsequently changed from the juvenile court to the youth court with the Criminal Justice Act 1991 when the age of criminal majority was raised from 17 to 18 years. As also noted in earlier chapters, its role developed in line with the major changes to the Youth Justice System (YJS) brought about by the Crime and Disorder Act 1998 and later statutes.

CONSTITUTION AND MEMBERSHIP

The youth court has a pivotal role in the YJS. Not only does it deal with varying and sensitive issues around children; it also has to apply complex legal provisions and has powers of imposing custody of up to 24 months (see also *Chapters 15* and *17*).

Although district judges (magistrates' court) can sit alone as a youth court, the largest part of youth court work is still undertaken by part-time, volunteer magistrates (also known as 'justices of the peace' (JPs)).

The youth court bench, like its adult equivalent, nowadays has a nationwide jurisdiction. Its local youth court panels are drawn from applicants from the local adult court bench. Such applicants will have sat in court on the adult bench for a minimum of 18 months or more and will have been sitting to hear adult cases. They will already have been appraised in respect of three basic 'competences':

- **managing yourself**, covering, e.g. how he or she manages his or her own learning and development as a magistrate and prepares ahead of a court hearing
- **working as a team**, covering, e.g. how he or she interacts with fellow magistrates, with the court legal adviser and criminal justice services (potentially quite significant re the youth court and local youth offending team (YOT)); and
- **making judicial decisions**, covering, e.g. how he or she structures decisions, takes account of the views of others, avoids prejudice, preconceptions and so on.

Prior to first appointment as a magistrate, all applicants for the bench will have been assessed against what are known as the 'six key qualities':

- good character
- understanding and communication

- social awareness
- maturity and sound temperament
- sound judgement; and
- commitment and reliability.

With this background, applicants from the adult bench seeking to join the youth bench are then assessed against three additional factors:

- **understanding**, e.g. of basic issues around youths and their reasons for offending
- **aptitude**, e.g. for working with such issues in a judicial environment; and
- **commitment**, e.g. to further training for, and sittings in, the youth court.

Applications are made to the local Bench Training and Development Committee (BTDC) or, in the Metropolitan part of London, to the Inner London Youth Training and Development Committee (ILYTDC). Such committees have the option of interviewing applicants (this will be all applicants and not just individual ones).

Such committees (known generically as TDCs) comprise local magistrates chosen by their colleagues and, in recruiting and appointing colleagues to the youth bench, they act as agents for the Lord Chief Justice (they also act in their own right as managers of the local appraisal scheme for all types of magistrates: adult, youth and family).

There is considerable initial and continuing training for youth panel members (including visits to youth penal establishments and community-based projects) and there is regular additional appraisal against the three competences noted above but as they apply in a youth court setting.

The minimum overall sittings requirement of a magistrate (as set by the Lord Chancellor[1] in consultation with the Lord Chief Justice) is the equivalent of 26 half-days a year. But, where a magistrate sits in both the adult and youth jurisdictions, this changes to a minimum of 15 half-days in each jurisdiction (this time fixed by the Lord Chief Justice in consultation with the Lord Chancellor).

However, such is the dedication of many volunteer magistrates and the need to develop their skills and competences that such minima are routinely exceeded.

The route to chairmanship in the youth court is via chairmanship in the adult court, both of which, in their respective terms, require application to the local TDC plus extra training and appraisal against a fourth competence known as 'Managing a Team'.

The youth court is technically a magistrates' court, but is a distinct and specialised part of it. Its basic remit is provided for by section 46 Children and Young Persons Act 1933 which provides that where a charge against a youth is to be heard summarily it must be heard by a youth court and not an adult court (although many

---

1. This is the Justice Secretary and Lord Chancellor. In this context the convention is to refer to him or her as the latter due mainly to the fact that that is how many court-related responsibilities are cast by statute.

lawful exceptions to this have already been noted in *Chapter 13*).

Section 46 also enables rules to be made to provide that various types of applications in respect of youths can also only be heard by a youth court.

No such rules have been made in relation to certain matters, hence the argument noted in *Chapter 13* that applications such as those for a bind-over or anti-social behaviour order (ASBO) in respect of a youth can (or perhaps even must) come before an adult court, although youth panel magistrates might then be rostered to sit in the adult court in such circumstances in any event. The youth court does however have power to make a criminal anti-social behaviour order (CRASBO) following any conviction in that court.

However, those court areas which list ASBO matters before a youth bench presumably argue that a youth court is nonetheless a magistrates' court and that section 46 is prescriptive as to what *must* go before a youth court but not exhaustive as to such matters. This awkward jurisdictional point has already been mentioned in *Chapter 6*.

SPECIAL ETHOS OF THE YOUTH COURT

Given the quite special nature of youth justice, related legislation and good practice have provided special features for youth courts, such as:

- the bench (like the adult court, never comprising more than three magistrates) generally has to comprise at least one man and one woman
- many areas of the country now provide dedicated youth court buildings
- if dedicated youth courtrooms cannot be provided, then furniture will, as far as possible, be laid out in a less formal manner, often with everybody remaining seated at the same level round a large table (see the example on page x)
- youth cases are usually listed on special days to separate them from other types of work that may be dealt with in the particular courthouse concerned[2]
- in any event, courts must take steps in the court building to keep youth defendants separate from adult defendants (unless the latter are, e.g. the youth's co-defendants, defence witnesses or relatives)
- the court must generally require (including by summons, or warrant if necessary) at least one parent or guardian to attend with a youth defendant aged 10-15 years, inclusive
- equally, the court has the option of requiring a parent or guardian of a youth defendant aged 16 or 17 years to attend court

---

2. A former 'one hour rule' requiring youth work to be separated from other types of work by at least one hour either side was repealed although suitable arrangements continue to be made where possible.

- not only should parents or guardians be aware of the orders made against their children but, on occasions, orders can be made against them as well (*Chapter 15*)
- presence at youth court hearings is restricted to members and officers of the court, parties to the case being dealt with and other persons directly concerned with it such as YOT members and representatives of a local authority where the youth is in its care or subject to involvement in its other youth justice services
- *bona fide* representatives of news agencies may also be in attendance (but see below as to what they can report)
- the court may specially authorise others people to be present (e.g. students, social workers or lawyers in training) and there is now a national, government-prompted 'opening-up' agenda in respect of court proceedings against youths so that youth courts are encouraged to be more ready to allow in other appropriate people[3]
- youth court chairmen receive special training in 'engagement', i.e. how to speak directly to youths (usually using their forename) so as to encourage them to 'open up' in court about their offending and response to the situation they find themselves in
- youth courts will explain to youths and parents or guardians what orders they propose making and will invite comments from the youth and these others
- if sensitive matters are raised, the court can require the temporary withdrawal of the youth, parent or guardian
- the terms 'finding of guilt' and 'order made on finding of guilt' are, by statute, to be used in place of 'conviction' and 'sentence' respectively, although this appears to be honoured more in the breach than the observance
- all witnesses giving evidence in the youth court take a different form of oath in which they 'promise' to tell the truth and not 'swear' so to do; and
- all those under 14 years-of-age (whether defendants or other witnesses) give their evidence unsworn (something which applies to children in any court).

SOME EVERYDAY PROCEDURES

Although criminal proceedings against youths have many special features to reflect the age and circumstances of those being prosecuted, there are, as in the adult court, certain broad areas of decision-making and responsibility:

---

3. The Criminal Procedure Rules 2005 provide that unless a court otherwise directs, only the following may attend a youth court: (i) the parties and their legal representatives, (ii) a defendant's parents, guardians or another supporting adult, (iii) witnesses, (iv) anyone directly concerned in the case, and (v) a representative of a news-gathering or reporting organization: see later in the chapter. The government's informal 'opening-up' agenda (which also applies to family courts) has not pleased everyone. Some critics claim it could breach human rights, especially those re family and private life in Article 8: see *Chapter 2*.

- case management
- remands
- arriving at a verdict; and
- enforcement of orders.

Certain other common procedures are noted in other chapters, such as that in relation to mode of trial (*Chapter 13*), anti-social behaviour orders (*Chapter 6*), assessment by a YOT and those affecting sentencing, including the giving of reasons and explanations for decisions and determinations made therein (*Chapters 15, 16* and *17*).

Case management

The need to progress cases against youths quickly through the criminal courts is well established and the former special arrangements in relation to persistent young offender (PYOs) have already been mentioned in *Chapter 6*.

Many modern-day processes reflect the work of the Criminal Procedure Rule Committee headed by the Lord Chief Justice. The Criminal Procedure Rules 2005 (as amended) now make extensive provision for the management of criminal cases against both adults and youths, with special additional factors relating to cases against youths. The stated overriding objective of the 2005 rules is that all criminal cases be dealt with 'justly', which expressly includes:

- acquitting the innocent and convicting the guilty
- dealing with the prosecution and the defence fairly
- recognising the rights of a defendant, particularly those under Article 6 of the European Convention On Human Rights ('fair trial': *Chapter 2*)
- respecting the interests of witnesses and victims and keeping them informed of the progress of the case
- dealing with the case efficiently and expeditiously
- ensuring that appropriate information is available to the court when bail and sentence are considered; and
- dealing with the case in ways that take into account matters such as gravity, complexity, the consequences for the defendant (including the severity of any sentence) and other people affected and the needs of other cases.

In furtherance of the overriding objective of dealing with cases justly, all participants in criminal proceedings are required to:

- prepare and conduct the case in accordance with the overriding objective
- comply with the rules, practice directions and directions made by the court; and
- inform the court and all parties at once of any significant failure (whether or not

that participant is responsible for that failure), to take any procedural step required by the rules, any Practice Direction or any direction of the court (a failure is significant if it might hinder the court in furthering the overriding objective above).

Further special provisions in respect of criminal proceedings against youths in the 2005 Rules include matters such as:

- the right of a parent or guardian (or possibly a relative or other responsible person) to assist an unrepresented youth
- a specific duty on the court to explain (in simple language suitable to the youth's age and understanding) the nature of the proceedings, the substance of the charge and, if found guilty, how the court proposes to deal with the case and the effect of any order or proposed order
- a specific duty on the court to make sure, at the end of the prosecution evidence, that there is a case to be answered by the youth
- specific rights, at various stages, for the youth and parents to address the court and make a statement or representations; and
- a specific obligation on a court, before sentencing, to consider, and if needs be call for, information about general conduct, home surroundings, school record, and medical history (see also the note on pre-sentence reports (PSRs) in *Chapter 15*).

A youth-specific criminal case management framework (i.e. a practical guide to operating the 2005 Rules in respect of youths) to follow that already in place for the adult court is still awaited, although, for the present at least, many aspects of the existing adult framework can readily be applied to youth cases.

Reporting restrictions

Although, as noted above, the press has the right to be present at youth court hearings, the Children and Young Persons Act 1933 places automatic restrictions of what may be reported in respect of such hearings and prohibits:

- anything which reveals the name, address or school of not just any youth defendant but also of any youth concerned in the proceedings be it as victim, witness and so on
- any particulars likely to lead to the identification of the above; and
- the publication of any picture relating to any of the above.

Youth courts are given the power to dispense, to a specified extent, with the prohibitions relating to youth defendants once convicted, if satisfied that it is 'in the public interest'. The parties to the proceedings, and the press, may make representations in this regard. This form of dispensation is increasingly being sought or used as the youth court 'opens up' its doors.

Equally, dispensation can be given in respect of any other youth 'concerned' in the proceedings, particularly if it is necessary to avoid any injustice to them.

Where youths appear in adult courts, be it as a defendant, victim or witness, then no such automatic restrictions apply but section 39 Children and Young Persons Act (CYPA) 1933 enables that court to impose (and subsequently remove) similar restrictions if and when it considers this to be appropriate. The same applies to proceedings in relation to anti-social behaviour (ASB) by youths where the general rule against reporting has been removed so as to allow general 'naming and shaming' unless the court actively bars this, in line with the government's Respect agenda.[4]

Revised guidance on 'Reporting Restrictions in the Criminal Courts' was published in 2009 jointly by the Judicial Studies Board, Newspaper Society, Society of editors and Times Newspapers Ltd: see jsboard.co.uk.

Remands

Effective case management should serve to reduce delays and thus the time youths spend remanded on bail or in custody pending finalisation of the case. Mostly speaking, the Bail Act 1976 applies equally to defendants of all ages:

- there is a general presumption in favour of bail
- similarly that such bail will not have any conditions placed on it
- conditions can be placed on bail only if justified within the criteria set under the 1976 Act (e.g. the likelihood of failure to surrender to custody, of committing offences on bail or of interfering with witnesses); and
- bail can be refused only if justified within the criteria set under the 1976 Act (as amended)(e.g. likelihood of failure to surrender to custody, of committing offences on bail or of the defendant interfering with witnesses).

The provisions of the 1976 Act (as amended by the CJIA 2008) are complex, lengthy and depend whether the offence charged is:

- an indictable only or either way offence
- a summary only imprisonable offence; or
- a summary only non-imprisonable offence.

It is not possible here to cover the minutiae of the Bail Act 1976,[5] but some special features relating to youths need to be highlighted:

---

4. See section 1(10D) and 1C(9C) Crime and Disorder Act 1998. This concerns the so-called CRASBO (see *Chapter 15* and the *Glossary*). The youth court proceedings themselves still cannot be reported on.
5. See specialist works on criminal procedure and bail.

- it has already been noted (see *Chapter 10*) that youths aged 17 years are generally treated as adults for remand purposes (so, for instance, if remanded in custody, they will always go into a remand centre or young offender institution in the prison system and not any form of local authority accommodation)
- whereas it is possible to refuse bail to adults for their 'own protection' the corresponding test for youths is (the wider) their 'own welfare'
- any youth aged 10-16 years inclusive will, if refused bail, *prima facie* be remanded to local authority accommodation
- bail-type conditions can be placed on those remanded to local authority accommodation
- in the case of those aged 12-16 years (inclusive) remanded to local authority accommodation, such conditions can include electronic tagging in certain situations
- for girls aged 12-16 years (inclusive) it is possible, in certain circumstances, for the court to add a 'security requirement' to a remand to local authority accommodation which will result in the girl being placed in a secure children's unit
- for boys aged 12-14 years (inclusive) it is possible, in certain circumstances, for the court to add a 'security requirement' to a remand to local authority accommodation which will result in the boy being placed in a secure children's unit
- if the 'security requirement' considerations are satisfied in respect of a boy aged 15-16 years (inclusive) this will result in the boy going into a remand centre or young offender institution unless deemed to be 'vulnerable'.

In addition, for certain repeat or serious offenders it is possible to impose an intensive supervision and surveillance (ISS) programme at the remand stage.

The ISSP is not a creature of statute but a package of measures created by the Youth Justice Board (YJB) against its own criteria, which is then offered to the court in appropriate circumstances.[6]

It comprises 25 hours of supervision per week with special surveillance measures (which can involve electronic tagging where available) in addition to any other bail conditions or even a remand to local authority accommodation.

It will be seen then that the non-bail remand regime for youths is progressive and based on a number of factors including risk, age, sex and personal needs. It is, at the same time, rather like the mode of trial provisions, somewhat labyrinthine.

Arriving at a verdict

The core process for determining whether or not a criminal charge against a youth is established is, for most purposes, identical to that in respect of an adult, albeit subject to the various embellishments, safeguards and protections noted elsewhere

---

6. ISS programmes in fact pre-dates the YJB and were a common local practice by 1998.

in this book. Centrally, the prosecutor must prove the case against the youth and to the required standard of proof, beyond reasonable doubt. The order of events (as laid down in the Criminal Procedure Rules 2005, as amended) can be summarised as follows. The court legal adviser (or in some places the court chair) will:

- read the allegation to the youth
- explain the allegation and the procedure for the hearing to the youth in terms that he or she can understand
- make sure that the youth has been advised about the potential (beneficial) effect on sentence of a guilty plea, i.e. in terms of credit: see *Chapter 15*
- ask whether the youth intends pleading guilty or not guilty; and
- formally take the plea accordingly

If the plea is one of guilty (and it appears to be clear and unequivocal) then the court will proceed to consider sentence (technically, courts do not 'sentence' youths but, rather, make 'an order on a finding of guilt': above).

If the plea is one of not guilty then the procedure will be broadly as follows:

- the prosecutor may summarise the prosecution case and identify any relevant matters of law or fact
- any facts formally agreed between the two parties, prosecution and defence, may be introduced by the legal representatives (or later as appropriate)
- prosecution witnesses will be called in turn by the prosecution, examined in chief by the prosecutor, cross-examined by the defence and then if applicable, re-examined by the prosecution
- any agreed written statements of witnesses will be received when appropriate
- at the end of the prosecution case the court will deal with any consideration as to whether there is a case to answer (or alternatively whether there is no evidence at all of a particular ingredient of the offence, or whether the prosecution evidence has already been discredited by this stage through, e.g. cross-examination)
- assuming that there is a case to answer, the legal adviser (or court) will explain the youth's right to give and call evidence and the possible effect if the youth does not give evidence or refuses to answer a question if giving evidence[7]
- if the youth is to give evidence himself or herself then he or she will give evidence before any other defence witnesses
- he or she and any other defence witness will be called in turn and examined in chief by the defence, cross-examined by the prosecution and then, if applicable,

---

7. Since 1998, appropriate inference can be drawn from silence at or before the trial.

re-examined by the defence

- the defence may then make a closing address, dealing with any matters of fact or law which are relevant to the case
- the prosecution has a right of reply on matters of law only (which may include the argument that there *is* evidence to prove the case beyond reasonable doubt)
- the defence has a right of reply to any such matters raised by the prosecutor; and
- the youth court will then, having considered the evidence and submissions, and having received any necessary advice from its legal adviser, either find the case not proved, and acquit the youth or will find the case proved beyond reasonable doubt and find the youth guilty (when it will then consider 'sentence': *Chapter 15*).

Enforcement of youth court orders

Relevant enforcement provisions are noted against specific orders in the following two chapters but, for the present, the enforcement of financial orders (fines, compensation and costs) against youths merits some immediate consideration.

An original financial order of the youth court will also state who is to pay:

- if the youth was aged 10-15 years (inclusive) then the court is required to order the parent or guardian to pay unless he or she cannot be found or it would otherwise be 'unreasonable' in the circumstances (if the youth is in local authority care then the order will be against the authority); and
- if the youth was aged 16-17 years (inclusive) then the court has a discretion whether or not to order the parent, guardian or local authority (as appropriate) to pay.

In any case then, where the obligation to pay has remained with the youth in person and there is a subsequent 'wilful and persistent' failure to pay on the youth's part (which would have permitted committal to custody for default in the case of an adult) then it possible for the court to order:

- the parent or guardian to enter into a recognizance to ensure payment of the sum outstanding; or
- the transfer to the parent or guardian of the duty to pay the outstanding amount.

Schedule 7 to the Criminal Justice and Immigration Act 2008 introduced, with effect from 30 November 2009, a new youth default order (YDO). By such an order the court may, instead of proceeding as above (and subject to certain provisions and any age criteria) make one of the following requirements which could otherwise be found in the new youth rehabilitation order (YRO) (see generally *Chapter 16*):

- an unpaid work requirement
- an attendance centre requirement; or
- a curfew requirement.

As with an order for committal to prison for default re an adult, it is possible to postpone imposition of the above requirements on such terms as the court, having held a formal enquiry into the defaulting youth's means, thinks appropriate. Any such requirements can also be enforced, amended or revoked much as if made under a YRO. This new YDO fits in with the 'young adult offender' approach to some older youths as per the note on *Age-related Terms and Terminology* (page xiii).

THE YOUTH COURT BENCH BOOK

A *Youth Court Bench Book* is provided to all youth court magistrates and their court legal advisers. This loose-leaf resource is provided by the Judicial Studies Board (JSB) in consultation with interested parties. It contains a wide range of advice, guidance, materials and sample procedures which can all be accessed at jsboard. co.uk.[8] Readers should be aware that in view of the substantial changes described in this book updating of this bench book is understood to be under way and a new version is expected as soon as this is complete.

APPEALS AGAINST DECISIONS OF THE YOUTH COURT

Youths have a right of appeal against a finding of guilt or order made on such a finding. This is to the Crown Court, where a judge and two youth court magistrates hear and determine the case afresh.[9] There is no ordinary appeal in respect of case management or venue for trial, but an application for judicial review by the High Court is possible, or a 'case stated' for the opinion of that court on a point of law.

At the Crown Court, the judge will have precedence in respect of matters of law although the youth court magistrates sitting with him or her have an equal say on matters relating to the facts, general merits and sentence. The final decision is by a straight majority but, in the case of a tie, the judge has a casting vote.

Clearly, magistrates will not sit on a case which they personally heard first time round in the youth court (i.e. out of fairness: see generally *Chapter 2*) but they can sit on cases heard by their local colleagues. The Crown Court will, however, hear appeals from a number of youth courts and not just those from the court from which a particular magistrate sitting on an appeal might come.

---

8. It follows the format of the *Adult Court Bench Book* given to all magistrates (see jsboard.co.uk).
9. *De novo* as it is often described.

CHAPTER FIFTEEN

'Sentencing'

Despite the existence diversionary measures of the kind discussed in *Chapter 11*, in England and Wales the official response to offending behaviour by people aged 10-17 years (inclusive) is still predominantly by way of a criminal prosecution. However, many youth court sentencing outcomes, whilst often involving sanctions, of the kind described in this and the following two chapters are intended to be rehabilitative, supportive and aimed at preventing re-offending.

Orders made on a finding of guilt

The youth court tones down the criminalisation and punishment of youths by avoiding the words 'conviction' and 'sentence' in favour of (the more cumbersome) 'finding of guilt' and 'order made on a finding of guilt'. Hence 'sentence' appears in inverted commas in the title to this chapter. Although the word sentence is routinely used by judges, magistrates and youth justice practitioners,[1] the underlying distinction serves to remind all concerned that, although a criminal prosecution model is being followed, its application is significantly different in a youth justice context. For the most part, this book uses the term 'sentence' as others do for ease and convenience, but readers should always bear in mind that what is really under discussion are orders of the kind described.

OVERARCHING CONSIDERATIONS

Certain wider considerations come into play when courts are making such orders:

- the 'principal aim' of the YJS, which is to prevent offending: *Chapter 3*
- the 'just deserts' approach based on 'seriousness' which stems from the Criminal Justice Act 1991 (and is now contained in the Criminal Justice Act 2003)
- the 'welfare' of children and young persons as provided for by section 44 Children and Young Persons Act 1933 which is set out in *Chapter 3*; and
- the new statutory purposes of sentencing youths described in this chapter.

At first sight it is not that easy to reconcile or blend these sometimes competing considerations. Fortunately the SGC's *Overarching Principles*: Sentencing Youths (2009)[2] and a new section 142A Criminal Justice Act 2003 (as added by the Criminal

---

1. Section 59 CYPA 1933. 'Sentence' is still often (mis)used in legislation (and by the SGC). The effect of s.59 is to 'construe' all such references as 'findings' and 'orders'. But it applies only to cases 'dealt with summarily'.
2. As noted elsewhere these are usually abbreviated in the text to the SGC's *Overarching Principles*.

Justice and Immigration Act 2008) show how this can and should occur.

Leaving aside for the present those special sentencing considerations which may apply in relation to certain cases heard by the Crown Court (*Chapter 13*), the general position concerning cases coming before the youth court for sentence is that:

- the 'seriousness of the offence' (and any associated offences) including considerations around 'culpability' and 'harm' (see below) effectively sets the 'sentencing ceiling', i.e. whatever else may come into play, the restrictions on liberty (whether or not the sentence is a custodial one or a community-based one) cannot be greater than is commensurate with the seriousness of the offence or offences concerned
- the court will then, taking into account the SGC's 'Youth Sentencing Guidelines', balance the principal aim of the YJS, welfare and statutory purposes; and
- it will adopt a structured approach to such decision-making (see later in the chapter).

Although following a structured approach is essential to ensure fairness and completeness and to underpin the formulation of reasons in support of sentencing decisions, the SGC guidelines (see further below) reflect the widely recognised position that orders against youths should be 'individually tailored' to the individual's offending and personal circumstances (including aspects of maturity). This is so even if this might otherwise challenge some conventional considerations around parity of sentencing and general consistency from case-to-case.

The SGC guidelines also stress that the sentence on a youth will generally be significantly *less severe* than that imposed on an adult for comparable offending, although as age and maturity advance that difference will generally be reduced.

AGE-RELATED SENTENCING POWERS

Age-related provisions are a recurring feature of this work including in relation to terminology (see *Age-related terms and Terminology* at page xii), jurisdiction and a range of powers, including sentencing powers as the chart at the end of this chapter demonstrates. They can also give rise to many procedural and other issues in respect of youths and particular care should always be taken to check the relevant statutory provisions and any guideline cases.

Where age-related criteria affect the availability of a given sentence or outcome[3] the basic statutory rule is to focus on the date of 'conviction' (i.e. that on which the youth was found guilty after a trial or on which a plea of guilty was formally entered and accepted. However, the stance of the SGC's *Overarching Principles* is to reiterate earlier case law to the effect that the *starting point* for sentencing should be the

---

3. e.g. in relation to sentence-related powers vis-a-vis parents or guardians: see later in the chapter.

sentence the youth would have been likely to have received at the time the offence was committed by him or her. But this is only a starting point and in appropriate circumstances, courts may use sentences available as at the time of conviction.

Where a youth becomes an adult during the course of the case

Where a defendant was convicted whilst still a youth but has already reached the age of 18 years by the time sentence falls to be imposed, then as already explained in *Chapter 13*, the youth court has power to remit the offender to the adult court for sentence. This may be of particular relevance if new and later offences are before the adult court. The adult court will then have available to it the full range of adult sentencing options in respect of the youth court matters (although it will no doubt still wish to take account of the fact that the offender was a 'mere youth' when he or she committed the offence). Alternatively, the youth court may retain jurisdiction and exercise its own youth court sentencing powers (but cannot use adult powers).

THE REFERRAL ORDER

Before looking at the structure of youth sentencing as such, it is necessary to consider the referral order. This provides a form of quasi-sentencing disposal which has its own fixed rules. It applies at the lower of the overall scale and involves the otherwise structured approach to sentencing being by-passed in favour of the application of its own criteria by a youth offender panel (YOP) of the kind noted in *Chapter 3*.[4]

Referral orders were introduced by the Youth Justice and Criminal Evidence Act 1999 but are now found in the Powers of Criminal Courts (Sentencing) Act 2000. Essentially they involve the youth court in referring the offender to the YOP. The relevant powers were significantly amended by the Criminal Justice and Immigration Act 2008.[5] They apply where:

- the offender is aged under 18 years
- the sentence is not fixed by law
- the court does not propose ordering an absolute discharge
- the court does not propose ordering a custodial sentence; and
- the court does not propose making a hospital order.[6]

In the following additional circumstances the compulsory referral conditions will be satisfied and the court *must* make a referral order, i.e. where:

4. See also that chapter for some variations in terminology concerning YOPs and YOP members.
5. Since 30 November 2009. See generally CJIA, sections 35-37.
6. i.e. under mental health legislation: see specialist works. Such orders are uncommon in the youth court.

- an offence before the court is an imprisonable offence
- the youth has pleaded guilty to that offence and also to all of any connected offences (i.e. offences falling to be dealt with at the same time); and
- he or she has no previous convictions in the UK other than for any offences now connected and falling to be dealt with at the same time.

Discretionary referral order

Even if the compulsory referral order conditions not be met, the court still has a discretion to consider making one (and irrespective of whether or not an offence is imprisonable). These discretionary powers apply where the youth has pleaded guilty to the offence (or, under these conditions, to at least one of the offences if there were more than one) and *any one* of the following criteria is also met, i.e. he or she has:

- no previous convictions in the UK other than for any offences now connected and falling to be dealt with at the same time
- been dealt with by a court in the UK for an offence on only one previous occasion and was then not made subject to a referral order; or
- been dealt with by a UK court for an offence on one or more previous occasions but has been made the subject of a referral order on only one previous occasion and a YOT or probation officer now recommends a referral order and the court is satisfied that there are 'exceptional circumstances'.[7]

The referral decision, the process from here on and its general effect

It can thus be seen that in straightforward cases the court might very quickly and easily be able to conclude that it either must make a mandatory order or will not make a discretionary one. It can then move straight to addressing the referral conditions (above) without the need to embark on a full sentencing exercise.

In discretionary cases its task may be more complex, particularly where a substantial sentence might be the alternative. There are also cases where it will lose or may need to consider declining jurisdiction altogether. These situations or potential situations and their complexities have already been addressed in *Chapter 13*.[8]

However and in general, given that the court must send the panel details of the offence or offences concerned, it will no doubt wish to make sure of the basic facts of the case and, where appropriate, of any mitigation that would be put forward had there been a trial and sentence, so that these can be passed on to the YOP.

---

7. This third (tightly drawn) criterion may give rise to some confusion given how it is expressed in statute (see section 35 CJIA 2008 which amends section 17 Powers of Criminal Courts (Sentencing) Act 2000). Presumably, the court could still make a referral order under it even if a referral order had not been made on any of two or more previous occasions, so long as it is now duly recommended and the circumstances are exceptional. Case law or guidance is however awaited.
8. The considerations in *Chapter 13* will in some instances need to be 'cross-fertilised' with those re referral orders.

If there is any doubt (particularly where the discretionary conditions apply) then the court may well consider it advisable to follow the fully, structured sentencing approach and to obtain a pre-sentence report (PSR) if and as necessary.

On making a referral order the court may add ancillary orders such as compensation and costs against the youth but cannot also make the youth subject to most other sentencing disposals. The parent may also be made subject to a parenting order but cannot be bound over to take and exercise proper control over the youth.

The effect of a referral order is to require the youth to attend meetings with the youth offender panel (YOP).

Save where it would be 'unreasonable', parents or guardians must also be required by the court to attend the YOP if the youth is aged 10-15 years (inclusive), with a discretion for the court to order parental attendance in the case of 16 or 17-year-olds.

Having been ordered to attend, parents who fail to do so can, if not otherwise subject to a parenting order, be referred by the YOP to the youth court which can then make a parenting order if satisfied that the failure is without reasonable excuse and that making an order would help prevent further offending.

Youth offender contract

At the first meeting of the youth, his or her parents or guardians and the YOP an attempt will be made to agree with the youth what is known as a 'youth offender contract', i.e. a programme aimed largely, but not necessarily exclusively, at preventing further offending and which may include matters such as reparation, mediation with the victim, unpaid work, school attendance, restrictions on movement and association and so on.

The contract will take account of the circumstances of the offence or offences that gave rise to the order and will ensure that any programme does not become disproportionate or interfere with school or religious considerations.

The contract will take effect for such period between three and 12 months as originally stipulated by the court. Its length will be based largely on the seriousness of the offence or offences concerned but may, while still in force and if originally for less than 12 months, be referred back to the court for an extension of up to three months, but not so as to take the overall period over 12 months. The SGC's *Overarching Principles* (see the *Appendix* to this work) suggest bands of:

- three to five months (low seriousness)
- five to seven months (medium seriousness)
- seven to nine months (relatively high seriousness); and
- 10-12 months for case of particularly high seriousness (possibly some of this being kept 'in reserve' in case an extension should be required: above).

The SGC makes reference back to the seriousness levels suggested in the *Youth Court Bench Book* (which is mentioned in *Chapter 14*).

If at the first YOP meeting, or after any subsequent attempts, agreement cannot be reached, then the matter will be referred back to the court, whereupon the order could be revoked and the youth sentenced in the normal way.

The YOP may, in the light of circumstances which arose after any contract was made (particularly if the contract is not adhered to), also refer the matter back to the court either for straight revocation or for revocation followed by dealing with the youth afresh for the original offence.

This then encompasses matters such as failure to abide by the contract, changes in personal circumstances or alternatively good progress under the contract.

Commission of a further offence during the currency of the referral order may, in exceptional circumstances, allow the court to extend the original order (but as already noted not so as to take it beyond 12 months in total), or to revoke it and resentence for the original offence or offences.

THE STATUTORY PURPOSES OF SENTENCING YOUTHS

It has already been noted that the seriousness of the offence will usually set the ceiling above which an order against a youth on a finding of guilt must not go, no matter how great any other considerations might be.

Thereafter, section 9 Criminal Justice and Immigration Act 2008 introduced (with effect from 30 October 2009), a new section 142A Criminal Justice Act 2003. This provides that on sentencing a youth the court must initially consider three things:

- the principal aim of the YJS (which is to prevent offending: *Chapter 3*)
- the welfare of the offender (as provided for in section 44 of the Children and Young Persons Act 1933: again see *Chapter 3*); and
- the new purposes of sentencing youths (below).

Surprisingly perhaps, this is the first time that legislation has provided clear statutory aims in respect of the sentencing of youths (the earlier section 142 of the 2003 Act was, likewise, the first occasion in respect of adults).

The new section 142A reproduces four of the five sentencing aims for adults found in section 142, i.e. the:

- punishment of offenders
- reform and rehabilitation of offenders
- protection of the public; and
- making of reparation by offenders to people affected by their offences.

It does not, however, reproduce the fifth (the reduction of crime, including by its deterrence). However, the principal aim of the YJS already covers similar ground, albeit in slightly different terms (see *Chapter 3*).

For this reason, crime prevention will, in the case of youths, generally take priority over the four statutory purposes of sentencing and this is reflected in the SGC's guidance document.[9] It is also to that document which is outlined below that courts must look for similar guidance.

There are certain, rare but significant, circumstances where the sentencing of youths will fall outside the usual sentencing approach and these are covered at the end of this chapter.

It should be noted that the statutory purposes of sentencing do not apply in certain circumstances, e.g. where the sentence is fixed by law or certain minimum or extended forms of custody fall to be considered (mainly in the Crown Court), or where a hospital order is appropriate.

The Sentencing Guidelines Council's *Overarching Principles*

The sentencing structure in respect of youths that emerges from this document is covered below and in its full form in the *Appendix* to this work. But before looking at a summary it is worth noting certain other documents which exist in relation to adult sentencing which can also have relevance to youth sentencing:

- The SGC's guideline *Overarching Principles: Seriousness* (December 2004). This document was primarily aimed at assessing seriousness in the case of adult offenders but it did, in its Foreword, state ' ... there are some aspects that will assist courts in assessing the seriousness of offences committed by those under 18.' Although, as will be seen, events have moved on, the SGC's 2009 guidance on sentencing youths, whilst obviously covering matters of 'seriousness', does not address it as a subject in itself and its 2004 guideline may thus retain some incidental or occasional relevance to youths.

- For cases sentenced on or after 23 July 2007 reference must be made to the SGC's revised guideline on *Reduction in Sentence for a Guilty Plea*. This guideline is not age-specific and therefore has relevance in respect of youths, although the effect of giving credit in respect of youths may, because of the overall different sentencing environment, need special consideration.

- The SGC's *Magistrates' Court Sentencing Guidelines* which relate to sentences imposed on adults on or after 4 August 2008. These expressly relate only to adults

---

9.   As with the adult purposes of sentencing, no hierarchy or order of priority is applied to the four youth aims even though punishment is mentioned first on the list. It is perhaps surprising that the opportunity was not taken to make a clearer distinction with adult sentencing when enacting the new provisions for youths.

but much of the ground covered (e.g. seriousness, starting points, aggravating and mitigating factors, offence guidelines, assessing fines, ancillary orders etc.) will also need to be covered in respect of youths and the adult guidelines will provide a useful point of reference. In particular, reference can be made to suggested periods of custody which are then generally reduced in respect of youths (see below). They also contain a pull-out card which lists statutory factors that, if they exist in a given case, serve to aggravate an offence, common aggravating features and items of offender mitigation. The first of these apply to youth by law, the other two by analogy. The adult guidelines also suggest periods in custody which the SGC has now advised should be appropriately reduced in the case of youths. A youth version of the *Magistrates' Court Sentencing Guidelines* does not appear to be envisaged, certainly not for the present, and it remains to be seen how far the adult guidance will, in practice, be transposed so as to to have broad application to youths.10

- The Judicial Studies Board's *Youth Court Bench Book*. As noted in *Chapter 14*, this book contains reference and guidance materials, including youth sentencing guidelines. Many of the materials are now to be revised by the JSB in the light of the SGC's *Overarching Principles* and the sentencing guidelines contained in it (especially re 'seriousness') will to a large extent be rendered inapplicable. However, the SGC has expressly made reference to the various levels of seriousness suggested in that book when looking at periods for referral orders (above).
- The SGC has previously published definitive guidelines that are offence-specific and which apply wholly or partly to youths of specified ages as well as adults, see, e.g. breach of an ASBO, robbery and sexual offences.

Although there will now be considerable new SGC guidance (to which all courts will have to have regard: below) there will also be an obvious gap in that there will not be any direct youth-specific equivalent of the *Magistrates' Court Sentencing Guidelines*. It remains to be seen whether this will be a problem in practice or whether courts will find it easy to take what is necessary or appropriate from those guidelines when applying the SGC youth-based principles.

The duty of courts in this respect is governed by section 172 Criminal Justice Act 2003 which provides that every court must:

- in sentencing an offender, have regard to any guidelines that are relevant to the offender; and
- in exercising any other function relating to the sentencing of offenders[11] have regard to any guidelines relevant to the exercise of that function.

---

10. The adult guidelines can be accessed at www.sentencing-guidelines.gov.uk
11. e.g. on breach of an order.

Where a court goes outside any relevant guidelines it must give its reasons for doing so in open court; which provides an impetus for them to follow a carefully structured decision-making process as explained below. Some of the salient points of the SGC's *Overarching Principles* include:

- 'seriousness' is the usual starting point
- 'culpability' and 'harm' will be major factors when assessing 'seriousness'
- restrictions on liberty must always be commensurate with the seriousness of the offence (but need not always seek to be used to this full extent: see below)
- it is important not to 'criminalise' youths unduly
- even more than with adults, youths need to be sentenced according to their individual circumstances
- the youth's level of maturity is more important than chronological age (especially when assessing culpability)
- the sentence for a further offence does not have to be more severe just because it follows a previous conviction
- the need for the sentencing court to consider a youth's 'welfare' includes concepts such as 'well-being' and 'best interests'
- mental heath issues may be particularly relevant when dealing with youths[12]
- special attention should be paid to learning difficulties or disabilities in youths
- speech, language and understanding issues need to be taken account of when trying to engage with youths about their offending
- courts must bear in mind that many youths feel that 'authority' will inevitably discriminate against them
- the danger of self-harm must be borne in mind, particularly in a custodial environment
- youths will generally be sentenced less severely than adults, although this differentiation will diminish with age (subject to corresponding increased maturity)
- youths must be given the opportunity (and a greater one) to learn from their mistakes
- youths tend to act impulsively and under the influence of others and often do not fully understand the consequences
- family and other environmental factors are heavy contributing factors to youth offending
- offending by children is often a phase that will pass
- the effectiveness of a criminal conviction and resulting sentence on a youth can have a disproportionate effect on future prospects (see also below in respect of the

---

12. Often they will be dealt with using diversionary schemes; although many such people are in custody.

Rehabilitation of Offenders Act 1974)

- youths may be more receptive to changing their behaviour than adults
- youths may be particularly vulnerable to contaminating influences in a custodial environment
- custody should be a 'measure of last resort'; and
- sentencing youths is, more than ever, a balancing exercise.

YOUTH-BASED SENTENCING POWERS IN OUTLINE

It is long standing practice for magistrates' courts and youth courts in particular to use structured decision-making guides to help with their main areas of work. Nowhere, perhaps, is this more important than when sentencing youths.

A structured approach

By following an agreed structure, courts not only ensure that all relevant matters are considered and weighed in the eventual balance but that they are taken into account in an appropriate order. Another feature is to guarantee that material factors and considerations are given appropriate weight. This in turn promotes consistency and correctness of approach and assists with the formulation and announcement of reasons for decisions. These should flow naturally out of this process rather than be rationalisations of hunches and intuitive conclusions.

Structure guides for sentencing youths draw heavily on the Criminal Justice and Immigration Act 2008 and SGC's *Overarching Principles*. As noted above, reference may also, on occasion, need to be made to other sources. The Criminal Procedure Rules 2005 give guidance as to practical matters, such as making sure all necessary information is obtained and considered, involving the youth, parents or guardians in the court process, making explanations and disclosing copies of reports.[13] A diagrammatic representation of a sample youth sentencing structure is given at at the end of this chapter.

Where punishment is 'inexpedient'

If, taking into account the nature of the offence and the youth's character, the court thinks that punishment is 'inexpedient' it may make either of the following orders:

Absolute discharge

The offence and guilt are marked but no penalty is imposed and the matter will not be deemed to be a finding of guilt for any purposes other than in those proceedings.

---

13. See Part 44 of the 2005 rules.

Conditional discharge

The offence and guilt are marked but no penalty is imposed on the (sole) condition that the youth commits no further offences for any period of up to three years, as stipulated by the court. Conviction for an offence committed within that period then renders the youth liable to be sentenced for the original offence (along with the new offence).

The matter is not be deemed to be a finding of guilt for any purpose other than those proceedings or related breach proceedings. Save in exceptional circumstances, a court may not impose a conditional discharge for an offence committed within two years of a (final) warning (see *Chapter 11*) nor can one be given for breach of an anti-social behaviour order (ASBO): see generally *Chapter 6*.

Sentencing where no formal seriousness threshold test needs to be met

In certain circumstances the court may decide that some form of punishment is appropriate or expedient. The following orders can then be made without the need for the court to find that any formal seriousness threshold has been reached:

Reparation order

This is a comparatively simple and immediate way to mark the offence, to enable the youth offender to make reparation either direct to the victim or indirectly to the community, and hopefully for the youth to learn from the experience and move on from his or her offending. Although it requires no specific seriousness or threshold test to be met, there are certain other hurdles.

Such an order cannot be made where a referral order or the new youth rehabilitation order (YRO) (*Chapter 16*) is ordered (both will address reparation in their own way), or when a custodial sentence is ordered (*Chapter 17*).

Reparation can be ordered as a free-standing disposal or alongside say a fine, although it would probably not sit easily with an absolute or conditional discharge (above) where punishment will, of necessity, have been found to be 'inexpedient'.

The reparation itself will typically range from sending a letter of apology to the victim of the offence to undertaking some unpaid work for the victim (if the latter agrees) or for the local community. Any such work must not exceed 24 hours and must be completed within three months.

The court must obtain a report as to suitable methods of reparation and the victim's attitude, but this need not be a full pre-sentence report (PSR): see further and generally below.

Legislation requires that courts sentencing youths must make a reparation order where they have power to do so unless they give reasons for not so doing.[14] Breach of the order makes the youth liable to a fine of up to £1,000 (£250 in the case of a

---

14. Powers of Criminal Courts (Sentencing) Act 2000, section 73(8).

child aged 10-13 years, inclusive). Alternatively, the order can be revoked and the youth can them be re-sentenced for the original offence.

Fine

By inference a fine will be considered where punishment is 'expedient' (i.e. an absolute or conditional discharge have been ruled out). The maximum fine that magistrates can impose on a youth is £1,000 (£250 if aged 10-13 years, inclusive). There is technically no maximum if the fine is imposed by a Crown Court other than general considerations of reasonableness and proportionality. However, when dealing with a youth appeal or breach of a youth court conditional discharge, the normal youth court £1,000 or £250 limits will apply as appropriate.[15]

Fines are generally intended to reflect the seriousness of the offending, to be based on the offending youth's 'financial circumstances' (a concept wider than that of 'means' which prevailed before the Criminal Justice Act 1991) and to have roughly the same proportionate impact on people with differing financial circumstances.

An immediate issue arises in respect of the financial circumstances of youths in that many have only pocket money or modestly paid part-time work, or they may be in receipt of the education maintenance allowance (EMA) grant. Many will, for most practical purposes, be financially reliant on parents, especially if still at school or college, unless they have started work (when their wages are likely to be equally modest in most cases).

The SGC's *Magistrates' Court Sentencing Guidelines* contain detailed guidance on the assessment of the financial circumstances of adults and, in particular, allow courts, where the offender is wholly dependent on the income of another person, to take into account the extent that, e.g. household income and assets are available to meet any fine imposed. Given that the SGC's *Overarching Principles* do not address in detail the issue of fining youths, there may be scope for transposing the standard adult guidance to youth cases in a modified form. Important however, is the SGC's advice that only rarely will the EMA grant be taken into account when the youth is living independently or in a household primarily dependent on state benefits.

Although there is probably considerable scope for academic discussion in respect of the fining of youths, it is likely that, given all the other factors applying, fines will not be imposed as frequently as in the adult court and are perhaps likely to be more of a token punishment. In any event, priority must always be given to ordering compensation (below), if it arises, out of available financial resources, so the scope in such cases for a fine in addition to compensation is likely to be even less.

The SGC's *Magistrates' Court Sentencing Guidelines* also provide for fines on adults to be assessed in bands (A, B and C) according to seriousness, which are then effectively multipliers of the offender's 'relevant weekly income' (RWI) to give the

---

15. All figures October 2009.

final amount of the fine. Again, this has not been specifically applied to the fining of youths but may be a useful comparison.[16]

Fines on adults are expected to be paid (and are normally made payable) within 12 months (or less for those on lower incomes). The anticipated period over which a youth could be expected to maintain payments is then, given all that has been said above, likely to be towards the lower end of this 12-month period in many cases. This then effectively serves to keep down the size of fines on youths.

Ordering payment by parents or guardians

No matter how the fine has been assessed, legislation requires the court to order fines imposed on 10-15-year-olds (inclusive) to be paid by their parent or guardian unless this would be 'unreasonable'.

Previously courts may have found it 'unreasonable' where a 10-15-year-old youth, say, had distinct and reasonable resources (e.g. generous pocket money or income from a weekend job) and could thus be expected to make payments therefrom.

The advent on 30 November 2009 of the youth default order (YDO) (see further below) may result in more orders being made for 10-15-year-olds to pay fines, etc. themselves given that there is now a clear and direct sanction against them as individuals if they do not pay. In respect of youths aged 16 or 17 years the requirement to make the parent or guardian pay becomes a discretion so to order.

Any parent or guardian ordered to pay their child's fine or other financial penalty has a right of appeal against that part of the order (but not against the penalty itself) to the Crown Court.

Enforcement of youth fines

Whenever a youth of any age has been ordered to pay in person and subsequently 'wilfully and persistently' defaults, the court can, subject to certain requirements:

- require the parent or guardian to enter into a recognizance[17] to ensure payment of the sum outstanding; or
- order that the sum outstanding now be paid instead by the parent or guardian; or
- since 30 November 2009 make a youth default order (YDO).

A YDO can make the youth defaulter subject to an attendance centre or curfew requirement as found in the new youth rehabilitation order (YRO) (*Chapter 16*) and in the case of 16 or 17-year-olds to a YRO-style unpaid work requirement.

Where a local authority has parental responsibility for a youth and the youth is in care or being provided with accommodation by the local authority then the

---

16. See *The Magistrates' Court: An Introduction* (2009), Gibson B, Waterside Press.
17. See the *Glossary*.

authority will be classed as a parent in relation to the payment and enforcement provisions (but not in relation to the assessment of financial circumstances).

Victims surcharge and order of priority

The compulsory victims surcharge (currently £15)[18] to be imposed in addition to any fine applies equally to youths and any fine must not be reduced because of this if the offender has the financial ability to pay both. The surcharge is intended to be directed towards helping victim and witness support services.

However, where the court considers the youth's financial circumstances are insufficient to meet all potential financial impositions, the order of priority must be:

- compensation
- victims surcharge
- fine; and
- costs (which in the case of a youth must not exceed the amount of any fine).

If the total financial order (fine, penalty, compensation and any additional forfeiture) does not exceed five pounds then costs can only be ordered if the court considers it 'right to do so': section 18(4) Prosecution of Offences Act 1985.

Compensation order as a sentence in its own right

Great emphasis is placed in all sentencing decisions on requiring offenders to compensate victims financially for the direct results of their offence or offences whenever relevant and feasible and this applies equally with regard to youth offenders.

Compensation can thus be ordered both as an ancillary order (see further below) or as a sentence in its own right (where it does not need to pass any formal seriousness threshold). It can relate to:

- personal injury
- loss
- damage; and/or
- funeral expenses.[19]

Compensation can be ordered for substantive offences or offences taken into consideration (TICs) but the limit is £5,000 multiplied by the number of substantive offences being sentenced for, irrespective of reference to which offence the injury, loss or damage arose from; a limit unlikely to be approached when sentencing most youths. Determining the amount of compensation to be paid is based on the

---

18. October 2009.
19. Other than 'in respect of a death arising from the presence of a motor vehicle on a road'. Restrictive provisions apply to road traffic accidents as these are usually matters for civil courts and insurers.

amount as assessed by the court on the information immediately available to it and the offender's ability to pay. In most respects the latter consideration in relation to youths is similar to that in respect of fines.

Where the issue of compensation arises and the court has power to order it but does not do so, it must give reasons for this, which could include say a lack of financial ability to pay, or the court's inability to make a proper assessment on the information provided to it. Ordering part payment (based, say, on ability to pay) is permissible but it may often complicate any other routes to compensation and is thus commonly avoided by both magistrates' courts and youth courts.

Community sentencing where the 'serious enough' threshold test is met

Section 148 Criminal Justice Act 2003 contains the sentencing threshold test for a community sentence, i.e. that the offence (or the combination of offences being dealt with at the same time) is (are) 'serious enough' to justify such a sentence.

In respect of youths, the only community sentence for offences committed on or after 30 November 2009 is the youth rehabilitation order (YRO): see *Chapter 16.*

The court must order and consider a pre-sentence report (PSR) (see further *Reports in the Youth Court* below) before deciding that this threshold test has been met unless it thinks such a report 'unnecessary' (probably a rare event when sentencing youths, especially given the 'scaled approach' to PSR writing: also below).

Section 10 Criminal Justice and Immigration Act 2008 amends section 148 Criminal Justice Act 2003 to provide specifically that, just because the 'serious enough' test is satisfied, it is not necessary to impose a community order or to impose restrictions on liberty as great as are indicated by the overall seriousness level.

In this way, it is possible for sentencers to reduce the level of sentence or its inherent severity in appropriate circumstances.

Custodial sentencing when the 'so serious' threshold test is met

The basic threshold test in respect of youths for the imposition of a custodial sentence is essentially as for adults, i.e. that the offence (or the combination of offences being dealt with at the same time) is 'so serious' that neither a fine alone nor a community order can be justified. The court then has the custodial powers which are outlined separately in *Chapter 17.* Note also however that that chapter also looks at 'alternatives to custody' (usually based on the use of community sentences, above).

ORDERS ANCILLARY TO SENTENCE

Most of the standard ancillary orders for adults apply when dealing with youths. It is not possible here to consider each in detail. The following list identifies some of the more common such orders:

- compensation
- endorsement and penalty points
- disqualification
- costs
- victims surcharge
- restitution
- forfeiture.

Deferment of sentence

It should also be noted that the youth court can, as the adult court may, defer sentence for up to six months. Given the nature of youth court proceedings and the general move towards speedy expedition and attending to the needs of youths this is perhaps likely to be an unusual course of action.

REPORTS IN THE YOUTH COURT

Before sentencing, magistrates can, and in some cases must, request information from YOTs to inform their sentencing decisions. As noted above, this is by way of a pre-sentence report (PSR). That report can take one of the following forms:

- **fast delivery report** – which is requested on the day of sentence and requires a short adjournment to enable the YOT court officer to interview the young person and parent(s) to make assessment of the level of intervention required to reduce the risk of re-offending. This is then presented to the court, usually in a locally agreed written format; or
- **written PSR** – which must be requested in cases where custody is likely or inevitable and is also desirable in the more complex sentencing decisions.

Assessments for a written PSR will normally require a ten working days adjournment including time to allow full enquiries by YOT practitioner. Assessment will include the seriousness of offences, motivation to change, risk of re-offending and harm, suitability for different interventions and these will be recorded in the ASSET assessment framework.[20]

The report writer will use the assessment to advise the magistrates or the Crown Court Judge about the level of risk of re-offending and harm to others, factors that may have contributed to the offending behaviour and the level of intervention required to reduce these risks. This assessment will follow the 'scaled approach' guidance by the YJB about managing risk.

---

20. For details of the ASSET framework, see www..yjb.org.uk Full PSRs are aka 'standard delivery reports'.

CREDIT FOR A GUILTY PLEA

The SGC's revised guideline on 'Reduction in Sentence for a Guilty Plea' (2007) has already been mentioned above.

The underlying intention is that by indicating an intention to admit guilt (and as early as possible) defendants can, for example, save witnesses the ordeal of giving evidence, save public and court resources and indicate contrition.

The guideline is relatively straightforward if a little lengthy but can, in appropriate circumstances, provide for up to a third reduction in the final sentence where the indication has been 'timely' (i.e. on the earliest appropriate occasion, which may well have been at interview) .

A 'graded' form of approach is provided for indications given at later stages in the proceedings to provide reduced credit.

Furthermore, especially where there is room to question whether the 'serious enough' or 'so serious' thresholds have actually been met, credit for a timely guilty plea can, instead of reducing the severity of any particular level of sentence, bring it down a whole sentencing level.

REMITTAL TO YOUTH COURT

There are statutory provisions enabling the Crown Court (save in the case of homicide) or an adult magistrates' court to remit a youth who has been found guilty to the youth court (including, in the case of a magistrates' court, to the youth's 'home' youth court if more appropriate).

Generally such a court must exercise that power unless it considers it 'undesirable'. In the case of the Crown Court it would clearly be 'undesirable' if that court definitely wishes to exercise any of its powers to order custody, especially those custodial powers not available to a youth court. A magistrates' court can itself make any of the following orders (and appropriate ancillary orders) re a youth:

- an absolute or conditional discharge
- a fine
- a compulsory referral order (*Chapter 15*); or
- a parental recognizance.

But, even then, it may feel that it is a youth court that has the appropriate experience to consider sentence and that it would be more appropriate to remit

There is also power to remit from one youth court area to another, say, to bring several matters together, or to let a 'home' youth court consider local circumstances and sentencing programmes with first-hand knowledge of their use.

ENFORCING RESPONSIBILITIES OF PARENTS/GUARDIANS

The SGC in its *Overarching Principles* reinforces the need for courts, particularly at the sentencing stage, to address the responsibilities of parents and guardians in relation to the offending of their children.

Parental bind-over

There is a statutory requirement (save where a referral order is made) that when a youth aged 10-15 years (inclusive) is sentenced, the parent or guardian will be required to enter into a recognizance[21] of up to £1,000 (as set by the court) to take proper care and to exercise proper control of their child (and to ensure compliance with any youth rehabilitation order).

However, this applies only if the court is satisfied that it would be desirable in the interests of preventing further offending by that child. The recognizance will last for any stipulated period up to three years or until the youth reaches 18 years if earlier.

Where the youth is aged 16 or 17 years there is a corresponding *discretion* to order a parental recognisance.

In all cases the parent or guardian must consent and an unreasonable refusal to consent can lead to the imposition of a fine of up to £1,000.

Where, in the case of a youth aged 10-15 years inclusive, the court is not satisfied that it would not be in the interests of preventing further offending it must state why in open court.

Parenting order

The sentencing court also has the power to make a parenting order in respect of the parent or guardian.

There is again a statutory requirement (including now also where a referral order is made) that when a youth aged 10-15 years (inclusive) is sentenced, the parent or guardian will be made subject to a parenting order.

However, this again also applies only where the court is satisfied that it would be desirable in the interests of preventing further offending by that child. Where the youth is aged 16 or 17 years there is a corresponding discretion to make a parenting order. Such orders, unlike a parental bind-over, do not require parental consent, although the parent's preparedness to engage with such order is often looked for as this may be a prime indicator of whether the order is likely to prove worthwhile.

The SGC's *Overarching Principles* (see *Appendix I* to this work) give further guidance on the kind of factors which need to be considered in respect of such orders.

The involvement of parents or guardians in respect of financial orders has already been covered above.

---

21. See the *Glossary*.

THE REHABILITATION OF OFFENDERS ACT 1974

The need not to over-criminalise or over-stigmatise youths is fundamental in the balancing exercise that has to take place when sentencing youths.

This was formally recognised as long ago as 1974 with the introduction of rehabilitation periods and the idea of 'spent' convictions which cannot be referred to once spent except in certain contexts such as court proceedings (when they must also be marked as spent). One effect is that the individual is in many circumstances not obliged to disclose such a conviction, e.g. in a job application or interview. The 1974 Act also provided that certain rehabilitation periods be halved in respect of offenders under 18 years of age.

The Criminal Justice and Immigration Act 2008 brought cautions, conditional cautions, reprimands and (final) warnings within the ambit of the 1974 provisions:

- the new conditional cautions for youths (*Chapter 11*) become 'spent' three months after they are given (save where the youth is later prosecuted, convicted and sentenced for the offence when the period is that applicable to the substantive sentence then imposed); and that
- a reprimand or (final) warning (*Chapter 11*) will become spent immediately.

MENTAL HEALTH CONSIDERATIONS IN SENTENCING

Mental health considerations are complex, especially when relating to youths, and are outside the remit of this book. However, in addition to the various safeguards applicable right through from investigation to courts stage, certain factors are worth noting at sentence stage. This is a specialist area as to which appropriate works should be consulted but in outline, if a court is considering imposing a custodial sentence on a youth who is or appears to be suffering from mental impairment:

- it must call for a medical report unless it considers one to be 'unnecessary'
- it must expressly consider any relevant information before it about the youth's mental condition
- in addition, it must consider the likely effect of such a sentence on the youth's medical condition and any treatment that may be available for such a condition
- hospital orders (including interim orders) and guardianship orders are available subject to certain complex provisions; and
- a requirement for medical treatment can be included in a youth rehabilitation order (YRO) (see generally *Chapter 16*).

SENTENCING OF OFFENDERS AGED 10-17 YEARS, INCLUSIVE
(In the youth court: other and varied provisions may apply in the Crown Court)

AGE*	10	11	12	13	14	15	16	17
Absolute discharge	√	√	√	√	√	√	√	√
Conditional discharge Only in exceptional circumstances if final warning given in preceding 2 years. Not for breach of ASBO.	√	√	√	√	√	√	√	√
Referral order See compulsory and discretionary conditions	√	√	√	√	√	√	√	√
Compensation As sentence in own right or as an ancillary order	√	√	√	√	√	√	√	√
Fine Note from text when parents must and may be ordered to pay	√ Max £250	√ Max £250	√ Max £250	√ Max £250	√ Max £1,000	√ Max £1,000	√ Max £1,000	√ Max £1,000
Reparation order Note from text when such an order cannot, or *prima facie* must, be made	√	√	√	√	√	√	√	√
Youth rehabilitation order (YRO) Imprisonable and non-imprisonable offences but only if 'serious enough': *Chapter 16*	√	√	√	√	√	√	√	√

YRO with ISS programme or fostering Imprisonable offences only and only if 'so serious': *Chapter 16*	√ **	√ **	√ **	√ **	√ **	√	√	√
Detention and training order (DTO) Imprisonable offences only and only if 'so serious': *Chapter 17*	x	x	√ **	√ **	√ **	√	√	√
Committal to Crown Court for sentence ('Dangerous offenders' only): *Chapter 13*	√	√	√	√	√	√	√	√

* Note commentary in text as to when age is to be taken for sentencing purposes
** Only if a 'persistent offender'

A STRUCTURED APPROACH TO THE INDIVIDUALISED SENTENCING OF YOUTHS

DETERMINE SERIOUSNESS OF OFFENCE(S)
Consider any offence-based factors that make it more or less serious of its type
Consider any statutory or other aggravating features
Consider harm caused and harm risked
Determine culpability
(Harm intended/appreciated but ignored risk/appreciated risk but did not intend it/should have appreciated risk)
Restrictions on liberty cannot now exceed this level of seriousness of offence(s)

CONSIDER ANY OFFENDER MITIGATION

BALANCING EXERCISE
Age and maturity
Seriousness of offence(s)
Likelihood of further offending and its possible harm
Reports and 'scaled approach'

Principal Aim of Youth Justice System

To prevent (re) offending by persons under 18 years

Welfare of Offender
1. Best interests
2. Wellbeing
3. Education/training
4. Removal from undesirable surroundings
5. Mental health issues
6. Learning difficulties/disabilities
7. Understanding and communication
8. Young people's anticipations of 'authority'
9. Vulnerability
10. Passing phase
11. Effects personal circumstances and experiences
12. Age and maturity
13. 'Best option'

Statutory Purposes of Sentencing Youths
1. Punishment
2. Reform and Rehabilitation
3. Protection of Public
4. Reparation

No stated order of priority

SENTENCE
1. Consider threshold tests
2. Credit for Guilty plea if and as appropriate
3. Generally less severe than for adult (level of sentence and also length/intensity within level)
4. Re-offending does not necessarily require higher sentence of itself
5. (Greater) opportunity to learn from mistakes
6. No undue penalisation
7. Obligations based on welfare must not exceed seriousness of offence(s)
8. Custody is last resort (with YRO with ISSP or Fostering as a specific alternative)
9. Engender the taking of personal responsibility
10. Tackle factors that might suggest further offending
11. Reinforce positive factors
12. Reparation
13. Reinforce parental responsibility
14. Ancillary orders

CHAPTER SIXTEEN

The New Youth Rehabilitation Order

As noted in *Chapter 15*, three major changes to the sentencing of youths were scheduled to come together on 30 November 2009:

- the introduction of statutory sentencing purposes for youths;
- the introduction of the new single (or 'generic') youth community order known as the youth rehabilitation order (YRO) (which mirrors the single community order approach for adult offenders introduced in 2003[1]); and
- the SGC's new *Overarching Principles* for the sentencing of youths.

The new YRO is available only in respect of offences committed (as opposed to convictions or sentences occurring) on or after that date. There is therefore a transitional period during which:

- some old-style, pre-YRO orders of the kind listed below (made before the YRO start date) will still be in force under the old law until these are exhausted, even though new-style YROs are 'up and running' (for cases committed on or after that date: see next point)
- old-style, pre-YRO orders of the kind listed below may still fall to be imposed in respect of offences committed before 30 November 2009
- old-style orders will fall to be managed and enforced by YOTs under and in the light of the former provisions; and
- aspects of the new SGC guidance (which is effective immediately on 30 November 2009) will need to be 'interpreted' in the light of this twin-track approach.

However, once the new YRO provisions do apply in any particular case, then the YRO is the only community sentence available. Ultimately, the following old-style youth community orders will cease to exist:

- action plan order
- curfew order
- supervision order

---

1. The adult generic community order was introduced by the Criminal Justice Act 2003. Old-style (i.e. pre-2009) youth community orders in fact reflect certain pre-2003 adult community orders. The youth sentencing provisions have only now been updated and effectively 'leapfrog' the 2003 Act.

- community punishment order (CPO)
- community punishment and rehabilitation order (CPRO)
- attendance centre order
- drug treatment and testing order (DTTO)
- exclusion order; and
- community rehabilitation order (CRO).

The changes also mean that any existing intensive supervision and surveillance (ISS) 'packages' will, in respect of the new YROs, need to be in line with the new statutory ISS provisions outlined below.

The youth sentencing framework: a note

The overall sentencing framework is described in *Chapter 15*. Readers should note in particular that a community sentence can only be imposed as a sentence where the 'serious enough' threshold for such a sentence is met. Equally, a court does not have to impose a community sentence for that reason alone, something emphasised by the Sentencing Guidelines Council (SGC). It can always 'do less', just as when it makes a community order, it can at its discretion and taking account of the overall circumstances of the offence and the youth concerned, use less restrictive requirements than are suggested by looking solely at the seriousness of an offence.[2]

Also as noted in that chapter, before deciding that the serious enough test is met, a court must consider a pre-sentence report (PSR) unless it thinks this 'unnecessary'.

BASIC FEATURES OF THE YRO

Unlike the existing adult community order, the YRO is generally available and not dependent on the offence concerned being imprisonable.[3] It is also available for those in the entire 10-17 years inclusive age range, subject to certain age-related provisions affecting the use of given requirements. These are noted in the chart at the end of this chapter.

The fifteen basic requirements

Once a YRO has been settled upon by the court, there is a basic 'menu' from which (subject to further criteria) any of 15 possible requirements can be selected and added to the YRO. There are also a further three features which arise in certain circumstances (including, as described below, as an 'alternative to custody'). The 15 basic requirements are summarised in the chart at the end of this chapter. For a fuller understanding of the situation, reference must be made of the lengthy and

---

2. Section 10 Criminal Justice and Immigration Act 2008.
3. See the *Glossary* for the use of this formula.

often complex provisions of the Criminal Justice and Immigration Act 2008 which sets out further and detailed considerations in relation to each.[4]

The YRO approach can be (and is, indeed, designed to be) used on more than one occasion if and when appropriate, with requirements being reconsidered where necessary to meet changed circumstances. This adaptability of the order to changing situations also means that custody can be viewed as even more a 'sentence of last resort' (see *Chapter 17*). However, where a YRO is already in force, a court cannot make a further YRO without first revoking the earlier one. This is not only a matter of practical tidiness and convenience but it also ensures that any current and ongoing requirements meet the then circumstances of the youth.[5] Such requirements may, then, possibly be less demanding than those which existed before, particularly if there has been significant compliance so far with a YRO.

General nature and extent of YRO requirements
When considering the nature and number of requirements, courts (and reports writers preparing PSRs) always need to bear in mind the follow demands:

- restrictions on liberty must not exceed the seriousness of the offence or offences
- the requirements must relate, as appropriate, to the new statutory sentencing aims, to the prevention of re-offending and also the youth's welfare: *Chapter 15*
- if there is more than one requirement they must be compatible with one another
- the effect of the requirements on the youth's family circumstances must be examined and taken into account
- so far as practicable, the requirements should not conflict with the offender's religious beliefs, or interfere with any work or education arrangements[6]
- the court must 'have regard' to any time previously spent in those proceedings on custodial remand (including to local authority care, with or without a security requirement: *Chapter 17*) which may thereby call for some appropriate reduction in the intensity of the requirements imposed.[7]

YROs generally take effect the day after being made,[8] save that, e.g. where:

- the offender is currently serving a detention and training order (DTO) (*Chapter*

---

4. Especially sections 1 to 8 and Schedules 1 to 4 of that Act.
5. As noted in *Chapter 1*, the lives and perceptions of young people tend to move on relatively quickly.
6. CJIA 2008 Sch. 1 Part 3.
7. Section 149 Criminal Justice Act 2003.
8. As this book was going to press it was learned that paragraph 30(1) of Schedule 1 of the CJIA 2008 was to be amended via the Coroners and Justice Bill to make YROs take effect immediately they are made. This change is likely to be in place in time for the commencement of the main YRO provisions. That Bill also gives courts a *general discretion* to defer the start of a YRO.

17), the YRO can be made to take effect either when the supervision part of the DTO commences on release or at the end of that supervision period; and

- two or more YROs are made on the same occasion with similar requirements the effect of such requirements can (subject to significant exceptions relating to fostering: below) be made to run consecutively up to any statutory maximum even though YROs technically and ordinarily take effect the day after sentencing.

Further points that the court or report writers must bear in mind are that:

- the court must state a date, not more than three years from the date of commencement (above) by which all requirements must have been complied with;
- where the new ISS provisions (below) are included, the date for compliance must not be earlier than six months from the commencement of the YRO; and
- the CJIA 2008 allows the Secretary of State by order to enable or require courts making a YRO to order periodic reviews of the YRO by a court (Schedule 1, paragraph 35) (re which trials are in progress).

THREE SPECIAL YRO FEATURES

As noted above, the 15 basic requirements are described in the chart at the end of the chapter. The further three special features also mentioned above are as follows:

Electronic monitoring

This requirement is not a freestanding requirement but an optional ancillary one which can be imposed to ensure compliance with such other of the 15 basic requirements as may have been imposed. However, the court *must* make an electronic monitoring (EM) requirement where it has made a curfew or exclusion requirement. Note also that (in summary):

- someone of a kind specified in an order made by the Secretary of State must be made responsible for the monitoring[9]
- the co-operation of any necessary third parties must be obtained
- EM will be by tagging the offender with an ankle or wrist bracelet and the court must be satisfied that arrangements exist for this in any relevant geographical area and in respect of the requirement or requirements to be so monitored
- the period of the monitoring will be fixed by the court or determined by the responsible officer in accordance with the court order (i.e. the YRO's 'responsible

---

9. Note that this is not the same as the 'responsible officer' mentioned later in the chapter (see CJIA 2008, Schedule 1, para 26(4)). See generally the *Glossary*.

officer': see later in the chapter and also the *Glossary*); and

- the responsible officer must give notice of the commencement of the monitoring to the offender, the person carrying it out and any third party before it can begin.

Intensive supervision and surveillance (ISS) or fostering

It has already been noted that, in respect of youths, custody is expressly to be seen as a sentence of last resort, even if the 'so serious' test for custody might otherwise be met *Chapters 15* and see also *Chapter 17*. The ISS and fostering provisions were added by the 2008 Act with this aim in mind. The ISS and (separate) fostering provisions are perhaps best seen not as ordinary YRO requirements but as a special 'high end statutory package' that can be used in quite specific circumstances. The circumstances, all of which must exist before the order can be made, are set out in section 1(4) of the 2008 Act (summarised):

- the court must be dealing with the offender for an offence that is imprisonable (as already noted above, the YRO itself and other requirements can generally be made whether or not the offence carries a maximum sentence of imprisonment); and
- it must be satisfied that the 'so serious' custody threshold test (*Chapters 15* and *17*) has been met (even though custody will not then be used: see next point); and
- but for the availability of the ISS or fostering provisions, custody would be appropriate (or, in the case of offenders aged ten or eleven, custody would have been appropriate had they been aged 12 years); and
- if the offender is under 15 years-of-age at the time of his or her conviction, he or she must be a 'persistent offender' (see later in the chapter and *Chapter 17*).

The effect is to create a form of direct alternative to custody for those who could by law receive a detention and training order (DTO) (as described in *Chapter 17*) and who are now actually at such risk (where they are aged 12-17 years, inclusive).

It also provides a significant 'preventive justice' option for those still too young by law to receive a DTO (offenders aged ten and eleven years) but who offend at a level of seriousness or frequency that, if they were marginally older, custody would be available and a likely outcome.

If the above circumstances exist and the court makes a YRO with ISS then in addition to any other requirements:

- the activity requirement must be in excess of the usual maximum of 90 days but not more than 180 days (now called an 'extended activity requirement')
- any such requirement must be accompanied by supervision and curfew requirements and, save where it is inappropriate or precluded, EM (above)
- a fostering requirement cannot be included (but see below); and

- it would appear that the only time that a YRO can include such activity, supervision, and curfew (plus electronic monitoring where applicable) as a 'package' is under these statutory ISS provisions.

YRO with fostering

If the court, in the basic circumstances listed above, instead makes a YRO with fostering (with or without any other permitted requirements):

- it must be satisfied that the offending behaviour was to a significant extent due to the circumstances in which the youth was living; and
- it must be satisfied that the fostering requirement would assist rehabilitation; and
- the offender's parents or guardians must have been consulted unless it is impracticable to do so; and
- the local authority must have been consulted.

A supervision requirement must also be added, arrangements must be in place in the relevant local authority area for fostering, and similar provisions apply concerning prior legal representation as for a DTO (see *Chapter 17*).

The fostering will be with a local authority foster parent for the area in which the offender resides or is to reside. It will be for up to 12 months (or up to 18 months from original imposition on breach of such a requirement) as specified by the court. But it cannot, in any event, extend beyond the offender's eighteenth birthday.

Where, subsequently, a suitable foster parent is no longer available and the responsible officer proposes to apply for revocation or amendment, then the youth is required to live in accommodation provided by or on behalf of the local authority pending the new court hearing to determine what is to happen.

It should be emphasised that the *only time* that a fostering requirement can be included in a YRO is when all the basic criteria noted above are met and that YRO and ISS packages are mutually exclusive.[10]

Where a court does impose a DTO then it must, in addition to giving any other reasons such as why it found the offence or offences 'so serious', also state why a YRO with ISS or fostering was not made rather than a DTO.

---

10. It has already been noted that, where the compulsory criteria in respect of a referral order apply (*Chapter 15*), the option of a YRO is effectively precluded. This may present sentencers with a dilemma where, say, a first time youth offender admits a particularly serious offence such as robbery. The court may, in accordance with the underlying approach to youth sentencing, wish to try to avoid custody but may feel that a referral order would be inadequate or uncertain (even despite the more demanding referral order contracts being considered by YOPs in response to such situations). However, it might be argued that the court can 'propose' making a DTO and then make a YRO with ISS or fostering as an alternative to custody under these provisions.

Custody for refusal to indicate willingness to comply with YRO requirements

It can be seen from the table at the end of this chapter that certain YRO requirements demand that the offender express his or her willingness to comply with them:

- mental health requirements
- drug treatment requirements
- drug testing requirements; and
- intoxicating substance requirements.

In the absence of an expression of willingness, section 152 Criminal Justice Act 2003 allows for the imposition of a DTO (*Chapter 17*) even though the 'so serious' threshold test for custody (*Chapter 15*) has not been met. Nonetheless, efforts should always be made to ensure that the youth has made a fully informed decision about whether or not to indicate a willingness to comply with the requirement.

In any event, this does not mean that custody should, or must, automatically follow. Courts should look at any reasoning behind a youth's lack of willingness and consider other YRO requirements (or even other sentencing options altogether) albeit without allowing the offender to dictate the contents of the sentence.

In any event, it might be considered generally inappropriate to use custody for a youth with mental health issues merely because of an unwillingness to comply with treatment requirements, especially where the offence was not 'so serious' in itself.

REPORTS TO COURTS

It will be recalled from *Chapter 15* that courts must generally, except where they think it 'unnecessary', call for and consider a pre-sentence report (PSR) before deciding that the 'serious enough' test is met. Also, certain YRO requirements themselves require a specific recommendation (or the court must be satisfied that certain criteria are satisfied) that will often come via the PSR.

Pre-sentence reports can take the following forms:

- a **fast delivery report** (FDR): this is provided on the day of sentence and requires a short 'stand-down' adjournment to allow the YOT court officer to interview the youth and, as applicable, his or her parents or guardians, to make an assessment of the level of intervention required to reduce the risk of him or her re-offending. This is then presented to the court, usually in a locally agreed written format; or
- a **written PSR**: this must be requested where custody is under active consideration and is, in any event, desirable with regard to all the more complex sentencing decisions.[11]

11. Written PSRs are also known as 'standard delivery reports'.

The more detailed assessments carried out for a written PSR will normally require at least a ten working day adjournment to enable a full assessment to be undertaken and enquiries to be made by the relevant YOT practitioner. Assessment will involve such matters as looking at the seriousness of offences, motivation to change, risk of re-offending and harm, suitability for different interventions, all using the ASSET framework mentioned in *Chapter 5* (and see also the *Glossary*).

The report writer will use the resulting assessment to inform sentencers about the background and circumstances of the offender, his or her attitude and response to the offence and any matters relating to physical or mental health, substance misuse and so on (when specialist expert reports may also be provided). The PSR will inform the court about the assessed level of risk of re-offending and harm to other people, factors that may have contributed to the offending behaviour and the level of intervention being suggested to reduce these risks. Critically, it will follow the 'scaled approach' to managing risk noted in *Chapter 5*. Suggested interventions linked to a YRO will accordingly reflect the level of risk identified in the PSR.

Earlier reports

It is common practice for existing written PSRs prepared, say, within the previous three months to be used with an oral update if sentencers request information about a defendant who is already subject to a community sentence and do not want to adjourn the case for more detailed reports unless absolutely 'necessary'.

PROMOTING COMPLIANCE OR 'BREACHING' A YRO

The SGC guidelines make it clear that youths should be given appropriate opportunities and support to comply with YRO requirements and that the primary objective of any breach proceedings for failure to do so is to ensure that the youth completes the order. Also, any sanction which the court thinks is necessary on breach should generally emphasise or intensify any punishment aspects of the YRO, rather than failures to comply resulting in a court moving straightaway to consider custody.

This again reinforces the 'last resort' approach to the custody of youths and signals that the YRO approach should not be jettisoned just because compliance with the order proves difficult to achieve or something of a challenge.[12] The SGC approach thus reflects the YRO enforcement and breach provisions in Schedule 2 of the Criminal Justice and Immigration Act 2008.

Where there has been an apparent failure to comply with a YRO requirement the responsible officer must first form an opinion as to whether or not the failure is 'without reasonable excuse'. If he or she considers that there is no reasonable excuse then a warning must be given (unless he or she is required to commence breach

---

12. If youth offenders were not sometimes 'difficult' then the point of the YRO might be lost altogether.

proceedings in any event as described below). Such a warning will:

- describe the failure
- state that it is unacceptable
- state that, where an earlier warning has been given in the preceding 12 months, any further failure could result in formal breach proceedings in the courts; and
- where no previous warning has been given, state that any subsequent failure on one or more occasions could result in formal breach proceedings before a court.

Essentially, those who have been warned on two occasions within a 12 month period for a 'without reasonable excuse' failure will not receive a further warning and, on any subsequent such failure in a 12 month period, the responsible officer must commence breach proceedings unless he or she is of the opinion that 'exceptional circumstances' exist. There is also a discretion to commence breach proceedings on a second failure without reasonable excuse within the period.

The court's powers in breach proceedings
The court dealing with any breach of a YRO will be the youth court, or the adult court if the offender is aged 18 years or above, when the breach proceedings are commenced, or the Crown Court as described below.

Adult court magistrates may not have been trained in respect of YROs and their breaches, or otherwise have detailed knowledge of youth sentencing. Although this type of situation is not new, the ability, in effect, to restructure a single, generic youth order with its 15 basic requirements, will, especially in the adult court, require very careful consideration at this stage. The decision might then be taken locally either to roster youth panel magistrates for that sitting of the adult court or, possibly, to list the breach on a youth court day but temporarily sit as an adult court.

It should also be noted that, where the Crown Court has made a YRO the application for a summons or warrant in connection with the breach will still be made to a magistrate, who will then require the offender to appear before the Crown Court unless at the time of sentence the Crown Court directed that any further proceedings (amendment, revocation or breach) come before a youth or adult magistrates' court. That might well, but not necessarily, have been so directed if the YRO was made on an appeal to the Crown Court (see generally *Chapter 14*).

Where a breach is proved to the satisfaction of the relevant court the following statutory options exist:

- a fine of up to £250 if the offender is under 14 years of age
- a fine of up to £1,000 if he or she is aged 14 years or over
- adding or substituting requirements (capable of being complied with within the

period of up to three years originally specified for the YRO)

- re-sentencing for the original offence (and revoking the YRO); and/or
- where the YRO was made by the Crown Court, but further proceedings in the case were handed to the youth or adult court (as described above), those courts have a power on breach to refer the offender back to the Crown Court.

Arguably (as suggested by the SGC) it is also possible to 'take no action' in appropriate circumstances as the above options are expressed as being permissive rather than mandatory or prescriptive.

The extent of compliance must be taken into account and courts will, doubtless, wish to check that full opportunity and support for compliance have been given, especially if custody is now a possible consideration.

There is a particular additional issue for adult courts dealing with breaches of YROs. The youth court may well have made the YRO in respect of offences that might otherwise have carried up to 24 months custody (*Chapter 17*) or even for an indictable-only offence such as robbery. In such cases the re-sentencing powers of the adult court might be inadequate (see *Chapter 13*) or, in the case of an indictable-only offence, non-existent. In such cases it would appear that paragraph 7 of schedule 2 to the Criminal Justice Act and Immigration Act 2008 will allow for committal to the Crown Court so that court may exercise its breach powers.

Adding or substituting requirements in or to a YRO

It appears that the straightforward removal of YRO requirements is not provided for on breach, although the substitution can presumably occur of a similar requirement but with different specifications (but note the existence of the power to revoke the YRO, and completely re-sentence, thereby readdressing all of the requirements).

It is not possible on breach to include an extended activity or fostering requirement if one is not already included in the YRO. However, it would be possible to re-sentence and include such requirements if the relevant criteria were then met.

If an unpaid work requirement was not originally included but is now added, then the minimum period is reduced to 20 hours instead of 40 hours so as to give some flexibility and not to intensify the overall YRO unduly, particularly where the breach was maybe less serious or there are other, more demanding, requirements still to be complied with by the youth.[13]

Since the underlying aim is, as per the SGC guidance, to ensure completion of a YRO it will be down to the skill of PSR writers and sentencers to manage the breach options accordingly. Also, unlike the provisions applicable to the adult version of

13. It would appear from section 1(1)(c) CJIA 2008 that the ability to include unpaid work on breach (as well as initially) only applies where the youth was aged 16 or 17 years at the time of conviction as opposed to at the time of the breach or the time when the court comes to deal with it.

the community order, there is no statutory obligation to intensify a YRO on breach if it is allowed to continue. So, the YRO approach might well then continue despite breaches although it may, on occasions, be more appropriate to re-sentence to a new YRO as already indicated.

Re-sentencing for the original offence

The statutory provisions for youth and adult courts allow them to deal:

> ... with the offender, for the offence in respect of which the order was made, in any way in which the court could have dealt with the offender for that offence (had the offender been before that court to be dealt with).[14]

The use of the term 'that court' towards the end of the above extract makes it clear that, if the offender appears before the adult court for breach, then that court will use its adult sentencing powers if it decides to re-sentence.

However, looking closely at the situation where the offender is still under 18 years of age when breach proceedings commenced, re-sentencing could include:

- a new YRO with such of the 15 basic requirements as are more suited to present circumstances
- a new YRO with ISS or a fostering but only if the relevant criteria are met; or
- a new YRO with ISS where the breach was found to be 'wilful and persistent', even if the original offence was not imprisonable and regardless of the general ISS criteria otherwise to be satisfied before making such an order (see above) .

The SGC guidelines suggest that the 'wilful and persistent' test be applied broadly along the lines of that for persistent offenders (i.e. with at least three breaches demonstrating a lack of willingness to comply with the order), thereafter allowing the further re-sentencing options of:

- a DTO (*Chapter 17*) for any of the permitted periods if the 'wilful and persistent' breach was of a YRO with ISS (including where the YRO with ISS was made on breach as above) without further reference to the 'so serious' test but only where the original offence was imprisonable
- a DTO for four months where, as above, it was a YRO with ISS made on an earlier breach but for a non-imprisonable offence and the current breach was found to be 'wilful and persistent'; or
- a DTO if the relevant statutory criteria are otherwise met.

---

14. CJIA 2008 Schedule 2, para6(2)(c).

In special circumstances, possibly some lesser form of order (such as a fine) might even be appropriate on re-sentencing.

It will be recalled that a YRO with ISS or a fostering requirement can be made in respect of 'persistent offenders' aged ten or eleven years even though they could not otherwise have received a DTO. On breach they still cannot receive a DTO since the relevant age for making such an order remains the date of their conviction.

Re-offending during the currency of a YRO

The SGC guidelines state that '… a sentence that follows re-offending does not need to be more severe than the previous sentence solely because there has been a previous conviction'. It should be recalled that re-offending, of itself, does not constitute a breach of the earlier YRO and, in such circumstances, it will be necessary to take stock again of all the factors relevant in sentencing youths as they apply at that particular time.

The existing YRO can be left in place or, in the interests of justice and having regard to circumstances since the making of the original YRO, it can be revoked with or without re-sentencing for the original offence. The extent of compliance so far with the YRO must be taken into account in any re-sentencing.

Amendment and revocation of a YRO

Schedule 2 to the Criminal Justice and Immigration Act 2008 provides the usual sort of powers to cancel or replace requirements in a YRO as well as to revoke (with or without re-sentencing) in the light of subsequent circumstances. In addition, it is possible for the time for compliance with an unpaid work requirement to be extended beyond 12 months.

PRE-EXISTING YROS (OR OTHER ORDERS)

Where there is a YRO already in force, a further YRO is not permissible unless the earlier one is also revoked at the same time (this can be done without specific application in such circumstances).[15]

This then reflects the SGC guidance that the YRO approach can and should where appropriate be used more than once and also ensures that the youth's current circumstances are always fully reviewed. It also keeps the overall order of events clearer and avoids cumulative requirements in different order and possibly confusing signals to a youth.

The position is similar where there is a pre-existing reparation order.

Technically speaking, it is possible to impose a YRO where there is already in force one or more of the nine 'old-style', stand-alone community orders noted at

---

15. CJIA Sch. 1 para 30(4).

the start of this chapter. Good practice and the tenor of the new provisions would suggest that the pre-existing community order should be revoked. Former requirements might then, where appropriate, be reproduced in the new YRO.

CONCLUDING REMARKS

The YRO provisions provide the widest range of, and flexibility in, community-based options to keep youths out of custody whenever possible.

However, in so doing, the legislation has inevitably become lengthy and complex and sentencers and other practitioners should always consider the source legislation and related SGC guidance noted above with the greatest of care.

OVERVIEW OF THE FIFTEEN BASIC YRO REQUIREMENTS

REQUIREMENT	AGE	NATURE OF REQUIREMENTS	NOTES
ACTIVITY	10 years or over	One or more of following: • participate in activities at specified place • participate in activities specified in YRO • participate (with parental consent) in residential exercise(s) for up to 7 days	Number of days to be specified in YRO (max 90 but up to 180 where part of intensive supervision and surveillance (ISS): see text). Responsible officer (see the *Glossary*) can give general instructions. Instructions given by person in charge to be complied with. Can include reparation.
SUPERVISION	10 years or over	Attend appointments with responsible officer or person nominated by responsible officer as determined by such people	Aimed at securing rehabilitation.
UNPAID WORK	Only if 16 years or over on conviction	Unpaid work for the benefit of the community (or even directly for the victim where appropriate) in the local justice area in which offender resides	Expressed in hours as specified by the court and in aggregate: • minimum 40 hours • maximum 240 hours. To be completed within 12 months but remains in force until work completed Offender to be 'suitable person' for such requirement. Managed by responsible officer.

PROGRAMME	10 years or over	'Systematic set of activities' at specified place(s), including (part) residential programme	Court to specify number of days. No minimum or maximum requirements. Programme to be suitable for offender. Responsible officer can give general instructions. Instructions given by person in charge to be complied with. Parental consent not required if residential.
ATTENDANCE CENTRE	10 years or over	Attend at attendance centre and engage in occupation or receive instruction under supervision of person in charge	Periods (age as on conviction): 10-13 years – max 12 hours (in practice minimum 2-3 hours) 14-15 years – min 12 hours, max 24 hours 16-17 years – min 12 hours, max 36 hours. Centre to be reasonably accessible to offender. Court fixes first attendance. Only one attendance per day and max 3 hours per day.
PROHIBITED ACTIVITY	10 years or over	Refrain from specified activities either on day(s) specified or for specified period	Court can include prohibition on possessing, using or carrying a firearm
CURFEW	10 years or over	Remain in specified places at specified times over a specified period	For up to 6 months. Min 2 hours and max 12 hours on any day. Must also include electronic monitoring (EM) unless inappropriate or is precluded by, e.g. the lack of any necessary third party cooperation. Court must consider information about place(s) to be specified and attitude of any others affected by the offender's enforced presence.
EXCLUSION	10 years or over	Prohibition on entering specified place(s) or area(s) for specified period(s)	Max overall length is 3 months. Must also include electronic monitoring (EM) unless inappropriate or is precluded by, for e.g. the lack of any necessary third party cooperation.

RESIDENCE	10 years or over in respect of a) Only if 16 years or above on conviction for b)	Reside with: a) with specified individual (with that person's consent) or b) at specified place.	Order can provide for responsible officer subsequently to agree that offender can reside elsewhere. Court to consider offender's home surroundings. Hostel placement (16 years and over) only if recommended by YOT, probation officer/provider or local authority social worker
LOCAL AUTHORITY RESIDENCE	10 years or over	Reside for period specified in specified accommodation provided by or on behalf of local authority	Court to be satisfied that offending behaviour due to significant extent to circumstances where offender is living *and* that local authority residence requirement will assist rehabilitation. Local authority and parent (unless impracticable) to be consulted. Court can stipulate who youth cannot reside with. Max 6 months or until 18 years old if earlier. Local authority can place with foster parent even if fostering requirement not made: see text. Similar provisions for legal representation as for a DTO.
MENTAL HEALTH	10 years or over	To submit for specified period(s) to treatment by or under direction of registered medical practitioner or chartered psychologist (or both, but for different periods) with a view to improvement of mental condition.	Can be as residential or non-residential patient at hospital or care home or as directed by the registered medical practitioner or chartered psychologist, but nature of treatment cannot otherwise be specified. Court must have written or oral evidence from registered medical practitioner approved under section 12 Mental Health Act 1983 as to the need for, and susceptibility of the offender to, treatment and that a hospital or guardianship order is not warranted. Arrangements have to be in place to receive the offender. Offender to be *willing to comply* with this YRO requirement.

DRUG TREATMENT	10 years or over	To submit during specified period(s) to treatment by or under the direction of specified person with the necessary qualifications, with a view to reduction or elimination of dependency on, or misuse of, controlled drugs.	Offender must have a dependency on (or propensity to misuse) controlled drugs that requires and is susceptible to treatment. Must be either residential at specified institution/place or non-residential at specified institution/place (at specified intervals) but nature of treatment cannot otherwise be specified. Only if recommended by YOT, probation officer/service provider. Offender to be willing to comply with this YRO requirement. Drug-testing requirement may be added.
DRUG TESTING	10 years or over	For period of drug treatment requirement, to provide samples in accordance with instructions given by responsible officer to ascertain whether there is any controlled drug in offender's body.	Only available if drug treatment requirement imposed. Court must specify minimum number of samples to be taken for each month and may specify the circumstances in which samples may be required and also what descriptions of samples. Offender to be *willing to comply* with this YRO requirement. If responsible officer is not the one to take the samples, court must order for test results to be communicated to that officer.
INTOXICATING SUBSTANCE	10 years or over	To submit during specified period(s) to treatment by or under the direction of specified person with the necessary qualifications, with a view to reduction or elimination of dependency on, or misuse of, controlled intoxicating substances.	Covers alcohol and any other substance or product (other than a controlled drug) which, or the fumes of which, can be inhaled or otherwise used for the purpose of causing intoxication. Offender must have a dependency on (or propensity to misuse) intoxicating substances that requires and is susceptible to treatment. Must be either be residential at specified institution/place or non-residential at specified institution/place (at specified intervals) but nature of treatment cannot otherwise be specified. Only if recommended by YOT, probation officer/service provider. Offender to be *willing to comply* with this YRO requirement.
EDUCATION	10 years or over (but not beyond compulsory school leaving age)	To comply, during period(s) specified, with education arrangements (made by parent/guardian *and* approved by local education authority (LEA)).	LEA must have been consulted and the court must be satisfied that appropriate full-time arrangements exist based on age, ability, aptitude and any special educational needs of the offender.

CHAPTER SEVENTEEN

Young People in Custody

As noted in *Chapter 15*, a custodial sentence can be passed on a youth as a sentence of last resort in prescribed circumstances. The court must have regard to the general sentencing considerations and guidance noted in that chapter. Notably, also, the threshold test for custody mentioned in that chapter (that the offence is 'so serious') must be met. Other safeguards include the fact that courts must normally obtain pre-sentence reports (PSRs) before passing this level of sentence and announce reasons generally for most sentence decisions. There is now an express statutory duty to announce the court's reasons if custody is used.[1] They need not use custody even when it is available and some specific instances are described under *Alternative to Custody* below.

Other routes to a custodial sentence

The 'so serious' threshold test leading to a DTO is not the only method by which youths can find themselves made subject to a custodial disposal on being found guilty. These are outlined in *Chapter 13* and are also matters relevant at the mode of trial stage given that the ultimate consideration will be for the Crown Court.

THE NATURE OF CUSTODY FOR YOUTHS

Ordinary custodial sentences given to youths (i.e. other than as noted in *Chapter 13* and *Children and Young People in Custody*, below) are known as detention and training orders (DTOs). It is the imprisonable nature of an offence in the case of an adult which determines whether a DTO can be used for a youth and because a DTO must be for a minimum of four months (below) it cannot be used where the maximum adult imprisonment for an offence falls below that level. [2]There are certain age (but not sex) restrictions:

- youths aged 10-11 years (inclusive) cannot be sentenced to a DTO (but see *Other routes to a custodial sentence* below; and
- where the 'so serious' test has been satisfied in respect of a youth aged 12-14 years (inclusive) there is an additional test, i.e. that the youth is a 'persistent offender'.

---

1. Road traffic cases apart, custodial sentences for youths were the first sentence decisions to attract such a duty in the then section 1(4) Criminal Justice Act 1982, which initially led to its lesser use. The current general provision is contained in section 174 Criminal Justice Act 2003.
2. There is thus a similar threshold with regard to a youth rehabilitation order (YRO) with intensive supervision and surveillance or fostering which can only be made in place of a DTO.

Persistent offenders

This term is not defined by legislation (and was expressly never linked to the former concept of the 'persistent young offender' (PYO) as described in *Chapter 6*). However, it has previously been held that a youth may still be a 'persistent offender' for present purposes even without any previous convictions if say there are previous relevant cautions or the current offending is in the nature of a determined spate or extended spree, although reference to the considerable body of continuing and somewhat involved case law on the subject is always necessary.

The SGC in its *Magistrates' Court Sentencing Guidelines* suggests that the definition, as previously explored in case law, must now be reviewed in the light of the relevant provisions of the Criminal Justice and Immigration Act 2008 and their effect on the youth sentencing framework. It suggests the following possible definition:

> In determining whether an offender is a persistent offender for these purposes, a court should consider the simple test of whether the young person is one who persists in offending. In most circumstances, therefore, the normal expectation is that the offender will have had some contact with authority in which the offending conduct was challenged before being classed as 'persistent'.

> A young offender is likely to be found to be persistent (and, in relation to a custodial sentence, the test of being a measure of last resort is most likely to be satisfied) where the offender has been convicted of, or made subject to a pre-court disposal that involves an admission or finding of guilt in relation to, imprisonable offences on at least 3 occasions in the past 12 months.

However, it is not clear whether this constitutes formal SGC guidance that all courts must have regard to or whether it remains a matter of statutory interpretation that will have to be the subject of future rulings in the higher courts.

Length of DTO

Any DTO imposed must be for a minimum of four months for each single offence. This ensures that, if a youth aged 12-17 years (inclusive) is to receive such a custodial sentence, it will only be imposed if, additionally, such a minimum period is justified. This then, effectively, raises the custody threshold for youths. Note that this minimum period of four months cannot be achieved by ordering shorter periods to run consecutively. It then increases upwards in set steps to six, eight, ten, 12, 18 or 24 months. However, the period cannot, by law, exceed the maximum term for which the Crown Court could imprison an adult for the same offence or offences.

DTO periods can be ordered to be served consecutively (up to the maximum of 24 months) using the set periods (section 101 Powers of Criminal Courts (Sentencing) Act) 2000). But the overall period cannot exceed 24 months,[3] so if the

---

3.　Although it is possible to achieve a longer overall period: see the last paragraph in this section.

result would otherwise be to take the overall period beyond 24 months, the balance is automatically treated as remitted.

The SGC now suggests that, subject to maturity considerations, the period of a DTO for offenders aged 15-17 (inclusive) should be half to three quarters of the period of custody applicable to an adult offender. It also suggests that the period of a DTO for offenders aged 12-14 years (inclusive) should generally be less than for their 15-17-year-old (inclusive) counterparts.

Unlike the position with imprisonment, there is no power to suspend a DTO, thereby further ensuring that it is truly a sentence of last resort.

It will be seen then that the youth court's powers of imposing custody far exceed those of the adult court (up to six months imprisonment in the case of the adult court, with six months and six months consecutive for two either way offences). This is why (as seen in *Chapter 14*) such great effort and care are taken in the recruitment, training and appraisal of youth panel magistrates.

The widening of the gaps as the sentencer moves beyond 12 months serves, perhaps counter-intuitively, to ensure that youth offenders generally receive shorter periods unless the circumstances demand a leap to the next higher one.

Before deciding whether or not the 'so serious' test has been met in the case of a youth, a written form of PSR must always be ordered and considered, although in appropriate cases the court may instead refer to a previous written report (or the latest of any previous ones) together with an oral update.

A DTO cannot be made unless the youth is legally represented or has been given the express opportunity to secure legal representation and has then failed to secure or apply for it or, having applied for publicly funded representation, has been found to be financially ineligible or has had such representation withdrawn on the basis of his or her conduct.

The first half of the DTO will usually be served in custody (although there are certain other early or delayed release provisions) and the second under supervision back in the community. Planning for release should have been considered at the original PSR stage and be implemented as soon as the youth goes into custody.

Failure to comply with the post-release supervision requirements can result in the youth being brought back to court, whereupon the court can either:

- impose a fine of up to £1,000 (£250 for somebody aged 12 or 13 years); or
- order a return to custody for up to three months, or for the balance of the original DTO if less.

The commission of further offences (but only if imprisonable) after release and before the time the DTO would otherwise have ended can result in the convicting court ordering such custody in relevant secure accommodation (which may take place in a different part of the youth secure estate if the youth is now older). This will be for a period equivalent to the time between the commission of the further offence and the date on which the existing DTO would otherwise have ended. This period of detention may be ordered to be served before any new custodial sentence begins, or concurrently with it. In these circumstances the usual maximum overall period of 24 months for any new DTO would not apply.

Time spent on remand

When imposing a DTO the court must 'take account of' (but not necessarily give automatic or direct mathematical credit for) any prior time spent on, e.g. secure remand or subject to a qualifying electronically monitored curfew bail condition (i.e. one for not less than nine hours a day): section 101 Criminal Justice Act 2003 as amended by section 22 of the CJIA 2008.

Credit is not given administratively for such matters after the imposition of the sentence, so that sentencers do need to pay particular attention to this aspect.

Given that half a DTO will be served in the community, it might, on occasions, be appropriate, in terms of fairness and proportionality, to equate the time spent on secure remand with double its length: see *R v. Eagles* [2006] EWCA 2368.

This might then serve to bring the length of the DTO down to the next permissible level. However, at the lower end, this might then suggest that a DTO should not be imposed at all as it might (notionally) fall below the four-month minimum period for a DTO (another example of the effective raising of the custody threshold for youths). Conversely, with a higher end DTO, the reduction might not be enough to bring the sentence down from, say, 24 months to 18 months.

The criteria relating to when youths can be placed on a qualifying electronically monitored curfew bail condition change when the youth becomes 17 years-of-age. Credit is, however, still given under section 101 in all cases. Opinions differ as to whether the credit here is automatically the *prima facie* 'straight half' of the appropriate bail period applicable to other custodial sentences for adults and youths or whether, given the set periods for DTOs, the half is merely to be 'taken account of' in general terms under section 101, by analogy and in terms of fairness.

Reference should be made to the somewhat complex provisions of the Bail Act 1976 and the amending provisions of the Criminal Justice and Immigration Act 2008 where a youth has been remanded on electronically monitored curfewed bail and is later sentenced to a custodial sentence.

ALTERNATIVES TO CUSTODY

Avoiding imposing custody, especially in the case of youths, by creating sentences expressed directly as an 'alternative to custody' is well established.

It has already been seen that, in determining that the 'so serious' test has been met, the court must have looked at the possibility of a fine alone or YRO (possibly with a fine added) as an appropriate disposal before finally deciding that the custody threshold has been met.

In respect of adults, the SGC expressly suggests the possibility of a fine (higher than the bands usually applicable) as an alternative to custody even where the 'so serious' test has been met and this approach might also apply to youths.

In respect of adults, the SGC's *Magistrates' Court Sentencing Guidelines* declare that 'passing the custody threshold does not mean that a custodial sentence should be deemed inevitable ... where there is a suitable intervention in the community' that will provide sufficient restriction and rehabilitation.

The SGC in its *Overarching Principles* echoes this by declaring 'Even where the threshold is crossed, a court is not required to impose a custodial sentence'.

There may well then be occasions when the court finds the above criteria for a custodial sentence met in the case of a youth, but is then persuaded to consider some other disposal as a more or less direct alternative.

Intensive supervision and surveillance (ISS) programmes are the most rigorous non-custodial intervention available for young offenders. As its name suggests, it combines intensive levels of community-based supervision and usually electronic surveillance with a comprehensive and sustained focus on tackling the factors that contribute to the young person's offending behaviour. ISSP packages target the most active repeat young offenders or most serious crimes.

The programmes seek to:

- reduce the frequency and seriousness of offending in the target groups
- tackle the underlying needs of offenders which give rise to offending, with a particular emphasis on education and training; and
- provide reassurance to communities through close surveillance backed up by rigorous enforcement.

To further refine this matter, section 1(4) Criminal Justice and Immigration Act 2008 now deals with an additional form of alternative to custody for youths with its own special threshold test.

Basically, where the 'so serious test' would otherwise have been met in respect of an imprisonable offence, the court may (and only in those circumstances) make a YRO which contains an intensive supervision and surveillance programme ('ISSP', as defined in Schedule 1) or which contains a fostering requirement. In addition, the 'persistent offender' test must be satisfied in respect of a defendant aged under 15 years.

This then provides a final practical safeguard before a youth is actually made subject to a DTO via the 'so serious' route.

Where such a YRO is available but custody is imposed nevertheless, the court must give its reasons for not adopting this form of alternative to custody.

The mere availability in certain circumstances of such YROs does not mean that they have to be imposed – the court can always look for other less severe forms of sentencing disposal which are more appropriate in all the circumstances and more likely to prevent further offending.

Such types of YRO are also available for those aged 10 or 11 years in similar circumstances even though they could not have been made subject to a DTO and although, on breach, they could still not receive a custodial sentence.

YROs are considered in greater detail in *Chapter 16*.

NATURE OF THE SECURE YOUTH ESTATE

As already noted above and in *Chapter 10* in relation to arrest detention and charge, young people aged 10-17 years (inclusive) can be remanded or sentenced to custodial institutions by criminal courts in England and Wales when the relevant criteria concerning mainly the seriousness or persistence of their offending are met. The range of secure facilities for this group is known as 'the secure youth estate'.[4]

The Youth Justice Board (YJB) is responsible for commissioning and purchasing places in this estate and for arranging the 'placements' of individuals. The following three main types of facility make up the secure juvenile estate:

- secure children's homes
- secure training centres (STCs); and
- young offender institutions (YOIs).

They are not subject to common legal frameworks or standards, thereby creating an array of considerations about the status of the detainee and the standards and regulations that apply in a given establishment.

Secure children's homes
Mainly provided by local authorities, these small units have a high staff to child ratio and are regulated by the Children Act 1989. Normally, they are used for 10-15 year olds (up to 16 years for girls) who have been either sentenced to custody or remanded into secure accommodation (under a court ordered secure remand (COSR)).

Secure training centres
STCs are larger facilities, run by private sector organizations. Apart from older girls,

4. Or sometimes the secure juvenile estate: see generally *Age-related Terms and Terminology* at page xii.

individuals making up their 'populations' are mainly below the age of 15 years when placed in the STC, on remand or by way of a sentence (above).

Young offenders institutions (YOIs)

These are HM Prison Service facilities which hold the large majority of the older male youth offenders. They cater only for young males aged 15-17 years, inclusive who are subject to custodial sentences or remanded into custody.

In addition, the YJB is developing a number of discrete units within prisons so that 17-year-old girls can be detained separately from adults.

Relatively few young people are detained through criminal proceedings under the Mental Health Act 1983 and they are placed in mental health facilities.

CHILDREN AND YOUNG PEOPLE HELD ON REMAND

Children and young people *held on remand* in a custodial institution in connection with criminal proceedings will be contained as follows:

- boys aged 10-14 years (inclusive) and girls aged 10-16 years (inclusive) who are subject to a court ordered secure remand (COSR) are held in a secure children's home or STC (above)
- boys aged 15 and 16 years are held in a YOI under children and young persons legislation
- boys aged 17 years are held in a YOI under adult legislation (*Chapter 10*)
- girls aged 17 years are held either in a separate unit in an adult prison or an STC.

CHILDREN AND YOUNG PEOPLE UNDER SENTENCE

Children and young people aged 12-17 years (inclusive) who are subject to a custodial sentence, usually a detention and training order (DTO) (above) will be held in the accommodation outlined above, according to their age. Those on a DTO will serve half the sentence in a custodial setting and half in the community, under licence, supervised by a youth offending team (YOT).

The majority of young people who are so sentenced will be subject to a DTO, but for serious and grave crimes (*Chapter 13*) other sentences may apply. Custodial sentences may be determinate or indeterminate in duration, In summary:

- detention and training orders (DTOs) are a **determinate** sentence given for a term of four, six, eight, ten, 12, 18 or 24 months
- long-term detention under section 91 Powers of Criminal Courts (Sentencing) Act 2000 is a **determinate** sentence for very serious and grave offences for all groups

from age 10-17 years, inclusive

- an extended sentence under section 228 Criminal Justice Act 2003 is a **determinate** sentence applying to 'dangerous' offenders aged 10-17 years inclusive
- detention for public protection under section 226 Criminal Justice Act 2003 is an **indeterminate** sentence applying to 'dangerous' offenders aged 10-17 years, inclusive
- detention for life under section 226 Criminal Justice Act 2003 is an **indeterminate** sentence for those aged 10-17 years, inclusive; and
- detention during Her Majesty's pleasure under section 90 Powers of Criminal Courts (Sentencing) Act 2000 is an **indeterminate** sentence for those aged 10-17 years, inclusive.

LOOKED AFTER STATUS OF YOUTHS IN CUSTODY

Legal status/event at point of custody	Effect of detention on young person's status
Looked after at the point of detention and subject of a full care order	No change – looked after status remains during and after detention.
Looked after – section 20 Children Act 1989 (this is a voluntary agreement between parents or guardians and the local authority).	Looked after status ends either on remand to custody or a custodial sentence. It is resumed post custody if parents, etc. and local authority agree.
Court ordered secure remand	Young person becomes looked after for the duration of the remand only. Looked after status ends on remand in custody or a custodial sentence.
Custodial sentence	No form of custodial sentence results in the child or young person becoming looked after. But those subject to a care order when sentenced retain their looked after status.

Most young people entering custody are not in the public care system, sometimes described as being 'looked after' by the local authority. However, young people who become the subject of a court ordered secure remand (usually 10-14 year olds (inclusive)) assume the status of being looked after for the duration of the remand.

The implications of this are that the local authority assumes responsibilities under the Children Act 1989 to fulfil their statutory responsibilities for contact with any children for whom they have parental responsibility who are placed in custody.

The table overleaf provides a basic overview of the status of children and young people who become subject to a custodial remand or sentence.

THE USE OF CUSTODY IN ENGLAND AND WALES

Youth justice workers, courts and a range of children's services support the government's stated aim of limiting the number of children in custodial provision, but the expansion in the use of custody which began in the early 1990s has continued since the implementation of the Crime and Disorder Act 1998.

The number of children and young people detained through criminal proceedings in England and Wales has attracted criticism from the United Nations Committee on the Rights of the Child which in October 2002 reported that the UK was in breach of its legal obligation to use custody as a last resort.[5] This continuing concern has been echoed by Barnardos, the children's charity, in August 2009, with particular emphasis on concerns about a rise in the number of 12-14-year-olds being held in secure settings.

The number of youths sentenced to custody in England and Wales more than tripled between 1991 and 2006. Proportionately, we lock up more youths than any other country in Western Europe (four times the rate in France, ten times that in Spain and one hundred times that of Finland). Concerns are not based solely on the numbers in custody, but also the implications of matters such as the following:[6]

- in April 2008 there were 3,012 youths in custody, 37 under 14-years-of-age
- by then, 48 children were serving indeterminate sentences
- 30 per cent of children in custody have been in the care of their local authority
- over 75 per cent of youths released from custody risk re-conviction within a year
- between 1992 and 2001 while the overall increase in custody was around 90 per cent, the equivalent rise for those under 15 years was 800 per cent
- there has been a disproportionate rise in the number of girls sentenced to detention, which has expanded by more than 400 per cent since 1992
- black children are five times as likely to be locked up then other 10-17 year olds
- the rise in custody is not predicated on any increase in youth crime (the 1990s witnessed a 20 per cent fall in recorded youth offending)

---

5. Article 37(b) of the United Nations Convention on the Rights of the Child.
6. Prison Reform Trust Briefing (2009), 'Criminal Damage: Why We Should Lock Up Fewer Children'.

- equal levels of concern are expressed about the level of remands in custody[7]
- the number of youths remanded in custody is up 41 per cent since 2000; and
- in 2008/9, the majority of youth remands to custody were for a week or less.

If the overall aim of the Youth Justice System (YJS) is to prevent offending (*Chapter 3*), it is apparent that with re-offending rates for those leaving custody being so high, the use of custody 'does not work' in terms of achieving that end.

The concerns about the use of custody for children and young people are many and varied but essentially they are centred on the contrast between the welfare needs of those detained and the capacity of custodial institutions to meet those needs. In 2007/8 a study by the children's charity Barnardos of children aged 12, 13 and 14 years old who had served a custodial sentence found that:

- just under 50 per cent had been abused
- more than 30 per cent were living with a known offender
- 38 per cent had witnessed violence in their family; and
- eight per cent had attempted suicide.

Common factors in the lives of those detained in custody are deprivation, low levels of numeracy and literacy, a history of care, high levels of mental impairment and they are often ill-equipped to cope with the custodial environment. Bullying is a feature in many institutions, and levels of self-harm, attempted suicide and suicide are worryingly high. Since the creation of multi-agency YOTS, the YJB has set ambitious goals for YOTs and others in meeting their responsibilities to:

- promote the safeguarding of children and young people in custody
- to plan for their release; and
- to implement a resettlement plan for children and young people re-entering the community.

Safeguarding children and young people in custody

Young people held in custodial institutions have historically been excluded from the mainstream services that most children in England and Wales are entitled to. On 29 November 2002, Mr Justice Munby ruled that the Children Act 1989 should apply to children detained in YOIs, that duties owed by local authorities continue to be owed to children in YOIs, and that human rights legislation applies to children in custodial facilities.[8] Following this judgement, local councils in areas where there is a YOI, prison or STC were asked to ensure that:

7. Prison Reform Trust Briefing (2009), 'Children: Innocent Until Proven Guilty?'.
8. 'The Munby judgement' (2002): *R v Secretary of State* EWHC 2497.

- they have agreed local protocols with custodial establishments in their area for referral, assessment and the provision of services to children in custody.
- the governor of the custodial establishment is invited to be a member of the Local Safeguarding Children Board (LSCB).
- the LSCB considers what arrangements they require to be put in place to ensure the safeguarding of children in custody; and
- local protocols are in place in the event of a serious incident, such as alleged assault by staff or a death in custody.

In 2003, the YJB and HM Prison Service implemented six initiatives in custodial settings designed to promote safeguards for children and young people in custody:

- safeguarding managers in establishments
- social workers in establishments
- advocacy services available to children and young people
- use of young people-specific policy and operational guidance
- child protection and safeguarding training for establishment staff; and
- consideration of building and cell design.

Planning for release from custody

Each year, 6,500 young people pass through custodial or secure settings, with about 2,700 young people in custody at any one time. Most young people who are subject to a DTO will serve half of their sentence in a custodial or secure establishment and the other half in the community, on licence, supervised by a YOT.

Planning for release from custody, secure accommodation or a secure training centre should start at the beginning of the sentence. It is the role of the YOT to undertake assessments to ensure that the level of vulnerability in a custodial or secure setting is understood by those who will be responsible for the safety and wellbeing of the young person; that any risks posed to others are fully understood; that links with family or carers are maintained; that education continues to meet the needs of the young person and that any health needs are met in the institution.

The aim of the YJB is that the transition from community to custody and back into the community is seamless, requiring all those concerned about the welfare and development of the young person to work collaboratively to an agreed plan.

REINTEGRATION AND RESETTLEMENT

Successful reintegration into and resettlement within the community is an essential element in helping to prevent offending by young people. A resettlement plan should enable young people leaving custody to realise the government's aims set out in the Green Paper, *Every Child Matters* discussed in *Chapter 1*,[9] for every child. Whatever their background or their circumstances, they should be given the support they need. To support this aim, the YJB responded to concerns raised by the Social Exclusion Unit's (SEU's) report of 2002, *Reducing Reoffending by Ex-Prisoners*[10] by developing a national youth resettlement framework. This reflected the aims of the 2004 Home office publication, *The National Reducing Re-offending Delivery Plan*[11] which sought to reduce re-offending by adults through greater cross-government collaboration and planning.

Successful transition from custody to the community requires a co-ordinated, multi-agency response that is sustained after release. The youth resettlement framework focuses on a number of areas, referred to as 'pathways':

- accommodation
- education, training and employment
- health
- substance misuse
- families
- finance, benefits and debt; and
- attitudes, thinking and behaviour.

The resettlement model emphasises the importance of what is known as sentence planning. The responsibility of the YOT in this regard is:

- **pre-sentence**: to gather information, make assessments concerning need, risk of re-offending and of harm to others, identifying key people to support plans
- **custody**: to assess response to sentence, assess vulnerability and alert the establishment to any concerns, check safeguarding plans, ensure education and health plans are being met, identify other resources, and facilitate links with the youth's family and community
- **community phase**: to implement plans for accommodation, education or employment, meet health needs, support family relationships, financial planning and so on; and
- **after the end of licence**: to identify continuing support from local services and the community.

---

9.   (2003). See dcsf.gov.uk/everychildmatters
10. Social Exclusion Unit (2002b)
11. Summary of a Social Exclusion Unit report: see cabinetoffice.gov.uk

These developments represent a considerable advance on the arrangements which existed in the past. They do however serve mainly to reinforce and normalise ideas concerning the custodial treatment of youths rather than raise questions about the the appropriateness of custody to begin with. Some other jurisdictions seem to have made greater progress in this regard.

CHAPTER 18

Youth Justice the Way Ahead

Youth justice has come a great distance since it first became a separate area of work and study within the broader sphere of criminal justice. It has also, in modern time, undergone seismic changes. No longer does the term Youth Justice System (YJS) (*Chapter 3*) trigger images of a court-based machine 'at the hub' routinely 'processing cases' in some disconnected way. Various strands now come together to create individualised outcomes for troubled youths through YJS networks. Indeed, a central feature is now the work of the Youth Justice Board (YJB), youth offending teams (YOTs) and youth offender panels (YOPs), which has come more to the fore.[1]

The work of the youth courts with their long traditions and special ethos also remains key, but it rests to a great extent on what the YJB and the YOTs can do and provide, the nature of their annual plans and the quality of their day-to-day work. As this book shows, the youth courts now have an enormous array of powers, whether of the preventive, punitive or rehabilitative kind. But the work of the YOTs, whose origins can be traced to philanthropic gestures of the early 1900s and initiatives taken at grass roots level by local 'juvenile justice units' from the 1980s onwards[2] has brought about a fresh sense of what youth justice involves.

At the same time, neither the YJB or YOTs can operate effectively without a thorough understanding of the stance being taken by sentencers. In this, the Sentencing Guidelines Council (SGC) *Overarching Principles* (which are reproduced in full in the *Appendix* to this work) represent a considerable step forward. As with the YJB's own 'scaled approach' discussed in earlier chapters, they represent a touchstone of youth justice for youth court magistrates, YOTs and YOPs alike.

CONTINUING AREAS OF INTEREST AND CONCERN

Just as it was hoped when the new YJS described in *Chapter 3* was set up under the Crime and Disorder Act 1998, it might now be anticipated that the changes of 2009 described in this book will settle the work of the courts and the YOTs for the foreseeable future. However, a number of areas of interest or concern could affect the direction of youth justice in the not to distant future, such as the fact that:

- the Justice Select Committee of the House of Commons, in responding to the SGC's draft guidelines, suggested that it might now wish to look at remand and

---

1. Or more 'centre stage' as it is sometimes put.
2. See generally the *Timeline* at the end of the book.

sentencing provisions for those aged 18-24 years, which it referred to as 'youth justice matters', possibly suggesting that, in criminal justice terms, the transition into adulthood (based on both chronological age and maturity) may come to be seen as covering a longer age span than at present

- there have been a substantial number of calls for the age of criminal responsibility to be raised and younger 'offenders' dealt with as welfare cases as has been the plan at least twice in the last sixty or so years, including at times for older youths also, as Chris Stanley's *Foreword*, explains; and

- demands for closer scrutiny of what is in fact achieved by some programmes, as brought to mind by a controversial report by researchers at Portsmouth University who in 2009 claimed to have found that intensive supervision and surveillance (ISS) programmes in place before the reforms of the CJIA 2008 were 'endangering the public and failing to stop criminal behaviour', on the basis that nine out of ten youths on such programmes, so the report said, went on to re-offend.

The causes of the events described in the last item were said to be related to levels of supervision and enforcement. The report suggested that the offenders concerned (and society) might be better served if they were 'removed from their environment, taught job-related skills and given supervision in the form of structured mentoring'.[3] It even suggested that some ISS programme offenders had also indicated that a custodial sentence might have deterred them more.

The research was criticised by some commentators who suggested that it sought to extrapolate the findings of a narrowly-based study in two geographical areas onto a wider canvass and, perhaps not surprisingly, the YJB expressed confidence in the existing (and forthcoming 2009) arrangements. It suggested that the research had not considered a wide enough range of ISS programmes, nor recognised that any re-offending might have been less serious and less frequent. Nonetheless observers are now likely to be carefully watching for how the new ISS provisions of the CJIA 2008 perform in terms of crime prevention generally and reducing re-offending in particular. Sound and timely monitoring and evaluations seem to be essential.

Returning to some further developments which are indicative of the need for continuing scrutiny:

- in 2009 the children's charity Barnardos suggested that 'children as young as 12 were being locked up too quickly and too easily' against the backdrop of a declared Government policy that custody should be used as a last resort;[4] and

- again indicative of the need for careful monitoring, evaluated and evidence-based

---

3. See port.ac.uk/news and events (accessed October 2009).
4. Barnardos press release, August 2009.

research of the impact of the new statutory criteria and Sentencing Guidelines Council (SGC) guidance, Barnardos chief executive, Martin Narey also, in September 2009, called for a greater focus on the removal of at-risk children from their home surroundings, including at birth where this is necessary.

This last suggestion appears to imply that some families and standards of parenting are not easily 'fixed' or 'repaired' and that there is a greater need for the State to step in, at least where children cannot be safely left with, or returned to, their own families. In a more general sense, this fuels other calls to strengthen the 'welfare' response to offending behaviour by youths rather than let matters gradually drift until a youth's difficulties are 'picked up on' in criminal proceedings.

Days before Martin Narey spoke, the media was reporting the case of two young brothers (aged ten and 12) from Doncaster, South Yorkshire, who had tortured and sexually assaulted two other young boys. Commentators suggested that the perpetrators were themselves at risk as a result of the abuse they had suffered, which in turn put them at risk of becoming abusers of others. It was suggested that it was a mistake not to remove them from their home situation and permanently 'disconnect' them from it (even if hindsight is always a valuable commodity).

The tensions between human rights considerations of respect for family and private life (*Chapter 2*) and the consequences of not taking appropriate action to remove a child before it is too late are patently obvious, but there is also a need for robust measures on occasion. What is clear is that debates on youth justice are far from over with the changes of 2009 and some quite fundamental issues concerning the whole approach to youth justice are likely to continue.

SOME GOVERNMENT MOVES

In mid-2009, Ed Balls, Minister of State at the Department for Children, Schools and Families (DCFS) and Alan Johnson, Home Secretary, jointly wrote to local authorities urging them to set up family intervention projects, targeted at 'problem families' with children who are at risk of becoming persistent offenders. Balls said that, thus far, only half of local authorities – a total of 75 – were taking part in the scheme. There were at that time 2,000 families in the intensive family support programme (IFS) with 42 new projects set up since the publication of the previous year's Youth Crime Action Plan (YCAP). He hoped that the IFS would rapidly expand to cover 20,000 problem families, hopefully 'within the next 18 months'.

The circular letter in question urged local authorities to expand and accelerate family intervention programmes in their areas or risk losing the extra money that was being made available. It uses a key worker to deliver intensive support to particularly 'chaotic' or 'challenging' young people and families, with certain non-negotiable elements and sanctions if behaviour does not change. The programme costs between £5,000 and £20,000 per family.

The same overall plan has seen the involvement of 26,000 young people in 'extra activities' on Friday and Saturday evenings and the introduction of street teams of youth workers in 65 local areas. Operation Staysafe is designed to remove vulnerable young people from the streets at night and to take them to a place of safety.

On a wider front, Ministers say they 'intend to clarify further' local relationships between childrens' trusts which bring together all services for children and YOTs. There has been talk of the possibility of 'youth crime budgets' becoming part of local authority funds, so that a geographical area has a vested interest in crime reduction and that there are thus greater incentives for the YJS to find ways of avoiding the consumption of expensive resources (such as custody or the more intensive youth rehabilitation order (YRO) schemes: *Chapters 16* and *17*). Budgets touching on local revenues can also be argued as more democratic in that it is perhaps easier for citizens to have their say or influence events. Other measures being looked at include simply making communities more aware of the costs of youth justice outcomes. In this regard, some areas of the country have already begun to publish relevant facts and figures in their information sheets and magazines for local citizens.

One pilot scheme involving 'custody panels' is run by the Local Government Association (LGA) and the Howard League for Penal Reform. It showed a 43 per cent drop in the number of children sent to custody as a result of the initiative. However, the revised YCAP makes it clear that Ministers do not intend to make it mandatory for a formal review process (such as that informal one) to take place before a child can be sentenced to time in a 'youth jail'. One key part of the YCAP was the promise of comprehensive packages of support, including housing and education, for young people leaving custody. Extra funding for this initiative was promised, over the next two years, but any details have yet to be announced and may be on hold as part and parcel of election-minded talk of public spending cuts.

As already indicated in *Chapter 6*, with a General Election on the horizon, a more punitive rather than welfare-based ethos has blown through Westminster. There has been a return to the 'Tough on crime' mantra of the late 1990s and Prime Minister Gordon Brown has also committed his party to a revival of the use of the anti-social behaviour order (ASBO), which for a time at least seemed to be more the butt of attacks concerning their high breach rates, apparent failure to stem subsequent offending and role in conferring 'badges of honour'. It is part of the tragedy of youth justice that it is an easy target for those who seek to make political capital out of the troubled lives of young people.[5]

---

5. The high watermark of which is perhaps the Bulger case noted in the *Glossary*.

A MATTER OF PERSPECTIVE

Whether or not events are moving in the right direction youth-justice wise can of course be a matter of perspective and sometimes of blind belief that people are 'doing the right thing'. Hence again the importance of evidence-based research, but also not to stifle the generation of ideas. Certainly the YJB see cause for optimism. The YJB's regular output of highly polished publications, include a periodic magazine, concisely titled *YJ*. According to the September 2009 edition which arrived as this work was about to go to press:

> Over a year on from the government's Youth Crime Action Plan, the number of young people entering the Criminal Justice System has fallen. And the youth restorative disposal (YRD), although still at its pilot stage, is still playing its part [see *Chapter 4*].

The same edition goes on, in a similarly positive fashion, to comment on new programmes, schemes, 'connections' to other parts of the YJS and resources, to deal with the life of police officers dealing with youth crime and anti-social behaviour (ASB) at 'street level', dealing with knife crime, youth inclusion programmes, educational support, vulnerable young people, 'fixing' broken family relationships and the experiences of young offenders 'in their own words'. Tellingly the editorial comment is headed 'Youth inclusion programme enters second decade of success' and the tone is, largely speaking, equally upbeat throughout the magazine. It is the kind of publication that some of the more progressive youth support and rehabilitation-based voluntary sector organizations have relied on for many years and indeed it is a welcome counter to the negative coverage by the popular press described in *Chapter 1*. It would of course be good to know that its tone will be matched by the results of the evidence-based research on the impact of the CJIA 2008 which can be expected in two to three years time. None of this coverage, of course, says anything about whether the system itself might be in need of more fundamental reforms of the kind suggested by Chris Stanley in his *Foreword*.

ONE NOTICEABLE AND RECURRING THEME

During the writing of this book it became necessary to speak with a range of practitioners and experts in youth justice. One recurring theme resonates through all their responses, 'If only matters were not so complex'. In presenting the picture of youth justice which appears in this book, references to complexity, difficult, matters of interpretation, technical arguments and the like have been largely avoided (except when this is impossible) in favour of a 'clean' and unhindered description of the subject matter. The main purpose was to present an accessible account which allows people to see at a glance how the various parts of the YJS and their main components fit together: what youth justice is all about. However, readers should be aware that there are many points at which further reference or research may be necessary. Neither may they always easily find reliable or definitive answers.

The complexity of youth justice law arises for several reasons. To begin with it is still, to an appreciable extent, 'bolted onto' the underlying laws and principles which apply in adult criminal justice situations. It is not possible to describe youth justice in pure isolation (and yet, at the same time, it is not possible at every juncture to stop and set out all the relevant and underlying adult law). Most practitioners, magistrates and others understand this. There are then the special or additional rules for youth that do exist and which may apply in all, some, or exceptional cases.

Finding those special rules or understanding dedicated youth-related criminal justice provisions is a challenge in itself in modern-times. The Criminal Justice and Immigration Act 2008 is just one example of the tendency of modern-day legislative draftsmen towards complexity, with the added difficulty of 'legislation by amendment' of existing Acts of Parliament. This in turn may refer to earlier legislation which of doubtful provenance in terms of its implementation or redundancy, whether in part, or sometimes under delegated powers which also allow for various (sometimes amended) applications of it in different parts of the country, including under pilot schemes which may or may not lead to the adoption of a particular law, provision or scheme nationwide.

It is probably no misrepresentation to say that both lawyers and others come, to a considerable extent, to understand youth justice by imbibing its workings and nuances as much from the myriad views and conversations that take place in day-to-day practice as they do their law books and internet-based reference tools. Hardly anyone can purport to be a master of all the chapter and verse involved without a particularly sustained effort.[6]

Youth justice is not simply a set of legal rules

The next problem of understanding youth justice stems from the fact it is not simply a legal construct or one that simply involves ordinary notions of justice (although again these have to be understood). It rests as much on general principles of the kind laid down by the SGC as on the powers of the courts.

Another way in which it is not 'legalistic' lies in the work of the YJB, YOTs and YOPs, who have developed their own tools, guidelines, 'scaled approach' and ethos. The powers of the courts only make sense in the light of the duties, responsibilities and remit of the arrangements whereby frontline youth crime prevention, youth crime reduction, diversion, intervention and much of their referrals or sentencing are put into practice. In summary, no one can really understand youth justice without:

---

6. One wonders what youths make of it. How much better a YJS which they can fully understand.

- a broad knowledge of the law (making allowance for its complexities)
- an understanding of the aims, purposes and work of the YJB, YOTs and YOPs
- the roles of other YJS practitioners; and
- a sense of the principles and values by which courts and practitioners operate, in which the work of the SGC is now paramount.

WAIFS, STRAYS AND OTHER PEOPLE'S CHILDREN

In the *Timeline* at the end of this work there is a reference to the Waifs and Strays Society founded by Edward de Montjoie Rudolf in London in 1881. This was one of the first organizations whose aims included tackling youth crime by presenting the offenders concerned with different choices. It is nowadays a quaint sounding name that serves to emphasise the way in which in the modern day we have learned to talk about youth offenders in an entirely different and, in some circles, as described in *Chapter 1*, outrightly condemnatory way.

Far better perhaps then to end this book on a counter-balancing note, by repeating, with a degree of licence, some words of wisdom. They are those of Baroness Barbara Wooton who after many years experience as chair of the Westminster juvenile court from the 1970s onwards emphasised that:

> The YJS should never forget that it is always dealing with other people's children.[7]

Other people's children, waifs, strays, feral youths, yobs or 'ratboys' it is the courts, practitioners, organizations and services described in this book which will make decisions that will affect them for the rest of their lives.

---

7. What she actually wrote was: 'Juvenile court magistrates should never forget that ... they are always dealing with other people's children'.

Glossary of Youth Justice-related Terms

With brief descriptions of a selection of youth-justice related organizations.

Bryan Gibson
© Waterside Press 2009

AA appropriate adult (who should be present, e.g. at a police interview of a youth or a court in place of a parent, etc): *Chapters 10, 14*

ABC acceptable behaviour 'contract', between a member of a **YOT** and an offender (or someone at risk of offending): *Chapter 6*

ABH actual bodily harm

abscond fail to surrender to bail, or to leave a court police station, crime scene, etc. without permission or excuse: *Chapter 14.*

absolute right one by virtue of the European Convention On Human Rights, that cannot be departed from. Contrast **limited right**s and **qualified right** as described in *Chapter 3.*

abuse of process improper or inappropriate use of laws, procedures, paperwork, etc

AC attendance centre Now one of the 15 requirements of a YRO (*Chapter 16*). Attendance centres marked their 60th anniversary in 2008: see *Timeline*, 1948. Junior centres cater for 10-17-year-olds; senior centres for those aged 16-24.

acquittal term used when someone is found 'not guilty' and **discharged**

action plan One by a **YOT** or **YOP** as concerning what action is to be taken in an offending or crime prevention scenario. See also **YCAP**

AD absolute discharge, i.e. where the offence is deemed to be trivial or technical, and where punishment is 'inexpedient'. Contrast CD below and see generally *Chapter 15.*

adjourn put off a hearing to: (1) a new date fixed by the court when adjourning; (2) later the same day (aka **standing down**); or (3) indefinitely (aka an adjournment sine die) (rare in criminal proceedings). Cases are adjourned, defendants are **remanded**.

advance disclosure See **disclosure**

affirmation as an alternative to swearing an **oath**, a witness is entitled to affirm, by stating:

I do solemnly and sincerely declare and affirm that the evidence I shall give will be the truth, the whole truth and nothing but the truth.

age see *Age-related Terms and Terminology: A Note* at the start of the book and the various references to 'age-related aspects' in the *Index*

aggravating factor one which makes an offence more serious (as per **sentencing guidelines**). Contrast **mitigating factor**.

ancillary order one additional to a basic sentence, e.g. **disqualification, costs**: *Chapter 15*

AOPM the Association of Panel Members which is working 'to establish a network for the 5400 community volunteers supporting **YOTs** in England and Wales, to share Good Practice in the administration of referral orders, and to provide a voice for communities to influence the effectiveness and development of restorative justice': see aopm.co.uk

appraisal a process via which magistrates', practitioners, staff, etc. are assessed to help them check on their progress, etc.

ASB/O anti-social behaviour/order: *Chapter 6*

assessment assessment for a report, scheme, suitability, or of seriousness, etc. A term widely used to signify the application of professional and/or expert opinion, advice or techniques to a problem or process, including in particular assessment for a **PSR** (*Chapter 15*), re mental impairment or drug treatment. Assessment models used by YOTs follow the **ASSET** and **ONSET** frameworks.

ASSET A YJB/YOT assessment tool: *Chapter 15*

Association of Panel Members See **AOPM**

backed for bail a warrant on which has been endorsed an instruction by the issuing court that the person arrested under it is to be released on bail (originally 'on its back')

Barnardos children's charity whose origins date from 1867 when Dr Thomas John Barnardo (1845-1905) founded a 'Juvenile Mission', 'The Earnest School, and first experimental Children's home in Stepney, East London; as part of a Crusade to rescue destitute children and young people – especially orphans and those who had been abandoned. This grew, over 140 years, into an international undertaking with 370 working centres in the UK alone. Barnardos' modern-day aims and visions include helping 'the most vulnerable children and young people to transform their lives and fulfill their potential'. The charity produces a range of related publications; its president is Cherie Booth QC; and its director (since 2005) the former first Commissioner of Corrections, Martin Narey. Contact details: Barnardos, Tanners Lane, Barkingside, Ilford, Essex IG6 1QG; Tel 0208 550 8822; barnardos.org.uk Note also **Barnardos' Videos** on a range of topics: see that same web-site.

BCS *British Crime Survey.* A key source of data concerning public perceptions of and attitudes to crime. See homeoffice.gov.uk/rds

best practice (or Best Practice) the finest way of dealing with a given matter, process, task, etc. as determined by senior management within an agency/service and/or experts and promulgated to managers, frontline practitioners, etc. Competing practices are considered to arrive at 'the best' method; sometimes after **multi-agency** consultation.

BME black or minority ethnic

Borstal a village near Rochester, Kent where the first 'experiment' in indeterminate training for young offenders aged 15-21 (23 from 1930) began; that gave its name to **borstal training** (1902 -1982); attributed to prison commissioner Sir Evelyn Ruggles-Brise (1857-1935). The play 'Borstal Boy' (1958) (and film 2002) by Irish playwright (and one-time terrorist) Brendan Behan (1923-1964) is set in a borstal and highlights the by then inherent brutality. In the short story, *The Loneliness of the Long Distance Runner* (1958) by Alan Sillitoe (and film 1962) a disadvantaged youth who turned to crime 'for relief' survives the **borstal regime** by pandering to the governor via athletic prowess; but deliberately stops short of the winning line in a key race: a metaphor for disaffected youth.

breach failure to comply with a court order or release licence, e.g. breach of bail, a community sentence, parole or an anti-social behaviour order (**ASBO**). Breach is associated with **enforcement:** see Chapters *15-17*. Note also breach of a **recognizance**.

British Association of Social Workers The largest association representing social work and social workers in the UK, 'whether qualified people or not, experienced, or just entering the profession'. BASW provides help and support, advice and campaigns on behalf of its members; who share 'a commitment to good social work practice' (see, generally, good practice) as outlined in the BASW's 'Code of Ethics for Social Work'. BASW, 16 Kent Street, Birmingham, B5 6RD; Tel: 0121 622 3911; info@basw.co.uk; basw.co.uk.

broken windows in the context of this work, an environmentally-based theory of criminology attributed to James Q Wilson and George Kelling (USA)(1960s) that crime, fear of crime and poor law enforcement are more likely to occur and be accepted as the norm in badly maintained areas, where 'windows get broken and and remain so', due, e.g. to low levels of respect, self-esteem, concern or motivation. There has been a resurgence of such thinking in modern times: see *Chapter 8.*

BTDC Bench Training and Development Committee: *Chapter 14*

Bulger case In 1992, James Patrick Bulger, a two year old child, was abducted and murdered in Liverpool, Merseyside by two 10-year-olds Jon Venables and Robert Thompson; leading to a public outcry, especially locally; triggering a firm new line on law and order and triggering further and increasing politicisation of criminal justice. Bulger disappeared from the New Strand Shopping Centre. His mutilated body was found on a railway line at Bootle. The accused (whose identities were disclosed in the interests of justice) were convicted at Preston Crown Court (1993) and ordered to be detained during Her Majesty's pleasure (see *Chapter 13*), with a judicial recommendation that they serve 'very, very many years'. Lord Taylor, Lord Chief Justice, then ruled that they should serve at least ten years. Media/press reaction (including a campaign by The Sun newspaper) led 300,000 people to petition Home Secretary Michael Howard. In 1995 he said that they should serve at least 15 years; but in 1997 the Court of Appeal found this unlawful and after appeals to the European Court of Human Rights (ECHR) (see *Chapter 3*), the Home Secretary lost to the judges the power to set tariffs for 'lifers' under 18 (and later adults: both, since 2007, Ministry of Justice-related matters). Thompson and Venables were released after eight years. An injunction safeguards their identities and locations. The case led to changes in the way trials of children at the Crown Court occur, then held in a highly formal way. There are more such cases of murder, etc. than most people realise, some 50 a year in the UK alone. Another notorious such case indicating the power of the media to demonise children is that of Mary Bell (1968). For a survey, see *Children Who Kill* (1996), Cavadino P (Ed.), Waterside Press.

burden of proof this term signifies where the onus of proving something lies, normally with the prosecutor in a criminal case except for special situations. Contrast **standard of proof** and see the further notes there below.

Butler Trust an independent charity which recognises 'excellence and innovation' by people working with offenders in the UK. Through its annual Butler Trust Award Scheme and associated Development Programme it helps to bring about effective care for offenders (including in the field of youth justice) by: identifying and promoting excellence and innovation by a range of criminal justice staff, contractors and volunteers; developing and disseminating best practice in the care and resettlement of offenders; and providing professional and personal development opportunities for award-winning staff. For further details, see thebutlertrust.org.uk

CAB Citizens Advice Bureau (a voluntary sector body): see citizensadvice.org.uk

Carpenter, Mary (1807-1877) Philanthropist who. after founding a girls school in Bristol (1829) and becoming superintendent of a Sunday School (1831-56), pressed for institutions designed to rescue youth offenders. She founded a boys reformatory (1852); girls reformatory (1854); and an industrial school (1859), all in Bristol (plus a 'ragged school' there). She published various works on penal reform. See also the *Foreword*.

case to answer a term used to signify that the evidence collected by the police or placed before a court by a prosecutor 'calls for an answer' from a suspect/accused person. In court it signifies that there is enough evidence for a court to convict, but whether it will do so depends an all the circumstances. An accused person does not have to provide 'an answer', but appropriate inferences can be drawn from silence.

case stated short for appeal by way of case stated: see generally *Appeals* in *Chapter 14*.

case management umbrella term for the processes by which cases are managed from start to finish, whether in a purely administrative way or judicially by the court itself. Hence, e.g. the **Youth Case Management Framework (YCMF)** and the YJB's own **'Case Management Guidance'.** See in particular *Chapters 7, 8* and *9*.

Catch22 (formerly **Rainer Crime Concern**). A nationwide charity working with young people 'in difficult situations'. Catch 22 works with their families and communities 'wherever and whenever young people need us most'. It is Catch 22's belief that as young people become more positive, productive and independent, the entire community benefits. It focuses on five key areas: learning, earning a living, somewhere safe to live, steering clear of crime and giving something back. The organization is based at Churchill House, 142-146 Old Street, London, EC1V 9BW (with branches elsewhere, including in Sheffield, Swindon, and Nottingham. Headquarters tel: 020 7336 4800; and for further information, see catch-22.org.uk

caution (1) a term used in relation to adults only, although youths can receive **'conditional cautions'** post-CJIA 2008: *Chapters 6* and *11*. Other uses of 'caution' include: **(2)** that by a **court legal adviser** re a youth's rights; and **(3)** a **police caution on arrest** (or before interview) re the 'right to silence' and the fact that inferences can be drawn from silence.

CBO civil behaviour order (of various kinds): see the brief note in *Chapter 15*

CD (1) conditional discharge: a sentencing disposal whereby the offender is discharged on condition that he or she does not commit another offence within a period of up to three years. Compare **AD** above. See generally *Chapter 15*. Also short for: (**2**) criminal damage.

CDRP Crime and Disorder Reduction Partnership

CDS Criminal Defence Service. Nationwide agency providing defence services to those on legal aid: *Chapter 12* and see legalservices.gov.uk

Centre for Crime and Justice Studies (CCJS) An independent charity based at King's College London (KCL) that informs and educates re all aspects of crime and the CJS, including youth justice: 'Our vision is of a society in which everyone benefits from justice, safety, economic and social security. Our mission is to promote just and effective responses to crime and related harms by informing and educating, through critical analysis, research and public debate'. The CCJS publishes a journal, *Criminal Justice Matters* and makes an annual **Una Padel Award** in memory of a former director. See crimeandjustice.org.uk

CEOP Child Exploitation and Online Protection Centre: see ceop.gov.uk

charge and requisition a new way of commencing criminal proceedings that it is planned to be phased in and that will replace informations and summonses re public prosecutors: *Chapter 12.*

child in a criminal context someone aged 10-13 (inclusive): see generally *Age-related terms and terminology* at the start of the book.

Children's Society a leading children's charity 'committed to making childhood better for all children in the UK ... [that takes] action to prevent, rescue and support children facing life trapped in a vicious circle of fear and harm. The society's origins lie in the Waifs and Strays Society of 1881: see the *Timeline* and for further details of its modern-day work with youths, see ChildrenSociety.org.uk.

Children Who Kill is the title of a collection of papers by eminent commentators including Gita Sereny, Allan Levy QC and Dr. Susan Bailey. It focuses on the scenario whereby up to 50 youths a year in the UK on average (and proportionately the same number in other countries) kill other human beings. The cases of Mary Bell and (victim) Jamie Bulger (see **Bulger case** above) thus represent a deeper, less visible and more thought-provoking, challenge. *Children Who Kill* (1996), Cavadino P (ed.), Waterside Press.

CJA Criminal Justice Act

CJIA 2008 Criminal Justice and Immigration Act 2008: see the implementation schedule in *Chapter 9.*

CJSSS Criminal Justice: Simple, Speedy, Summary (of which 'Simple, Speedy, Youth Justice' is a component.

'clip around the ear' The early-to-mid 20th century practice whereby low-level offenders (typically juveniles) were cuffed about the ears by a police officer as a warning (hence aka cuffing). It remains a metaphor for warnings, reprimands, conditional cautions or police advice. Hence the Tory Opposition's 'new generation clip around the ear' and promise tough (below) action following a poor response by offenders (2009) (contrast its approach to **hoodies** below in 2006).

competence magistrates' general levels of progress re aspects of their role are assessed by asking whether they have acquired certain competences *Chapter 14*. A similar approach may be used more widely in the YJS.

conferencing in effect 'sitting around a table to discuss a case, allegation, strategy, etc, especially multi-agency **case conferences** which focus on a particular individuals and his or her progress (now often within a **YOT** or, e.g. a **MAPPA** below). The term is also used in restorative justice circles in particular where the **family group conference (FGC)** (or **community conference**) has a central role. Meetings with a lawyer are sometimes called **a conference**, especially with a barrister.

connections usually a reference to making connections via networks of resources and facilities, so that they can be accessed by young people especially

ConneXions The ConneXions service was established in 2001 with the aim of providing a comprehensive service to meet young people's needs for information, advice and support. Using a **multi-agency** approach, ConneXions provides high-quality, impartial, information, advice and guidance, together with access to personal-development opportunities to help remove barriers to learning and progression and ensure young people make a smooth transition to adulthood and working life. As part of the service, a dedicated website, **ConneXions Direct**, is available for young people aged 13 to 19. See dcfs.gov.uk/everychildmatters

conviction in the youth court this term translates as 'finding of guilt': see *Chapter 15*.

costs (1) the costs of a criminal case, which may be ordered to be paid by the offender (or to the offender from public funds) according to the outcome of a case. In the case of a youth an order for costs must not exceed a certain limit: see *Chapter 15*. A **wasted costs** order can be made against a legal representative in some circumstances. **(2)** The **costs of youth justice** see generally *Chapter 5*.

contract see **ABC** and **YOC**. The term contract is also used in particular to signify the purchasing of private sector services.

COSR court ordered secure remand: *Chapter 17*

CPA (1) crime pattern analysis. **(2)** Child Protection Agency.

CPO (1) crime prevention officer; **(2)** child protection officer; **(3)** community punishment order (transitional cases): *Chapter 16*.

CPRO community punishment and rehabilitation order (transitional cases): *Chapter 16*.

CPR 2005 Criminal Procedure Rules 2005

CPS Crown Prosecution Service

CPRC Criminal Procedure Rule Committee

CRASBO a colloquial but widely used term for criminal anti-social behaviour order, i.e. an **ASBO** made on conviction for an offence rather than on a civil application

CRB Criminal Records Bureau. Enhanced CRB checks are nowadays routine for YJB practitioners and others working directly with children. See also **disclosure** below.

Criminal Classes: Offenders at School is the ingenious title of a work by Angela Devlin (1995), Waterside Press, in which the backgrounds of people who went on to enter the adult Criminal Justice System are traced through oral histories of their educational using headings such as 'Wagging and Sagging, Bunking and Skiving', 'New Kids on the Block', Teachers: Good, Bad and Boring' and 'Odd One Out'. The work also seeks to identify where things went wrong at school.

criminalisation a term with various connotations, focusing around the idea of 'turning people into criminals' or 'making criminals out of people'; either due to the way in which the law itself impacts on them, or the way that the CJS (or YJS) treats them, e.g. through targeting offences or law enforcement priorities. The term is also associated with the creation of an excessive number of crimes; as well as poverty, disadvantage and people 'on the margins of society; who are also vulnerable to **net widening** (below). The process is also nowadays associated with anti-social behaviour (**ASB**) (and civil behaviour orders (**CBOs**)), where behaviour which is not intrinsically criminal is criminalised if there is a breach of the original order: *Chapter 6*.

CRO (1) Criminal Records Office. **(2)** Crime reduction officer (police or local authority).

CRP crime reduction programme/partnership

CS custody sergeant: who oversees **PACE** related matters of youth detention: *Chapter 10*.

CYPA Children and Young Persons Act

DAT (multi-agency) drug action team

DCFS Department for Children, Schools and Families: see dcfs.gov.uk

deaths in custody generic head under which deaths in prison, police or other official custody (or detention) are discussed; whether from attack, natural causes, suicide, accident, or ill-treatment. Some 100 deaths per year are involved. Many cases have become rallying points, including those of Zahid Mubarek (d.1997) re whom a public inquiry made over 150 recommendations for improvements following his being killed by a cell-mate at Feltham Young Offender Institution; and Adam Rickwood (d.2004 aged 14) the youngest person to die in custody in the UK: at Hassockfield Secure Training Centre, County Durham (operated by the private sector). Arrangements exist for automatic referral for investigation. Further information about this topic is available from the lead organization INQUEST (inquest.gn.apc.org).

default usually a reference to fine default; and see, especially, the **YDO**

deferment postponement of sentence with some clear objective in mind: see *Chapter 15*

delegated legislation that made under delegated powers, e.g. by a Minister of State; aka Statutory Instrument (SI) or regulations, possibly bye-laws

demonisation styling, **labelling** or **stereotyping** (both below) individuals, or groups, as people whom the public should fear (who, in some cases, may be dubbed 'evil'); such as **hoodies** (below), immigrants, paedophiles and people from marginal backgrounds. Similarly, views or opinions, may be demonised; and 'monsters' created by the media/press and in popular culture. The process may often have political dimensions; and has connections to hate crime, discrimination and social exclusion. See works on criminology.

designated case worker a member of the **CPS** who is qualified and competent to deal with certain matters in court but not the full range of tasks falling to a Crown prosecutor

detention (1) police detention (or that of other authorised law enforcement agencies) of suspects as per the Police and Criminal Evidence Act 1984 (PACE); aka detention without charge. **Further detention** can be authorised by a court up to a maximum of 96 hours by way of a **warrant of further detention**: *Chapter 10*. **(2) Detention at Her Majesty's pleasure** (aka **detention for life** can (in some cases must) be ordered by the Crown Court instead of life imprisonment); or re a young offender, someone unfit to plead or who is insane: see generally *Chapter 13*. **(3) detention in a YOI**. **(4) Detention in a special hospital** (or other hospital): a Crown Court matter. **(5)** Other uses include **detention of foreign nationals** re border control; and **home detention curfew** (a form of prison release licence for adults only using **EM**). **Detention centre** is a former youth punishment institution before the creation of modern forms of custody for youths.

DI detective inspector

disclosure (1) revealing information, documents, reports etc. about aspects of a prosecution or defence case. Hence, e.g. **advance disclosure of the prosecution case** by the CPS. The Criminal Justice Act 2003 amended the Criminal Procedure and Investigations Act 1996 which contained certain pre-trial disclosure provisions relating to both **parties**; notably re **disclosure of the defence case** so that this now extends to the making and updating of a 'defence statement'

setting out the nature of the defence, any specific defence, points of law, evidence, abuse of process and a list of defence witnesses (including experts). The Lord Chancellor can prescribe further matters. A court may draw **inferences** from shortcomings in such disclosure; but cannot convict solely on that basis. **(2) disclosure of a pre-sentence report (PSR):** *Chapter 15.* **(3) disclosure of unused prosecution material**: since 2003 the prosecutor must disclose 'any prosecution material ... not previously ... disclosed to the accused person and which might reasonably be considered capable of undermining the case for the prosecution ... or of assisting the case for the accused'. **(4)** Since 2002, following the Police Act 1997, the **Criminal Records Bureau (CRB)** provides authorised access and disclosure of information via its **disclosure service**; allowing organizations in the public, private and voluntary sectors to make safer recruitment decisions. There are two levels of check depending upon the nature of the position, known as **standard disclosure** and **enhanced disclosure**: see crb.gov.uk **(5)** Note also **disclosure of information** under the Freedom of Information Act 2000.

discontinuance i.e. of a case by a Crown prosecutor where prosecution **threshold** or other tests are no longer met, including under a duty to review cases: *Chapters 11* and *12*.

DJ district judge. In a YJS context meaning a district judge (magistrates' courts)

dock The (usually) wooden and/or glass structure where an accused person stands in court; sanctified by tradition and the needs of security. Youth courts are less formal and hence there is no dock in the *Example of a youth courtroom* at the front of this book; but the metaphor 'in the dock' continues to signify being called to account generally.

doli incapax rule a rule of the Common Law whereby (as extended) someone between the ages of 10-14 could not be guilty of an offence unless, in addition to ordinary *mens rea*, he or she knew that what he or she did was seriously wrong. This rule was abolished by the Crime and Disorder Act 1998 (but the statutory rule that a child under ten does not have the capacity to commit crime survives).

domestic national not international: *Chapter 2*

DPP Director of Public Prosecutions

DrugScope national membership organization and leading, independent 'centre of expertise' in the drugs field. DrugScope provides drug information, publications and posters, promotes effective responses to drug taking, undertakes research, advises on policy-making, encourages informed debate and acts as a voice for member organizations working 'on the ground'. It publishes *Druglink* a bi-monthly magazine. The organization can be contacted at Prince Consort House, Suite 204 (2nd Floor), 109/111 Farringdon Road, London EC1R 3BW, tel: 020 7520 7550; and for further details, see drugscope.org.uk

DS (1) duty solicitor; **(2)** detective sergeant.

DTO detention and training order *Chapters 15, 17*

DTTO drug treatment and testing order (transitional cases): *Chapter 16*

DYO deter young offenders: *Chapter 5*

ECHR (1) European Convention On Human Rights; **(2)** European Court of Human Rights (but the latter is usually written **Eur. Ct. HR**).

EDR (or sometimes **ERD**) earliest date of release, i.e. of a youth from custody

either way offence one that can *in the case of an adult* can be tried in either the magistrates' court or the Crown Court according in the case of an adult. For the relevance of the term to youths, see mainly *Chapter 13*.

EM electronic monitoring: *Chapter 16*

enforcement Generic term for **(1) law enforcement** in general, e..g. by the police; or **(2)** the 'chasing-up' offenders through **breach** proceedings or, e.g. **fine enforcement** (*Chapter 15*), to ensure that sentences are complied with. Both are modern-day **YJS** priorities.

EPO emergency protection order: *Chapter 7*

EPQA Effective Practice Quality Assurance: *Chapter 3*

equivocal plea one where the **accused person** admits the offence but gives an inconsistent explanation ('I stole the goods but intended to give them back'); which cannot be accepted. The case is **adjourned** for him or her to consider matters, take legal advice, etc. and, if necessary, for a trial to be held.

Esmée Fairburn Foundation (EFF) grant-making body established in 1961 by Ian Fairbairn as a memorial to his wife Esmée; now one of the largest independent funders in the UK, including of youth justice-related projects. A key aim of EFF is 'to improve the quality of life for people and communities ... now and in the future'. EFF aims to commit £25 million annually towards a wide range of work; and is a member of the Association of Charitable Foundations. EFF, Kings Place, 90 York Way, London N1 9AG. tel: 020 7812 3700; info@ esmeefairbairn.org.uk; and for further details, see esmeefairbairn.org.uk.

ESS Extended Schools Service: *Chapter 6*

EWO either way offence

expert someone who a court accepts as qualified to give **opinion** evidence rather than simply evidence of fact. But the court will decide whether to accept that evidence. Not especially **expert reports** to accompany **PSRs.**

fair trial a fundamental requirement of the system as now underwritten by human rights: see especially *Chapter 2*.

FDR fast delivery report, i.e. a short form of **PSR**

FGC family group **conference**: *Chapter 4*

financial circumstances order one made in fine enforcement proceedings or at the sentencing stage for relevant means to be disclosed

foreign court one elsewhere, not necessarily abroad, such as the offender's **home court**

fostering Usually in a YJS context meaning fostering in the context of a **YRO**: *Chapter 16* (or possibly as a component of bail)

FPN/D fixed penalty notice/for disorder: *Chapter 6*

gatekeeping Keeping people out of the formal CJS, or away from more severe forms of punishment, including by using 'alternatives' and 'diversion'. A strategy often adopted within the **YJS** in particular: *Chapters 1, 11*.

GBH grievous bodily harm

Geese Theatre Company a team of actors and group workers who present interactive drama and hold workshops, training and consultation sessions within the CJS and YJS. Since 1987, the company has built up an international reputation for innovative work with offenders and youths at risk. Geese Theatre Company, Woodbridge House, 9 Woodbridge Road, Birmingham B13 8EH; 0121 4496222; info@geese.co.uk; and for further details, see geese.co.uk

G&R grounds and reasons, i.e. for refusing to grant bail to someone: see *Chapters 10, 15*

grave crime one re which an older juvenile can or must be sent to the Crown Court for trial: *Chapter 13, Which Court?*

Growing Out of Crime is the title of a seminal work by Andrew Rutherford, a former prison governor, in which he argues that offending behaviour is often a natural part of growing up, or maturation. Those families, schools and groups at the lower end of the social spectrum tend, generally speaking, to be less well-equipped to deal with troubled youths, whereas those with greater financial or personal resources can keep their children away from the YJS using a range of tactics and devices. This is about more than parenting, rather the inequalities of the social system and what is nowadays recognised as forms of exclusion. *Growing Out of Crime: The New Era* (3rd. Edn. 2002), Waterside Press argues that 'managing' such behaviour whilst recognising its relationship to 'growing up' is one key.

guardian in youth justice terms, rights and responsibilities are frequently cast on parents or guardians (or failing that the local authority where a child is in care or being 'looked after by the authority). References to parents in this work should be read in this extended way unless stated otherwise. Contrast **independent guardians** re family cases.

guidance advice or assistance pointing to how correctly or best to approach a task, decision or responsibility: of which countless examples exist across the courts and CJS, especially in a YJS context those of the **SGC** and **YJB**. Hence also **guideline** one which has been considered, ratified or sanctioned, as per the **SGC's** *Overarching Principles: Chapter 15*.

harm preventing harm is a general aim and priority of the YJS, re offences of violence and sexual offences in particular; whilst **repairing harm** or **reducing harm** is also a rationale of **restorative justice (RJ)**

hate crime term used to describe a range of **hate-related offences** and/or those with a **hateful motive**, including, e.g. **incitement to racial, or religious, hatred**. CJS measures have targeted a growing range of such conducts,

via police crackdowns and also the priorities of the CPS. Legislation means that all such offences are treated as generally more serious.

HM Her Majesty's as in detention at **Her Majesty's pleasure**; **HMCS** = Her Majesty's Court Service; **HMIP** = Her Majesty's Inspectorate of Probation; **HMPS** = Her Majesty's Prison Service (responsible for **YOIs** which are used for older youths: *Chapter 17*).

holding charge one on which an offender can be held pending further investigations, usually meaning a less serious charge than the main one being pursued, but still involving a criminal offence sufficient for this purpose.

home court that for the place where a youth normally resides, to which cases may be remitted for sentence: *Chapters 13* and *15*.

hoodie a (peculiarly British) phenomenon of the 2000s: a youth (typically) who wears a hooded top and who is thus hard to recognise or identify; and might be an offender or, perhaps more likely, a law-abiding young citizen sporting a modern fashion. Hence at one stage (ill-conceived) government plans to target the wearing of such clothing; countered by a 2006 Tory Opposition **'hug a hoodie'** campaign (so dubbed by Government). Clothing and lifestyle accoutrements have often been associated with similar stereotypes (below), including, e.g. Teddy Boys (1950s); Mods and Rockers (1960s) and Chavs (1990s). See generally, **labelling, stereotyping** (both below and see *Chapter 1*).

hooligan originally a 'rough-and-tumble sort of person'; not necessarily involved in offending; but gradually a term for a lawless person. In modern times it has been informally applied to a range of offenders, especially young offenders involved, e.g. in riots, public order offences or anti-social behaviour (**ASB**); including football hooligans. The word first appeared in popular culture in the late-19th century re a boisterous Gypsy family, the Houlihans, Irish people living in London in the 1890s; who feature in *The Hooligan Nights: Being the Life and Opinions of a Young and Impertinent Criminal* (1899), Rook, C, Victorian London Publications.

Howard League for Penal reform a leading UK penal reform organization taking its name from the 18th century prison reformer John Howard (1726-1790). Aka 'The League', it is the oldest such body in the UK (1866). It is independent of government and other spheres of influence and funded by donations. Its core aims/beliefs include (paraphrased): a safe society where fewer people are victims of crime; where offenders should make amends for their offences/change their ways; and where community sentences should be used to make people take responsibility. John Howard's influential works include *The State of the Prisons in England and Wales with Preliminary Observations, and an Account of Some Foreign Prisons and Hospitals* (1794). See generally howardleague.org

HR/HRA human rights/Human Rights Act 1998: see generally *Chapter 2*

ID identity/identification

'imprisonable offence' one which carries (or 'attracts') imprisonment *in the case of an adult*, not necessarily one where that sentence will be used in a given case. Many powers are referable to whether an offence is so imprisonable. Hence a 'surreal' situation which arises in the youth court of asking whether an offence is imprisonable in the case of an adult in order to determine whether youth court powers (which do not include imprisonment as such) apply. Note however, that, under the **CJIA 2008**, the **YRO** does not involve such a test: *Chapter 16.*

in camera in private, as when a court, exceptionally, sits 'behind closed doors'

indictable triable in the Crown Court 'on indictment'. Hence also **'indictable only offence'** (as opposed to and **either way offence (EWO)**) re more serious matters some of which can or must be tried there in the case of a youth also: *Chapter 13.* Contrast also **summary offence**: see that chapter.

information and summons the long standing method of commencing lesser (and some more serious) summary proceedings; that is scheduled to be replaced for public prosecutors by **charge and requisition**

INQUEST nationwide charity launched in 1981 to campaign against deaths in custody: the only organization in England and Wales exclusively concerned with such matters. It tracks and publishes information, including by way of an annual summary. INQUEST is also concerned with coroner's inquests. The organization also supports relatives, families, friends and advisers of people who have died in custody, and campaigns for improvements to reduce the incidence of such deaths. INQUEST, 83-89 Fonthill Road, London N4 3JH; Tel: 020 7263 1111; inquest.gn.apc.org

ISO individual support order: *Chapter 6*

ISS intensive supervision and surveillance (a special feature of a **YRO**): *Chapter 16.* Hence also common use of **ISSP** where P = programme.

IYO Inspection of Youth Offending. A programme over the five years 2003-2008 under the auspices of **HMIP**.

IYSS Integrated Youth Support Services: *Chapter 6*

John Paul Getty Foundation nowadays in the form of the **John Paul Getty Junior Charitable Trust**, this body funds 'well managed projects across the UK that help to relieve poverty, support disadvantaged people . . . and effect long-term change where help is not readily available from the public or private purse' (normally only through other charities). It has been involved in the sponsorship of various initiatives in the sphere of criminal justice and youth justice. It was endowed by the American Sir John Paul Getty II KBE (d. 2003). By 2008, it had assets approaching £60 million. JPG Charitable Trust, 1 Park Square West, London, NW1 4LJ; tel: 020 7486 1859. For further details, see jpgettytrust.org

JP justice of the peace (for practical purposes the same as a magistrate). Youth courts use youth court magistrates and district judges (magistrates' court): *Chapter 14.*

Joseph Rowntree Foundation (often just **Rowntree Foundation**). The origins of the foundation's work in the field of criminal justice are traceable largely to the work of Benjamin Rowntree (1871-1954), a member of the Rowntree confectionery family, who used his own funds and resources to encourage research in this field. He was the author of *Poverty* (c.1898), a groundbreaking investigation into working class conditions. In modern times the foundation has been concerned with such issues as anti-social behaviour (**ASB**) and in 2006 sponsored a symposium organized by the Association of Chief Executives of Voluntary Organizations (ACEVO) to discuss a range of public issues including those affecting the third sector.

JSB Judicial Studies Board

judicial appertaining to the **judiciary** and its **judicial decision-making** functions; and the prefix for each of several bodies to support the work of the judiciary, especially post-Constitutional Reform Act 2005.

just deserts The Old Testament principle of 'an eye-for-an-eye, a tooth-for-a-tooth'; as translated into proportionality and became an underlying rationale of the sentencing framework of the Criminal Justice Act 1991.

Keep Kids Safe a 'communication project' initiated by schools in Yorkshire, Humberside and Greater Manchester using latest technology as developed in partnership with school staff and a team of leading education, software and communication experts. The project was driven by the needs of schools, children and young people and their parents/carers, and was underpinned by the Every Child Matters (**ECM**) agenda. The project now operates in partnership with schools and local authorities nationwide. Keep Kids Safe Project, Globe II Business Centre, 128 Maltravers Road, Sheffield S2 5AZ; helpdesk tel: 0114 2250301; helpdesk@keepkidssafe.co.uk; and for further details and 'free trial' offers, see keepkidssafe.cu.uk

'Key Elements of Effective Practice' A YJB guidance document for YOTs (2009)

Kidscape a body committed to keeping children safe from abuse and protecting them from harm. The first charity in the UK established specifically to prevent bullying and child sexual abuse. Kidscape operates UK-wide to provide individuals and organizations with the practical skills and resources to achieve this, including by equipping vulnerable children with practical 'non-threatening' knowledge and showing them how to keep themselves safe. The organization works with those under the age of 16, their parents/carers, and people who work with them and has a helpline, publications and undertakes training, research and confidence building sessions. Kidscape, 2

Grosvenor Gardens, London, SW1W 0DH; tel 020 7730 3300; helpline: 08451 205 204; and for dedicated email addresses and further details, see kidscape.org.uk.

labelling a terms used to signify (various) theories of criminology which argue that given words can cause those to whom they are applied to be adversely stereotyped (below), also causing them, e.g. to have that same self-image/'act up to type', etc: *Chapter 1*

LCJ Lord Chief Justice (currently Lord Judge)

LCJB Local Criminal Justice Board

Liberty The National Council for Civil Liberties (NCCL) founded in 1934 as a cross party-political, non-party membership body 'at the heart of the movement for fundamental rights and freedoms'. See liberty-human-rights.org.uk

limited right See human rights: *Chapter 2*

list The daily list of cases in a particular court. Hence, e.g. **listing officer** or **listing manager.**

LJA local justice area

LO liaison officer: see also, e.g. **FLO** = family liaison officer, **VLO** = victim liaison officer

'looked after' looked after by a local authority, a status which can occur depending on the exact nature of a court custodial sentence or remand: see *Chapter 17*

MA Magistrates' Association. The MA was established in 1920 and incorporated by Royal Charter in 1962. It responds to Government on matters of mutual interest and initiates projects and proposals of its own. It publishes a regular journal, *The Magistrate*. It has a Youth Court Committee and provides a number of youth-related materials at its website: magistrates-association.org.uk.

mags/mags court magistrates/magistrates' court.

mandatory obligatory/compulsory. Certain sentences or orders are mandatory, in the sense that the court has no further (or only confined) discretion once certain basic facts are found to exist.

MAPPA Multi-agency Public Protection Arrangements to monitor dangerous and high risk offenders in particular

MC magistrates' court. Hence, e.g. **MCA** = Magistrates Courts Act'.

media panic One in which significant publicity is given to events of immediate concern to journalists, etc. often disproportionately to the problem or threat, thereby stirring-up possibly unjustified anxieties and fears.

mediation a non-conflict approach to the resolution of problems between, e.g. individuals, communities, the State, organizations; that has close connections to many aspects of **restorative justice (RJ)**, including re victim-offender mediation.

mentor Someone who acts as a guide and sounding board. Mentors may be used with youth offenders and those at risk of offending within a range of programmes or schemes. Magistrates also have mentors (as do other YJS practitioners). Hence, generally, the **Mentor Foundation** which focuses on 'the prevention of drug misuse in its efforts to promote the health and well-being of children and young people and to reduce damage to their lives'. Mentor and **Mentor International** can be contacted at 5 Forest Road, Loughborough, LE11 3NW; tel 01509 221622; secretariat@ mentorfoundation.org; and fir further details, see mentorfoundation.org

MHA Mental Health Act (various dates)

MIND (National Association for Mental Health) The leading mental health charity for England and Wales. Mind is a force for change: 'With one in four people likely to experience a mental health problem every year it is critical that we raise awareness and promote good mental health for the benefit of all members of society'. MIND, 15-19 Broadway, Stratford, London E15 4BQ; tel 020 8519 2122, F: 020 8522 1725; contact@mind.org. uk; Mind Cymru, 3rd Floor, Quebec House, Castlebridge,, 5-19 Cowbridge Road East, Cardiff CF11 9AB; tel 029 2039 5123, F: 029 2034 6585

mitigation a matter which makes an offence less serious than it might otherwise appear to be (**offence mitigation**) or which goes to the offender's individual personal circumstances so as to suggest some degree of leniency (**offender mitigation**). Hence terms such as **plea in mitigation** following conviction; and **mitigating factors** as opposed to **aggravating factors (above)**. Note also the term **mitigating circumstances** re **totting-up** in relation to road traffic penalty points cases.

mode of trial the procedure for determining whether **either way offences** should be tried locally or at the Crown Court: as described re its application to youths in *Chapter 13*

MOJ Ministry of Justice.

multi-agency involving more than one (and possibly several) YJS agencies or services, e.g. in a liaison, strategy or similar pairing, or working relationship. **YOTs**, e.g. are multi-agency, as are police/CPS Youth Justice Units (**YJUs**). Often associated with 'partnership' and 'working together', such arrangements are increasingly common and may involve the private, voluntary or charitable sectors.

Munby judgement see the explanation in *Chapter 17* under *Safeguarding children and young people in custody*

Nacro formerly the National Association for the Care and Resettlement of Offenders, having now adopted this acronym; a major crime reduction charity specialising in '[making] society safer by finding practical solutions to reducing crime'; that since 1966 has 'worked to give ex-offenders, disadvantaged people and deprived communities the help they need to build a better future'. It has over 200 projects in diverse locations across England and Wales including in relation to young offenders and youth justice. It also has a **Youth Justice Section**. See nacro.org.uk For Scotland see the similarly formulated Sacro: sacro.org.uk

NAI non-accidental injury. i.e. one that is unexplained and may well be suspicious, usually meaning to a child by a parent, etc.

naming and shaming (N&S) a concept with primitive appeal and traceable to Anglo-Saxon times at least; the notion that offenders may mend their ways (or at least be identified to other potential victims) if their names are made public; and they themselves feel shame, possibly leading to remorse and 'going straight'. In modern times, the media/press and some police forces have been to the fore in naming and shaming people, including by the publication of names, sometimes addresses and even photographs in local newspapers or on the internet; often re 'run-of-the-mill' offences. Note also the special rules in favour on such action by courts re anti-social behaviour (see *Reporting Restrictions* in *Chapter 14*). Such practices, however, risk the negative impact of, e.g. **labelling** (above), any mistakes and social exclusion. Shaming (as opposed to N&S and viewed from a more positive perspective) is often integral to **restorative justice (RJ)**.

Napo membership and representative body for probation officers and other staff working for the National Probation Service (**NPS**). Napo celebrated its centenary in 2007. It is a trade union, professional association and campaigning body which undertakes a range of activities, including training, representations to government and the publication of *Probation Journal* and *Napo News*. See napo.org.uk. There is also an **Association of Black Probation Officers (ABPO)** which works with staff of African, African-Caribbean and Asian origin, including to oppose the effects of racism.

National Association for Youth Justice (NAYJ) membership organization established in 1994 by a merger of the National Intermediate Treatment Federation (NITFed) and Association for Youth Justice. Members of the NAYJ work in relation to the youth courts and the Crown Court, with links to youth offending teams (**YOTS**) and other youth workers, educationalists and child specialists. From the late-1990s, the NAYJ undertook a review of its philosophy and policy concerning the YJS, leading to 'Working with Children: The Philosophical Base' (NAYJ) which offers a set of values and beliefs to 'underpin legislation, policy and practice'. NAYJ publishes *Youth Justice: An International Journal.* See nayj.org.uk

National Society for the Prevention of Cruelty to Children (NSPCC) Originally the London Society for the Prevention of Cruelty to Children (1884) but the NSPCC since 1889. It is the only non-statutory agency authorised to bring care proceedings in respect of children. NSPCC London Office, Weston House, 42 Curtain Road, London, EC2A 3NH; tel 020 7825 2500; and for Divisional Offices, email contact, helpline, telephone numbers and information, see nspcc.org.uk

National Treatment Agency (NTA) a 'special health authority' within the National Health Service, established by Government in 2001 to improve the availability, capacity and effectiveness of treatment for drug misuse in England. 'Our task is to improve the quality of treatment in order to maximize the benefit to individuals, families and communities'. The NTA works in partnership with national, regional and local agencies to deliver better treatment and outcomes. NTA, 6th Floor, Skipton House, 80 London Road, London SE1 6LH; tel: 020 7972 1999; and for further details, see nta.nhs.uk

National Young People's Substance Misuse Forum a body to actively promote and support provision of 'high quality, dedicated, comprehensive specialist treatment services' to young people as a key part of UK drugs strategy. The aims of the forum include (summarised): identifying and promoting good practice; influencing policy-makers and partner agencies; providing a voice for treatment providers and users of their services; raising awareness, maintaining a communication network; initiating and facilitating open, informed debate; providing expert advice; and promoting and supporting links with relevant organizations. For further information, see nypsmtf.org.uk

National Standards (NS) standards issued and applicable nationwide within an agency/ service, etc., including in particular NS for the work of the **YOTs.** Note the YJB's **National Standards for Youth Justice Services**.

National Youth Association See nya.org.uk

NAYJ See **National Association for Youth Justice** which is described above

NCJB National Criminal Justice Board

NDR normal date of release, i.e. from custody

NEO no evidence offered, i.e. by a prosecutor, thereby inviting the court to dismiss the case

net widening bringing a greater target group of people into contact with the CJS as suspects, offenders, prisoners, etc. whether via **criminalisation** (above), more active law enforcement or a wider range of punishments. Certain commentators argue that the more powers the courts or CJS agencies/services have, the greater the chance that they will make full use of them and at a more punitive level; the greater the range of sentences, the more they will be 'tested out'. Net-widening is also connected to the vested interest that some members of the CJS (and YJS) or private sector may have in increasing the numbers of people it 'processes' since profit is involved.

NFA (1) no further action (by the police, a court, etc), effectively where some matter is 'marked closed'; **(2)** no fixed abode/address.

NG not guilty

'nip it in the bud' simplistic notion heard in many a debate on crime and punishment (particularly re youths); the analogy being that early intervention is the way to cut down on offending. Opponents argue this is counter-productive, criminalising, and may in fact cause offending to escalate rather than stop.

no case short for 'no **case to answer**': above

NOMS National Offender Management Service. YJB services operate independently of NOMs, but there are various connections, e.g. probation officers are part of YOTs and the National Probation Service (**NPS**) part of NOMS. Note also (the independent) **HMIP**.

non-statutory not covered or provided for by Act of Parliament; whether a process, method or CJS agency. Hence the term '**non-statutory sector'** re those parts of the 'wider youth justice service': *Chapter 3*.

NPS National Probation Service

NS See **National Standards** (above).

NSP no separate penalty, i.e. when a court passes sentence for several offences and views matters 'in the round'. It may then decide that re some lesser matters further punishment would be disproportionate in all the circumstances.

NSPCC The **National Society for the Prevention of Cruelty to Children** (see above).

oath usually that of a witness giving sworn testimony in the courtroom (or alternatively after making an **affirmation** (above)).

offender someone convicted of a criminal offence, i.e. as opposed to a (mere) **suspect** or **accused person**, both of the latter being entitled to the presumption of innocence

ONSET a **YJB/YOT** assessment tool. Whereas **ASSET** is used for youth offenders, **ONSET** is used in preventive work: for details of the framework, see the YJB publication 'Prevention' (2009); or visit yjb.org.uk

openness a virtue demanded in justice-related matters along with accountability, visibility and transparency. Hence, e.g. **open court** and

'opening-up of the courts': *Chapter 15.*

opinion the general rule is that evidence must be as to facts not opinions; but **experts** (above) can give opinion evidence once they have been accepted as such by the court. However, it is the court and not the expert who will then decide whether to accept the opinion offered (and there may be disagreements between experts for the opposing parties).

ordinary language legal requirements mean that various explanations must be given in 'ordinary language', i.e. avoiding technical language and obscure or exclusive terms

original offence looking back, that which is the underlying offence in respect of, e.g. breach proceedings, enforcement, etc.

PACE Police and Criminal Evidence Act 1984. Hence also the **PACE codes** made under that Act relating to police **detention**, etc.

parent, guardian, etc. Normally speaking references to a parent should be read in the alternative as being to a guardian where the latter exists rather than the former.

parental responsibility/matters See *Chapters 7* and *15.*

Parents Against Drug Abuse (PADA) PADA was set up in Birkenhead in 1984. The concept of supporting friends and families of substance users was realised by Joan Keogh MBE, mother of two heroin-using children. Various organisations across the UK were helped to set up by PADA and the body now has links with more than 250 projects across the country. PADA is also now a Centre of Learning for National Open College, an alternative therapies programme. PADA, The Foundry, Marcus Street, Birkenhead, Wirral, CH41 1EU; tel 0151 649 1580; admin@pada.org. uk; and for further details, see pada.org.uk

party the **party to a case** in a criminal case the parties are the prosecutor and accused; although their lawyers and defence teams are sometimes loosely described using the same terminology. Those involved in other roles are often described as 'participants'.

PCSO police community support officer

penalty points those endorsed on a driving licence re 'totting up' in relation to road traffic (or some other) offences

plea the answer given by an **accused person**

when asked by the court legal adviser how he or she pleads to a charge, either a **guilty plea** or a **plea of not guilty**.

PNC Police National Computer

PN/D See **FPN/D**

P(O)PO prolific or (other) priority offender: *Chapter 5*

POYP Positive Opportunities for Young People

preliminary hearing one at the start of a case as part of **case management** above

previous usually short for **previous convictions** aka '**form**'

Prince's Trust (PT) a youth charity which 'helps change young lives'. It works with 14 to 30-year-olds who may have struggled in school, been in care, are long-term unemployed or have been in trouble with the law. Since 1976, the trust has given help and support to over 575,000 young people to which 100 are added each working day; most moving into work, education or training. It was founded by His Royal Highness The Prince of Wales. Head office: Prince's Trust, 18 Park Square East, London NW1 4LH; tel 020 7543 1234; webinfops@princes-trust.org. uk and for a list of programmes, projects and key events in the trust's history, see princes-trust.org.uk

Prison Reform Trust (PRT) a leading reform group, which holds, e.g. that custody should be reserved for those whose offending is so serious that they cannot serve their sentence in the community. For details and PRT publications, see prison-reform-trust.org.uk

pronouncement The announcement of a sentence, order or decision; usually following **forms of 'pronouncements'** such as those recommended by the **JSB**: see jsboard.co.uk

PRT see **Prison Trust** above

PSR pre-sentence report, meaning, re a youth, by a **YOT**: *Chapter 15*. See also **FDR** and **SDR**.

PYO persistent young offender: *Chapter 5*

QC Queen's Counsel (aka '**silk**'), i.e. a senior barrister who wears a silk gown, mostly seen in the Crown Court and above.

Quaker Crime, Community and Justice Group Quakers have worked for centuries to improve the CJS (and YJS), whether in a philanthropic, practical or optimistic way. Quakers were amongst those to promote restorative approaches (*Chapter 4*) in order 'to keep all those who are harmed by crime at the centre' of criminal processes. For further information, see quaker.org.uk

qualified right See human rights in *Chapter 2*

R Regina (or Rex), i.e. the Crown as in *R v. Smith and Jones*

RCC Rainer Crime Concern: see **Catch 22** above

reasons reasons for a decision; including **grounds and reasons** for refusing bail, etc: *Chapters 14*. Reasons must nowadays be given in various specific situations and generally under human rights law for many outcomes.

recognizance a formal promise to pay/forfeit a sum of money in the event of some future occurrence: re a bind-over or as with a surety for bail. Hence terms such as **taking a recognizance** for the process whereby the person concerned makes this promise to the Crown by signing a document, or **forfeiture of a recognizance** on breach of a bind-over.

referral a term used generally to signify referral to an agency or service, e.g. for assessment, treatment or an expert opinion. Hence more specifically re youths, the **referral order** to a **YOP** by a youth court: *Chapters 3* and *15*. For further details of referral in general, see the YJB's 'Prevention' (2009); or visit yjb.org.uk

Regina/Rex See **R**

register the official court record of outcomes

regulation usually one made under an **Act** and dealing with minutiae or detail not contained in or enacted at the time of the Act itself. However, regulations have increasingly included more significant content, including many new criminal offences.

rehabilitation a word that occurs repeatedly in contexts such as 'punishment and rehabilitation', to emphasise that the latter is also a key aim after (or during) a sentence. Rehabilitation is closely connected with other purposes such as **welfare, reintegration** and **resettlement**. It is also integral to **RJ.**

reintegration reintegration into a community following exclusion from it by, e.g. custody

remand whereas cases are **adjourned**, accused or convicted people are remanded (except in lesser cases when there can be a simple adjournment); either by way of a **remand in custody** or **remand on bail.** Hence also **remand centre** re young offenders (usually).

Hence terms such as **remand wing** at a prison.

remit transfer a case or matter to another court (or in other senses to 'someone else'), as with remission of a juvenile case by the adult court to the youth court: *Chapter 15*. Note also that fines can be remitted in some circumstances (meaning in this case wholly or partly 'written-off').

re-open a case to re-start it, usually meaning in order to put right an error (to which technical rules apply)

reparation 'putting things right', 'making good' or repairing harm, actually or metaphorically, re a victim or community. Various reparation schemes exist re youths. Note also the **reparation order** (*Chapter 15*) and **reparation as a requirement of a YRO** (*Chapter 16*).

representation usually a reference to **legal representation**, including **State funded legal representation**, aka legal aid

reprimand normally a reference to the scheme of **reprimands and warnings** for juveniles: *Chapter 11*. The term is also sometimes used to describe an admonishment by a court when someone is sentenced, in effect a 'telling-off', or similarly in a school setting.

requirement usually that of a youth rehabilitation order (**YRO**) or release licence (or as attached to some other forms of sentence): *Chapters 16, 17*.

resettlement a gradual process under which an offender is resettled in a community after being outside it due to custody (or other forms of social exclusion). **Reintegration** and resettlement usually go hand-in-hand.

responsible officer various statutory provisions cast duties on such an officer in relation to a given court order. In youth justice terms (much as for adult community orders) the 'responsible officer' will be the person given the responsibility by the sentencing court of overseeing, managing, applying for variation of, encouraging compliance with, or dealing with breaching, etc. certain court orders such as parenting orders and **YROs**. For parenting orders it will usually be a YOT officer but might, instead, be a probation officer (or person providing probation services under contract), or a local authority education welfare officer. For YROs it will usually be a YOT officer or possibly a probation officer

(or person providing probation services under contract) save where e.g. the only YRO requirements are curfew or exclusion and with **EM** - in this case it will be the private contractor responsible for the electronic monitoring; or if the only requirement is for attendance centre, in this case it will be the person in charge of the centre. There will be no 'responsible officer' for an **ASBO/CRASBO** - where the new CJIA 2008 duty to review falls on the police and local authority, possibly in conjunction with other specified persons

Restorative Justice Consortium (RJC) is a nationwide collective of **RJ**-based organizations and a good starting point for information. See the further details in *Chapter 4*. The organization can be contacted at RJC, Suite 50, Albert Buildings, 49 Queen Victoria Street, London EC4N 4SA; tel 020 7653 1992; info@restorativejustice.org; and for further details and a list of member organizations, see restorativejustice.org.uk.

restraining order an order to prevent harassment under the Protection From Harassment Act 1997

restriction a word with various YJS connotations: the lawful **restriction of liberty**. Since 1991 it has been a broad sentencing concept in England and Wales. Note also **restriction order**: one under a YRO (see Chapter 16). Magistrate may impose **reporting restrictions** pending the outcome of a trial or concerning a juvenile; and there are certain standing reporting restrictions as noted in *Chapter 14*. The term is also to be found in contexts such as **legal restriction** or **physical restriction** aka 'restraint' (as per 'control and restraint' of a youth in custody).

review is the reappraisal, revisiting or investigation of events, usually by an independent and/or higher or specially appointed authority that may exercise related powers or make recommendations. Hence, e.g. the **Criminal Cases Review Commission** (CCRC): see ccrc.gov.uk. Note, in particular, **review by a Crown prosecutor** of a case file under a continuing duty; **review of police detention** (*Chapter 10*); and **judicial review** (a form of appeal: *Chapter 14*), Note also the duty of the police and local authorities to review ASBOs (*Chapter 6*).

retiring room the magistrates' own quarters attached to the courtroom where they can 'retire' by way of an **adjournment** to consider their verdict, sentence, etc. in private.

revocation cancellation of a sentence or order

revolving door metaphor for the response to custody of offenders repeatedly sent there, who pass in and out of institutions as if via the revolving door of a store or hotel; as also used re other forms of institutional care (especially re mental impairment), or similar recurring scenarios such as those involving 'problem families' or aspects of social exclusion.

RIC remand in custody

RJ restorative justice: a form of justice which focuses on repairing harm rather than processes which increase conflict, distress, pain, formality, etc. See generally *Chapter 4*.

ROSH risk of serious harm

rule usually in a **CJS** context a reference to a statutory or Common Law rule

SSP Safer Schools Partnership: *Chapter 6* and see also above.

SDR standard delivery report, i.e. a written **PSR**

SE social exclusion. Hence **SEU** for Social Exclusion Unit (of government). Inclusive strategies are intended to reduce crime.

section The section of an Act of Parliament. Note **'being sectioned'** where someone is suffering from mental impairment, i.e. ordered into hospital: see specialist texts.

sentence In the youth court this term translates as 'order made on a finding of guilt': *Chapter 15.*

sentencing guideline nowadays a reference to one issued by the **SGC:** *Chapter 15*

'serious enough' the threshold test for a community sentence: see *Chapter 15*

SGC Sentencing Guidelines Council

SI statutory instrument (a form of **delegated legislation**), often containing **regulations**

silk See **QC**

social services usually a reference to the social services department of a local authority (now frequently combined with education duties)

'so serious' the threshold test for a custodial sentence: *Chapter 15*. This test should be distinguished from the more general and informal idea that an offence may be so serious that some other course should be taken, e.g. in relation to exceptions to the making of a compulsory referral order.

SOVA a leading national volunteer mentoring body started in 1975 by a group of volunteers working within the then Inner London Probation Service (ILPS). In 1982, SOVA began working with social services departments, recruiting, training and deploying volunteers to offer support and advice to young people within local communities. SOVA projects now exist across England and Wales and are developed in partnership with local agencies. SOVA Head Office and Southern Area Office, 1st Floor Chichester House, 37 Brixton Road, London, SW9 6DZ; tel 020 7793 0404; london@ sova.org.uk; and for other dedicated contacts, other areas of the country and further details, see sova.org.uk

specified activities, i.e. as an activity requirement of a **YRO**

specified offence one specified for a given purpose, particularly in an Act of Parliament, Schedule or instruction

SPO senior probation officer, usually

SSP Safer Schools Partnership: A working arrangement between schools, the police and possibly others to tackle crime prevention in school. For some further details,, see the YJB publication 'Prevention' (2009); or visit yjb. org.uk.

scheduled listed, but usually meaning in an Act of Parliament, as with a **scheduled offence** to which a particular power, jurisdiction or provision attaches. The term is also used to signify **scheduling** as it applies to **listing**, above

standard of proof The standard to which a criminal allegation must be proved, by the prosecutor i.e. 'beyond reasonable doubt'. The civil standard is lower, 'on a preponderance of probabilities'. But note that civil matters leading to criminal consequences attract the criminal standard of proof from the outset, such as **ASBOs**. See *Chapters 2, 6* and *14*.

starting point that within a **guideline**, especially a **starting point** for a sentence

State funded representation the full modern-day term for legal aid

statutory instrument See **SI**

STC secure training centre: *Chapter 17*

stereotyping categorising someone (or something) by reference to a preconceived notion of their (its) supposed type; by reference to features unlikely to be all-embracing or universally applicable; such that the stereotype may be misleading, prejudicial, or in some instances offensive.

structured decision-making making decisions following a pre-ordained structure within which all relevant considerations are identified and weighed at each stage and reasons developed in support as the process goes along.

submission a submission to the court, e.g. re a point of law or evidence or that there is **no case to answer**

summary (1) A word used in various contexts, most significantly re **summary justice**, usually meaning: in a technical sense, justice in the magistrates' court which can also be quite correctly described as a **court of summary jurisdiction**; hence also **summary offence** means one triable only in the magistrates' court and the **CJSSS** initiative (above). **(2)** Similarly in relation to military discipline in particular or that under the Young Offender Institution Rules; **(3)** Justice meted out speedily, simply and untrammelled by complex procedures or rules, whether in a court or, e.g. by way of a police **reprimand or warning, FPN/D**, etc., the term having been adopted in particular in modern times to describe 'justice' stemming directly from police or administrative action rather than judicial decisions of the courts. **(4)** More loosely, any form of 'justice' which occurs speedily whether officially (and lawfully) or not. Hence **summary trial** for trial before magistrates in the youth court. **(5) Summary of the prosecution case**: the outline given at the start of a trial or when making **disclosure**. **(6)** Any synopsis or brief version of events.

SureStart Launched in 1989, this is the government initiative to 'give children the best possible start in life', including through improvements, e.g. in childcare, early education, health and family support. The programme was originally intended to support families from before the birth of the child until he or she was four years old but was extended to cover an certain support up to age 14 (16 for those with disabilities). For further details, see surestart.gov.uk

sus 'suspicion'. Hence the **sus laws** allowing police to stop and search people 'on suspicion' of an offence (or generally re terrorism).

suspect someone suspected of a criminal offence and who may, e.g. be in police **detention**

TACT The Adolescent and Children's Trust is a charity set up in 1992 in response to changes in child care policy. Instead of local authorities continuing to place children in their care into large children's homes, they were encouraged to provide home-based care in the form of fostering. TACT is the UK's largest charity provider of fostering and adoption services. In recent years it has merged with other organizations, including the Independent Adoption Services (IAS) and Children Law UK (CLUK) (formerly the British Juvenile and Family Courts Society) and the charity Parents for Children (PfC). TACT seeks to influence opinion and raise awareness of all issues affecting children in care, including in the media/press; and to benefit children involved in the justice system as well as 'on the fringes of care'. Operating profits are re-invested in the provision of services. TACT Central Office, 303 Hither Green Lane, Hither Green, London, SE13 6TJ; tel: 020 8695 8142; enquiries@tactcare.org.uk; and for further details, see tactcare.org.uk

tag an electronic tag as for **EM**

tampering (1) tampering with a motor vehicle, e.g. interfering with the operation of its brakes, steering or to gain entry to it. **(2) tampering with a jury. (3)** Informally, any similar offending behaviour involving 'interference', e.g. with children.

tariff (1) The going rate as per a **sentencing guideline**; or **(2)** one set by a Crown Court judge re a life sentence or certain other sentences, i.e. the time to be served before the offender can be considered for release.

TDC training and development committee

testimony the oral evidence of a witness in the court room on **oath** or **affirmation**

threshold a hurdle to be surmounted before a

218 Youth Justice and The Youth Court

particular power, right, etc. can be exercised, particularly a **prosecution threshold** (*Chapter 12*) or a **sentencing threshold** (*Chapter 15*).

TIC take(n) into consideration

ticket usually a reference to a **FPN/D**

time limit one restricting events to a given time frame, such as a **custody time limit** or limit for bringing **summary proceedings**

totting-up that under the penalty points system re endorsement and disqualification.

Triage name of a project for the experimental placing of **YOT** members in police custody suites.

TWC or sometimes (the verb) **'twocking'**: taking a motor vehicle without consent of the owner.

UK Harm Reduction Alliance A campaigning coalition of drug users, health and social care workers, criminal justice workers and educationalists which aims to put public health and human rights at the centre of drug treatment and service provision for drug users. For further details and contact points, see ukhra.org

UN United Nations

unrepresented usually meaning a defendant who has **no legal representation**; when there is a duty on the court (discharged via the court legal adviser) to assist him or her

up-tariffing sentencing someone at a level higher than should be the case. Hence and because of this there will be less room for manoeuvre if an offender is later charged with a further offence as he or she will already be well up the sentence ladder. Compare **net widening** (above).

variation alteration of a sentence or order where applicable/permissible

verdict the decision as to whether someone is guilty or not guilty made by magistrates (or a jury in the Crown Court) at the end of a criminal trial: see *Chapter 14*

VFM value for money

VP vulnerable person/vulnerable prisoner

VPS victim personal statement, made to a police officer (or possibly a probation officer) and produced in writing to a court for its information before sentence is passed.

VS (1) Victim Support; and hence **VSS** for Victim Support Scheme. VS is a key example of the work of the voluntary sector and

volunteers. It is an independent charity helping people affected by crime. It provides free, confidential support to help victims deal with their crime-related experience, whether or not the crime is reported. From 2008, various local member charities across England and Wales began merging to form a single, nationwide body. VS is in contact with over 1.25 million victims and witnesses each year. See, further, victimsupport.org.uk. (2) Voluntary sector. (3) Voluntary service.

warrant usually a reference to court process issued by a magistrate or a judge requiring an arrest. See also **'backed for bail'** above. Note also **WFD** = warrant of further detention: see *Chapter 10*.

warning (1) any general warning by the police re a hazard or future conduct and sometimes re the latter by a court; but also **(2)** a reference to the system of **reprimands and warnings** for juveniles: *Chapter 11*.

welfare The YJS has long been associated with welfare aspects of offending and rehabilitation and many organizations operate in this field. See *Chapter 1*.

'what works' (or **'what works?'**) expression/ question encapsulating the notion that the CJS (and YJS) should look to methods/ approaches/outcomes that are shown by evidence-based research to have a predictable outcome, nowadays usually meaning in terms of crime prevention/crime reduction or other key CJS/YJS aims. A 'what works' Home Office initiative is described at crimereduction.homeoffice.gov.uk. What works has been linked to the delivery of services to a consistent standard which are effective for all groups of victims and offenders; but has other subtleties of meaning and became part of the mantra of the (New) Labour government in 1997 (when it was adopted by managers in many public services); together with an insistence on procedures for monitoring and evaluation. What works has long been associated with the realisation that some sentences work, others not so well. But contrast the pessimistic, **nothing works**; and the over-certainty of **prison works** (which was prevalent from 1993 onwards more as an exercise in blind political faith than on the basis of evidence). Variants include **what works for children**. In a criminological context, what works is associated with Robert Martinson who in 1974 published an essay: 'What Works? Questions and Answers About Prison Reform'; and since with various experts.

'Wiring-up' Youth Justice an exercise to recommend a programme of work that 'champions [the YJB's] investment in people, process and technology'. See generally *Chapter 5*

Wootton, Dame Barbara (1897-1988). Penal reformer, criminologist and magistrate who was made a life peer (1958). Her publications include *Social Science and Social Pathology* (1959), Wooton B et al, George Allen & Unwin and Crime and *Penal Policy: Reflections on Fifty Years Experience* (1978), Wootton B, Allen & Unwin. She is credited with various celebrated observations, including that which has been plagiarised at the end of *Chapter 18*, 'Juvenile court magistrates should never forget that ... they are always dealing with other people's children'.

working together working together with other agencies to a discernible, agreed aim

written statement one made in writing by a witness and that may be admissible as evidence in criminal proceedings provided that correct related procedures have been followed

WS Witness Service

YC youth custody

YCAP (or **Y-cap**) youth crime action plan (national or local): *Chapter 6*

YCMF Youth Case Management Framework (of the YJB)

YDO youth default order: *Chapter 15.*

YIP Youth Inclusion Programme: for some further details, see the YJB publication 'Prevention' (2009); or visit yjb.org.uk

YISP Youth Inclusion and Support Panel: *Chapter 3.*

YJ youth justice. Hence also, e.g. **YJB** = Youth Justice Board; **YJPF** = Youth Justice Planning Framework; **YJS** = Youth Justice System; **YJT** = Youth Justice Team.

YMCA leading Christian charity committed to supporting all young people, particularly in times of need. YMCA England supports and represents 135 local YMCAs nationwide, providing professional and relevant services that 'make a difference' to the lives of young people in over 250 communities. The YMCA agenda includes crime diversion and work in young offender institutions (**YOIs**). A **YMCA Offender Services Unit** started in 1994 as a joint initiative with Lancaster Farms Young Offender Institution and later spread elsewhere; to help prepare inmates for life on release. Formerly known as the Young Men's Christian Association (the first YMCA being founded by George Williams in 1844 in St. Paul's Churchyard, London); and Young Women's Christian Association (YWCA) (still YWCA). **YMCA England**, 640 Forest Road (registered office), London E17 3DZ; tel 020 8520 5599; enquiries@ymca.org. uk; and for further details, see ymca.org.uk.

YWCA England and Wales, Clarendon House, 52 Cornmarket Street, Oxford, OX1 3EJ; tel 01865 304200; info@ywca.org.uk; and see ywca.org.uk. YO young offender: one aged 18 to 20 inclusive

YOC youth offender contract: *Chapter 15*

YOI young offender institution: *Chapter 17*

YOP youth offender panel: *Chapter 3*. Note that YOPs may be referred to as 'referral order panels' or 'community panels' and their members simply as 'panel members'. Hence the **AOPM** above.

YOT youth offending team

YoungMinds a leading charity 'committed to improving the well-being and mental health of children and young people and empowering their parents and carers'. YoungMinds operates online and through conferences, workshops, education and publications, including its bi-monthly 'YoungMinds' magazine for 'everyone concerned with child and adolescent mental health. YoungMinds, 48-50 St John Street, London, EC1M 4DG; tel 020 7336 8445; email contact is via the organization's website where further information can also be found, see youngminds.org.uk

Young People in Focus (YPF) (formerly the Trust for the Study of Adolescence (TSA)) is a registered charity founded in 1989 (as the TSA); which helps individuals and organisations working with young people

and families to provide better services.
YPF Main Office, 23 New Road, Brighton
BN1 1WZ; tel 01273 693 311; info@
youngpeopleinfocus.org.uk; and for further
information, see youngpeopleinfocus.org.uk.

youth see *Age-related terms and terminology* at
the start of the book.

youth court panel The panel of youth court
magistrates: *Chapter 14*

youth offender panel (YOP) The panel of
volunteers that which deals with youth who
are subject to referral orders: see *Chapter 3*

YP (1) young person (14-17 years); **(2)** young
prisoner (18-20 inclusive).

YRD the experimental youth restorative disposal:
Chapters 4 and *18*.

YRO youth rehabilitation order: *Chapter 16*

zero tolerance (ZT) a law enforcement strategy
that relies on virtually automatic arrest,
charge, prosecution, etc. and pro-active
policing backed by a resolve on the part
of courts to deal firmly with offenders;
including re low-level offences and anti-social
behaviour (**ASB**). ZT tends to eliminate
or constrain discretion. It seeks to reassure
citizens via deterrence and by instilling
respect. Opponents argue that it merely
stifles disrespect, failing to create that deeper
form of respect which is a prerequisite to
changing attitudes; and that it leads to
displacement of crime. It began in the New
York Police Department (NYPD), USA under
Commissioner William Bratton (early 1990s).
In the UK, it is often linked to Cleveland
Constabulary (late-1990s), in particular to
initiatives by Superintendent Ray Mallon (later
the directly elected mayor of Hartlepool). ZT
may target offences of a given type, or ASB;
sometimes due to CPS strategies. Trends in ZT
have been towards community-based crime
prevention/crime reduction.

A Timeline of Youth Justice

Bryan Gibson
© Waterside Press 2009

1361	Justices of the Peace Act confers wide-ranging jurisdiction on magistrates who gradually acquire both a judicial and administrative tole
1700s	England's Bloody Code allows for draconian punishments, including of children. Instances of children as young as eight being executed.
1750s	Many destitute children end up in the workhouse or (adult) 'houses of correction', or are subjected to transportation.
1815	Society for Investigating the Alarming Increases of Juvenile Delinquency in the Metropolis formed. Elizabeth Fry founds 'schools' within prisons for children who at that time may be imprisoned with their parents.
1836	Charles Dickens reaches a wide popular readership by publishing his new work *Oliver Twist* in instalments in the newspapers, highlighting exploitation of young children and their vulnerability to criminal influences.
1837	Vagrancy Act targets rogues, vagabonds and beggars, many just children.
1838	Parkhurst Prison Act establishes the first dedicated custodial regime for young offenders, on the Isle of Wight. Many inmates simply learn a trade as a prelude to being transported to penal colonies. Young offender wings in other prisons make small inroads on the adult regime.
1843	Prison inspectors note that the treadmill (a large wheel turned by walking on it) is 'inappropriate for girls and for boys under the age of 14 years'.
1846	Overcrowding in communities and prisons causes the description 'academies of crime' to emerge (*The Times*, January 12).
1847	Select Committee inquires into juveniles and transportation. Sir John Pakington MP cites cases of juveniles held for long periods in custody without trial, alongside 'hardened adult offenders', for relatively minor offences. First stirrings of 'parental responsibility': parents to be fined 'if they can be found'. Juvenile Offenders Act gives magistrates power to sentence children under 14 to a whipping with a birch rod.
1850	Legislation follows a Bill for the Correction and Reformation of Juvenile Offenders. Summary justice by way of a whipping for a first offence of vagrancy or larceny (theft), with reprimands for girls; and whipping at the end of a prison sentence as a 'terror', but also to allow 'leniency' by compensatory early release. An era of 'media panics': *Chapter 1*.

1854	The first of several reformatory and industrial school Acts
1862	Whipping of Offenders Act restricts punishment to 12 strokes for juveniles
1865	The crank (a hand turned device for futile labour on which the resistance could be increased so as to demand greater effort by a prisoner and which had to be turned a set number of times per day), hard labour, disciplinary 'bread and water' and solitary confinement (the 'black hole' for older youths. Straightjackets used for children as young as 10 years of age.
1866	Industrial schools, with strict discipline and industrial training, including for orphans, children of prisoners and 'badly behaved' youths. Howard League for Penal Reform founded: see *Glossary*
1867	Barnardos formed: see the *Glossary*
1881	Lushingham Committee set up to examine reformatory and industrial school regimes for young people convicted of criminal offences. Waifs and Strays Society founded by Edward de Montjoie Rudolf (1852-1933), a civil servant, in the parish of St Anne's in Lambeth, London (for details see hiddenlives.org.uk/articles/history)
1870s 1880s	Education Acts provide schools for all children and make attendance compulsory, reducing crime by taking young offenders 'off the streets'
1900s	'Reformatory prisons' set up for young offenders
1906	Liberal Government with a reforming agenda
1907	Probation of First Offenders Act allows for the first time supervision for many, especially younger offenders: based on the work of Frederick Rainer and the London Police Court Mission, reflecting the origins of the modern-day charity sector organization Catch 22: see the *Glossary*
1908	Children Act (sometimes called the 'Children's Charter') deals with child protection; forbids the imprisonment of children; and establishes juvenile courts. Older juveniles can only be sent to prison if a court issues an 'unruly certificate'. Local authorities get power to keep poor children out of the workhouse and protect them from abuse (the genesis of social services). The Act abolishes the death penalty for under-16s. Children barred from dangerous trades and buying tobacco or alcohol. Prevention of Crime Act introduces borstal training based on an experimental scheme located in the village of Borstal in Kent: see *Glossary*.
1913	Children's Branch established within the Home Office. A plan to end the imprisonment of youths under-16 is placed 'on hold' due to the outbreak of the First World War (and not revisited until 1969).
1927	Departmental Committee on Young Offenders (1925-1927) reports.

1930s	The era of the 'clip around the ear' by 'local bobbies' for young people caught in the act of committing minor offences (which only gradually becomes metaphorical): see *Chapters 10, 11* and the *Glossary*.
1932	House of Lords case of *Woolmington v Director of Public Prosecutions* reaffirms the burden and standard of proof in all criminal cases: the prosecutor must prove his or her case beyond reasonable doubt.
1933	Children and Young Persons Act establishes the rule that all courts must always have regard to the welfare of children, whether as defendants or when attending court in other roles, such as as a witness: *Chapter 1*. Court reporting restrictions first introduced for youths: *Chapter 14*. Age of 'criminal capacity' increased from seven to eight.
1948	United Nations Universal Declaration of Human Rights follows the Second World War when many children perished in Nazi concentration camps, including on their way in 'child transports'. Criminal Justice Act 1948 introduces attendance centres run by the police, usually on a Saturday, a mix of education and physical exercises, which deprives youth offenders of their liberty and leisure time (*Chapter 16*).
1950s	European Convention On Human Rights and Fundamental Freedoms A post-war era of 'crackdowns' and 'strong' punishments: *Chapter 1*.
1959	UN Declaration of the Rights of the Child
1960	Ingleby Report on Children and Young Persons in Custody
1961	Criminal Justice Act. Detention centre powers and regimes for juveniles and young offenders modified.
1963	Children and Young Persons Act. Age of 'criminal capacity' raised from eight to ten years.
1968	In Scotland, juvenile courts are replaced with children's hearings
1969	Children and Young Persons Act revises the powers of the juvenile court, extends the 'welfare model' and introduces a twin-track system of care or criminal proceedings. The Act increases the age of criminal capacity (*Chapter 1*) from the ten (of 1963 above) to 14, the idea being that all younger children be dealt with under welfare legislation, but this is never implemented, leaving the age at ten in England and Wales: see now in particular for younger children *Chapter 7*. The 1969 Act also phases out borstals which, by now, have become 'universities of crime'.

1970	The Children's Society (see *Glossary*) realigns its work with children and young people. It gradually stops the routine use of children's homes. Its work begins to focus more on 'children and young people in need' within local communities, in partnerships with local authorities and in the youth justice sector as an integral part of this.
1974	Rehabilitation of Offenders Act leads to more generous rehabilitation periods for youths than for adults, normally half the time, after which convictions need not be disclosed to employers and the like
1976	Bail Act under which a juvenile may be held for his or her own welfare
1977	Criminal Law Act increases the powers of the then juvenile court
1980s	An era of (mainly) local initiatives to establish projects and programmes four youth offenders including as 'alternatives to custody'
1982	Criminal Justice Act abolishes borstal altogether, modifies detention centre orders and introduces youth custody. Section 1(4) is the first sentencing provision to require magistrates to give reasons, i.e. in juvenile custody cases. First Juvenile Justice Units (JJUs), forerunners of youth offending teams (YOTs), become influential through 'initiatives' with young people and schemes to divert them from prosecution or custody. Juvenile incarceration falls dramatically, but later begins to rise again as the wider political mood changes. Tory Government introduces a new regime based on youth custody and detention centre orders.
1983	The then Department of Health and Social Security injects an unprecedented sum of £15 million into the YJS to encourage local schemes of 'intermediate treatment' (IT). Dubbed 'treats' by some but lauded by others, IT (a form of supervision using proportionate interventions according to the seriousness of the offence) becomes the flagship for most juvenile alternatives to custody. In a few years the then detention centre population is reduced by 75 per cent from a high of 8,000.
1984	Police and Criminal Evidence Act (PACE) and PACE Codes in response to a number of high profile miscarriages of justice. Code C contains extra safeguards for youths, including 'appropriate adults': *Chapter 10*.
1985	Birth of the Crown Prosecution Service (CPS) which gradually adopts a dedicated and specialist approach to the prosecution of children and young persons: see generally *Chapters 11* and *12*. The 'Beijing Rules': seek to further safeguard children in the courts: *Chapter 2*.
1988	Criminal Justice Act introduces young offender institutions (YOIs) in place of youth custody and detention centre.

1989	Children Act splits the jurisdiction of the juvenile court so that it deals almost exclusively with crime. Family proceedings court now deals with child care, under 'public law' or 'private law': *Chapters 7* and *10*. UN Convention On the Rights of the Child: *Chapter 2*.
1990	'Riyadh Guidelines' to prevent juvenile delinquency and the UN Rules for the Protection of Juveniles Deprived of Their Liberty: *Chapter 2*. An era of restorative justice begins, much early work being youth-related.
1991	Criminal Justice Act introduces the first statutory sentencing framework (primarily) for adults, based on just deserts and proportionality. First directly CJS-related anti-discrimination laws introduced. The 1991 Act renames the juvenile court the youth court and extends youth jurisdiction and sentencing powers to include 17-year-olds. Adult criminal majority now in line with the age of majority in general: *Chapter 13*.
1992	Juvenile court becomes the youth court under the CJA 1991 above. Bulger case (see *Glossary*) ignites calls for a 'crackdown' on youth crime and opens the way for the 'prison works' mantra and era that follows.
1993	Sexual Offences Act abolishes the Common Law presumption that a boy under the age of 14 cannot commit rape.
1994	Criminal Justice and public Order Act introduces secure training centres which are to be mainly education focused and run by the private sector. National Association for Youth Justice (NAYJ) formed: see the *Glossary*.
1997	New Labour comes to power with a 'Tough on crime, tough on the causes of crime agenda' and corresponding plans to tackle social exclusion (SE). Home Office publishes *No More Excuses: A New Approach to Tackling Youth Crime*.
1998	Origins of the modern-day Youth Justice System (YJS). Crime and Disorder Act introduces the Youth Justice Board (YJB), youth offending teams (YOTS), Crime and Disorder Reduction Partnerships (CDRPs), a principle aim of youth justice (preventing offending) and the first anti-social behaviour order (ASBO) provisions which are directed at youths. Initially declared to be for use in a relatively small number of cases, ASBOs are used more and more and in a wide range of situations. Persistent young offenders (PYOs) targeted: *Chapter 5*. New system of reprimands and warnings: *Chapter 11*. Human Rights Act incorporates the European Convention of 1950 (above) into UK law. A new emphasis on parenting begins. Old doli incapax rule abolished so that there is no need to prove understanding that offending behaviour was seriously wrong re under-14s: *Chapter 7*. Referral order introduced: *Chapter 15*.

1999	Access to Justice Act revises legal aid and legal services. Youth Justice and Criminal Evidence Act.
2001	Crime and Disorder Act 1998 parenting orders begin: *Chapter 6.* Fixed penalty notices for disorder (FPNDs) under the Criminal Justice and Police Act.
2002	Child Exploitation and Online Protection Agency (CEOP) established. White Paper, *Justice For All.* Police Reform Act gives the Home Secretary stronger default powers re police forces, creates an Independent Police Complaints Commission (IPCC) and expands anti-social behaviour powers. allowing the police to issue fixed penalty notices for disorder (FPNDs). Bench Training and Development Committees (BTDCs) introduced. Munby judgement affects how children in custody are viewed: *Chapter 17.*
2003	Anti-social Behaviour Act extends the scope of ASBOs. It introduces dispersal orders and parenting contracts: *Chapter 6.* Green Paper, *Every Child Matters.* Criminal Justice Act 2003 changes many adult-based sentencing powers and some which are applicable to youths or reflected in youth sentencing, especially re more serious crimes and dangerous offenders. But youth court sentencers are left to use many 'old-style' community orders, a situation not corrected until the advent of the youth referral order (YRO) under the Criminal Justice and Immigration Act 2008 (below).
2004	Children Act 2004 reflects a preventative agenda whilst the Audit Commission criticises expenditure on youth justice *Chapter 6.*
2005	Youth Justice Board (YJB) identifies 'four' domains as risk factors in relation to youth offending: the family, the school, the community and 'personal or individual' factors: *Chapter 1.* It also publishes (one of several key documents) *Risk and Protection Factors Associated with Youth Crime and Effective Interventions to Prevent It.* New Criminal Procedure Committee and Criminal Procedure Rules. Green Paper, *Youth Matters.*
2006	Criminal Defence Service (CDS) Act. Police and Justice Act. Violent Crime Reduction Act. Road Safety Act. Racial and religious hatred legislation. ASBO breach rates reported to be running at 'over 60 per cent', in some areas of the country, with ASBOs seen by some young people as a 'badge of honour': *Chapters 6, 18.* Northern Ireland introduces an innovative restorative-based youth conferencing system as an alternative to prosecution (not unlike referral orders: *Chapter 15*).

2007 Ministry of Justice (MOJ) created. Home Office restructured after Home Secretary Dr. John Reid announces that it is 'not fit for purpose'. Prisons and probation join the courts under the umbrella of the MOJ (with judicial matters dealt with separately). Lord Chancellor becomes 'Justice Secretary and Lord Chancellor'. SGC publishes 'Reduction in Sentence for a Guilty Plea'. Department for Children, Schools and Families (DCSF) assumes key de facto responsibilities for juveniles and becomes a crime prevention partner alongside the MOJ and Home Office. Crime overall is falling as it has done, more or less, for some time: *Chapter 1*.

2008 MOJ issues 'HM Courts Service Framework' under which youth courts operate as an off-shoot of the administration of magistrates' courts. Criminal Justice and Immigration Act makes wide-ranging changes, including re the police, offender management, criminal law, crime and disorder, international fine enforcement, immigration status in certain cases involving 'criminality', automatic deportation of offenders and the maintenance of public order. It also introduces the 'youth conditional caution' (*Chapter 11*) and youth rehabilitation order (YRO) (*Chapter 16*) (among other things). It is estimated that some 3,000 criminal offences have been added to the statute book since 1997. A scaled approach to dealing with youth offenders is promulgated by the YJB with the support of others including as it transpires the SGC in its own guidelines. The PYO initiative of 1998 is discontinued in favour of 'deterring young offenders' (DYO): *Chapter 5*. Youth Crime Action Plan: *Chapter 6*.

2009 Implementation of the main youth justice reforms of the CJIA 2008. SGC publishes *Overarching Principles: Sentencing Youths*: see especially *Chapter 15*. Prime Minister Gordon Brown, speaking at the annual Labour Party Conference, announces a tough new line on anti-social behaviour (ASB). Controversial proposals to allow the Ministry of Justice to take over 'failing YOTs'. Various penal reform groups and others urge that there is general over-use of custody for lesser offences that should really attract alternative forms of sentence. Pilot schemes test out the idea of a 'youth restorative disposal' (*Chapters 4* and *18*).

Appendix

Sentencing Guidelines Council

Overarching Principles
– Sentencing Youths

Consultation Guideline[1]

FOREWORD

The Sentencing Guidelines Council was created in 2004 in order to frame guidelines to assist courts as they deal with criminal cases across the whole of England and Wales.

The Council receives advice from the Sentencing Advisory Panel which consults widely before tendering that advice. The Council then produces a draft guideline on which it seeks the views of a limited group as provided by the Criminal Justice Act 2003.

The background to these offences and the approach to sentencing are set out in the advice from the Panel (and the consultation paper that preceded it), which are published alongside this draft guideline.

All documents can be found at www.sentencing-guidelines.gov.uk or can be obtained from the Council's Secretariat at 4th Floor, 8-10 Great George Street, London SW1P 3AE.

Responses to the consultation should be received no later than 28 August 2009. When the consultation period is concluded, the Council will consider any responses received and then issue a definitive guideline to which every court is required to have regard in accordance with section 172 of the 2003 Act.

Chairman of the Council
June 2009

Contents

Foreword

General approach

A. **Statutory provisions**

B. **Sentencing principles**

   (i) Approach to determining sentence
   (ii) The principal aim of the youth justice system
   (iii) The welfare of the offender
   (iv) The purposes of sentencing

C. **Effect on sentence of the offender being a young person**

D. **Balancing the relevant considerations**

E. **Crossing a significant age threshold between commission of an offence and sentence**

F. **Persistent offenders**

G. **Enforcing the responsibilities of parents and guardians**

Sentences

A. **Referral orders**

B. **Financial orders**

C. **Youth Rehabilitation Orders**

   (i) Threshold and availability
   (ii) Effect of a guilty plea
   (iii) Approach to determining nature and extent of requirements
   (iv) Length of order
   (v) Determining the requirements and the length of an order
   (vi) Orders with intensive supervision and surveillance or fostering
   (vii) Breaches

D. **Custodial sentences**

   (i) Threshold and approach
   (ii) Length of sentence

Trial and sentencing of cases in the Crown Court

  (i) Homicide
 (ii) Statutory minimum sentences
(iii) Grave crimes
(iv) Dangerous offenders
 (v) Jointly charged with an adult
(vi) Remittal from the Crown Court

Annex A
Equality, human rights and areas of potential discrimination

GENERAL APPROACH

A. Statutory provisions

1.1 Offence seriousness is the starting point for sentencing. In considering the seriousness of any offence, the court must consider the offender's culpability in committing the offence and any harm which the offence caused, was intended to cause or might foreseeably have caused.[1] In imposing sentence, the restrictions on liberty must be commensurate with the seriousness of the offence.

1.2 Section 142A of the Criminal Justice Act 2003 sets out relevant considerations when sentencing an offender aged under 18; a court must[2] have regard to:

   (a) the principal aim of the youth justice system (to prevent offending (including re-offending) by those under 18);
   (b) the welfare of the offender; and
   (c) the purposes of sentencing.[3]

1.3 The purposes of sentencing listed for those aged under 18 are:

   (i) punishment;
   (ii) reform and rehabilitation;
   (iii) protection of the public; and
   (iv) reparation to those affected by the offence.[4]

1.4 In addition to the statutory provisions, a court sentencing a young offender must be aware of obligations under a range on international conventions which emphasise the importance of avoiding "criminalisation" of young people whilst ensuring that they are held responsible for their actions and, where possible, take part in repairing the damage that they have caused. This includes recognition of the damage caused to the victims and understanding by the young person that the deed was not acceptable. Within a system that provides for both the acknowledgement of guilt and sanctions which rehabilitate, the intention is to establish responsibility and, at the same time, to promote re-integration rather than to impose *retribution*. The young offender should learn the lesson and never repeat the wrongdoing.

B. Sentencing principles

2.1 Far more than with adults, the approach to sentence will be individualistic.

2.2 The youth of the offender is widely recognised as requiring a different approach from that which would be adopted in relation to an adult. Even within the category of "youth", the response to an offence is likely to be very different depending on whether the offender is at the lower end of the age bracket, in the middle or towards the top end; in many instances, the maturity of the offender will be at least as important as the chronological age.

2.3 However, the sentence must remain proportionate to the seriousness of the present offence (except in the rare circumstances where the criteria for a sentence under the dangerous offender provisions are met) and should not impose greater restrictions on liberty than the seriousness of the offence justifies simply to deal with the risk of re-offending. Particular care will need to be taken where a young person has committed a relatively less serious offence but there is a high risk of re-offending.

2.4 Whilst a court is required to aggravate the seriousness of an offence where there are previous convictions (if the court considers that to be reasonable taking account both of the offence and the time that had elapsed since the previous conviction[5]), a sentence that follows re-offending does not need to be more severe than the previous sentence solely because there has been a previous conviction.

(i) Approach to determining sentence

---

1. Criminal Justice Act 2003, s.143(1)
2. This section does not apply when imposing a mandatory life sentence, when imposing a statutory minimum custodial sentence, when imposing detention for life under the dangerous offender provisions or when making certain orders under the Mental Health Act 1983.
3. section 142A(2)
4. section 142A(3)

5. Criminal Justice Act 2003, s.174(2)

2.5 When determining sentence, the court will:

(1) Assess the culpability of the offender and the harm caused (or intended or foreseeable) taking into account aggravating and mitigating factors relating to the offence.

The assessment of offence seriousness will fix the most severe penalty that can be imposed and will determine whether an offence has crossed the necessary threshold to enable the court to impose a community or custodial sentence.

Even where the custody threshold has been crossed, a court is not required to impose a custodial sentence; similarly with the community sentence threshold.[6]

Harm may be to individual victims or to the community or society at large. Of the four levels of culpability for sentencing purposes, intention is the highest followed by recklessness, knowledge and negligence. Even within those levels there will be gradations of seriousness.

Statutory aggravating factors (including previous convictions) will be relevant in assessing the seriousness of an offence.

(2) Consider any mitigating factors that apply to the offender and any reduction for a guilty plea.

(3) Having taken account of all these factors, a court must then determine sentence including any relevant ancillary orders.

The overall impact of the sentence and the ancillary orders must be considered to ensure that the restrictions on liberty are no more than is commensurate with the seriousness of the offence.

(ii) The principal aim of the youth justice system

2.6 By section 37 of the Crime and Disorder Act 1998, the principal aim of the youth justice system is to prevent offending[7] by children and young people. For the offender, it incorporates the need to demonstrate that such conduct is not acceptable in a way that makes an impact on the offender whilst also identifying and seeking to address any other factors that make offending more likely. For any victim of the offence and society as a whole, it incorporates the need to demonstrate that the law is being effectively enforced and to sustain confidence in the rule of law.

(iii) The welfare of the offender

2.7 By section 44 of the Children and Young Persons Act 1933, "Every court in dealing with a child or young person who is brought before it, either as an offender or otherwise, shall have regard to the *welfare* of the child or young person, and shall in a proper case take steps for removing him from undesirable surroundings, and for securing that proper provision is made for his education and training".

2.8 In other requirements or obligations, different terminology – *best interests, well-being* or *welfare* – may be used. Generally, although there are shades of difference between the meanings, it is unlikely that different decisions will arise solely from those differences.

2.9 Accordingly, since "welfare" is the term used in the legislation applicable to England & Wales, that is the term used in this guideline. Welfare includes the obligation to secure proper provision for education and training,[8] where appropriate to remove from undesirable surroundings[9] and the need to choose the best option for the young person taking account of the circumstances of the offence.

In having regard to the "welfare" of the young person, a court should ensure that it is alert to:

• the high incidence of mental health issues amongst young people in the criminal justice system;

---

6. ibid., s.148(5)

7. including re-offending; s.142A(2)(a)
8. Children and Young Persons Act 1933, s.44
9. ibid.

- the high incidence of those with learning difficulties or learning disabilities amongst young people in the criminal justice system;

- the effect that speech and language difficulties might have on the ability of the young person (or any adult with them) to communicate with the court, to understand the sanction imposed or to fulfil the obligations resulting from that sanction;

- the extent to which young people anticipate that they will be discriminated against by those in authority and the effect that it has on the way that they conduct themselves during court proceedings;

- the vulnerability of young people to self harm, particularly within a custodial environment;

- the extent to which changes taking place during adolescence can lead to experimentation;

- the effect on young people of experiences of loss or of abuse.

2.10 In the light of the high incidence of these issues amongst young people in custody or subject to a community sentence, and taking account of the fact that the principal aim of the youth justice system is reducing offending, a court should always seek to ensure that it has access to information about how best to identify and respond to those issues and, where necessary, that a proper assessment has taken place in order to enable the most appropriate sentence to be imposed.

(iv) The purposes of sentencing

2.11 As set out in paragraph 1 above, a court sentencing a person under the age of 18 is obliged to have regard to the principal aim of the youth justice system, to the welfare of the offender in accordance with section 44 of the 1933 Act and to the four further purposes of sentencing. As with offenders aged 18 and over, no order of priority is given in statute to those purposes. There will be occasions when all these obligations point in the same direction but there will be other occasions when

they do not and a court will be required to determine the best balance following the approach set out in this guideline.

2.12 A difference from the purposes set out for adult offenders[10] is the omission of "the reduction of crime (including its reduction by deterrence)". As the principal aim of the youth justice system[11] is the prevention of offending by children and young people; the emphasis should be on approaches that seem most likely to be effective with young people who are before a court for sentence.

C. Effect on sentence of the offender being a young person

3.1 In addition to the distinctive range of penalties available for youths, there is an expectation that, generally, a young person will be dealt with less severely than an adult offender, although this distinction diminishes as the offender approaches age 18 (subject to an assessment of maturity and criminal sophistication). In part, this is because young people are unlikely to have the same experience and capacity as an adult to realise the effect of their actions on other people or to appreciate the pain and distress caused and because a young person is likely to be less able to resist temptation, especially where peer pressure is exerted.

3.2 Additionally, in most cases a young person is likely to benefit from being given greater opportunity to learn from mistakes without undue penalisation or stigma, especially as a court sanction might have a significant effect on the prospects and opportunities of the young person, and, therefore, on the likelihood of effective integration into society.

3.3 When sentencing a young offender whose offence involves sexual activity but there is no evidence of a coercive or abusive relationship or of anything other than consensual activity, a court will need to be aware that a desire to explore gender identity or sexual orientation may result in offending behaviour. Depending on the

---

10. Criminal Justice Act 2003, s.142
11. see para. 2.6 above

seriousness of the offending behaviour, offender mitigation may arise where that behaviour stems from sexual immaturity or confusion.[12]

3.4 Individual sanctions are likely to have a greater impact on a youth than on an adult, especially lengths of time spent in a custodial establishment, not least because of the exposure to influences likely to entrench criminal conduct (to which a young person may be more susceptible than an adult) and the greater risk of self harm than exists in relation to an adult.

3.5 There is some research evidence that suggests that, when youths are considering whether or not to commit an offence, "they lack the maturity to fully understand the consequences of their harmful acts" and, typically, they are viewed as "impulsive, inexperienced, emotionally volatile or vulnerable, and more easily influenced by negative family members, peers, negative culture values and poverty than older adolescents and young adults".[13]

3.6 Factors regularly present in the background of those juveniles who commit offences include: low family income, poor housing, poor employment records, low educational attainment, early experience of offending by other family members or of violence or abuse (often accompanied by harsh and erratic discipline within the home) and the misuse of drugs.[14] There is also some evidence that those young people who are "looked after" have been more at risk of being drawn into the criminal justice system than other young people acting *in similar ways*.[15]

---

12. The Sentencing Advisory Panel has previously stated that Crown Prosecutors and the court should take account of an offender's immaturity and normal juvenile experimentation: Sexual Offences Act 2003 – the Panel's Advice to the Council – page 4, para. 21, www.sentencing-guidelines.gov.uk

13. Corrado et al., Should deterrence be a sentencing principle under the Youth Criminal Justice Act (2006) 85 Canadian Bar Review at p.548

14. See, for example, the range of approaches in the Youth Crime Action Plan 2008 Chapter 5: www.homeoffice.gov.uk

15. See, for example, Care experience and criminalisation The Adolescent and Childcare Trust, September 2008 www.tactcare.org.uk

3.7 It is clear that these factors do not cause delinquency (since many who have experienced them do not commit crime); nonetheless, there is a strong association and any response to criminal activity amongst young people will need to recognise the presence of such factors if it is to be effective.

The following factors have led to a different approach to the sentencing of young people who offend (compared with the approach for adult offenders) and will affect the sentence imposed in an individual case:

• offending by a young person is frequently a phase which passes fairly rapidly and therefore the reaction to it needs to be kept well balanced in order to avoid alienating the young person from society;

• a criminal conviction at this stage of a person's life may have a disproportionate impact on the ability of the young person to gain meaningful employment and play a worthwhile role in society;

• the impact of punishment is felt more heavily by young people in the sense that any sentence will seem to be far longer in comparison with their relative age compared with adult offenders;

• young people may be more receptive to changing the way they conduct themselves and be able to respond more quickly to interventions;

• young people should be given greater opportunity to learn from their mistakes;

• young people will be no less vulnerable than adults to the contaminating influences that can be expected within a custodial context and probably more so.

D. Balancing the relevant considerations

4.1 This guideline sets out a process that will enable the various obligations and requirements to be applied consistently.

It is, however, only a framework and is intended to apply to the generality of cases.

In balancing the purposes of sentencing, the key elements are:

- the age of the offender (chronological and emotional),

- the seriousness of the offence,

- the likelihood of further offences being committed, and

- the extent of harm caused or likely to result.

Far more than with adults, the approach to sentence will be individualistic.

Proper regard should be had to the mental health and capability of the young person, and to any learning difficulties or disorders or speech and language difficulties, all of which are likely to affect the likelihood of those purposes being achieved.

4.2 The younger an offender (taking account of maturity and not just chronological age) the more likely it is that considering the welfare of the young person will be of greater significance. Since many young people "grow out of" crime, the obligation to have regard to the welfare of a young person who has offended might in some circumstances be best manifested by protecting that person from the adverse effects of intervention in his or her life rather than by providing for some positive action.

4.3 The requirement to have regard to the welfare of a young person is subject to the obligation to impose only those restrictions on liberty that are commensurate with the serious of the offence; accordingly, a court should not impose greater restrictions because of other factors in the young person's life.

4.4 In relation to custodial sentences, the reconviction rate is high and there are concerns about the effect on vulnerable young people of being in closed conditions. Risks commonly found are those of self harm and suicide and, in relation to female offenders, the additional impact on both the offender herself and on the child if the offender is the primary carer of a small child or is pregnant.[16] Since a court is obliged to have regard to the welfare of the young person, it must have regard to these issues when considering sentence.

4.5 Particular care should be taken where an offender has issues arising from mental health, from learning difficulties or from a disability. Research shows that there is a high incidence of these issues in young people in the youth justice system and, in particular, in custody. For reference, information about the level of incidence is summarised in Annex A.

4.6 Some young people may attend court believing that they will be discriminated against or otherwise unfairly treated; this might be for any of a wide range of reasons including ethnicity and sexuality. However unjustified that belief is, a court will need to be alert to the fact that the young person's behaviour in court might be affected by it.

4.7 These issues are not always able to be identified at an early stage in the proceedings leading to sentence. As a result, a court needs to be alert to the possibility that the conduct of the young person (and that of any adult accompanying them in court) might be affected by issues relating to mental health, learning or communication, or some other form of disability that has not previously been identified.

4.8 In such circumstances, care needs to be taken in ensuring that the young person is able to take a proper part in the court proceedings, is able to understand what the court requires as a result of the sentence imposed and that that sentence properly takes account of difficulties in compliance that may arise from those issues.

4.9 The obligations to treat the reduction of offending as the principal aim of sentencing and to have regard to the welfare of the young person both require a court to consider the issues noted above, not only in determining the sentence to be

---

16. The Corston Report – a review of women with particular vulnerabilities in the Criminal Justice System, March 2007, Home Office, www.homeoffice.gov.uk

imposed, but also in determining the length or content of that sentence.

The proper approach for the Crown Court, a magistrates' court or a youth court when sentencing a young offender is for the court, within a sentence that is no more restrictive on liberty than is proportionate to the seriousness of the offence(s), to seek to impose a sentence that fulfils the purposes of sentencing and other matters to which the court must have regard (see section A above) by:

- confronting the young offender with the consequences of the offending and helping the young offender to develop a sense of personal responsibility – these consequences may be experienced by the offender himself or herself, by the family of the offender, by the victim(s) of the offence and/or by the community;

- tackling the particular factors (personal, family, social, educational or health) that put the young person at risk of offending;

- strengthening those factors that reduce the risk that the young person will continue to offend;

- encouraging reparation to victims;

- defining, agreeing and reinforcing the responsibilities of parents.

E. Crossing a significant age threshold between commission of an offence and sentence

5.1 There will be occasions when an increase in the age of an offender[17] will result in the maximum sentence on the date of *conviction* being greater than that available on the date on which the offence was *committed*.

5.2 In such circumstances, the approach should be:

- where an offender crosses a relevant age threshold between the date on which the offence was committed and the date of conviction or sentence, a court should take as its starting point the sentence likely to have been imposed on the date on which the offence was committed;

- where an offender attains the age of 18 after committing the offence but before conviction, section 142 of the Criminal Justice Act 2003 applies (whilst section 142A applies to those aged under 18) and the sentencing disposal has to take account of the matters set out in that section;[18]

- it will be rare for a court to have to consider passing a sentence more severe than the maximum it would have had jurisdiction to pass at the time the offence was committed even where an offender has subsequently attained the age of 18;

- however, a sentence at or close to that maximum may be appropriate, especially where a serious offence was committed by an offender close to the age threshold.

F. Persistent offenders

6.1 Certain sentences are available only where the offender is a "persistent offender" - in particular, a youth rehabilitation order with intensive supervision and surveillance or with fostering in relation to an offender aged between 10 and 14[19] and a detention and training order in relation to an offender aged between 12 and 14.[20] This criterion does not have to be met before the Crown Court imposes long term detention (see paragraph 12 below) or detention for life.

6.2 Similarly, additional powers may be available to a court where a youth rehabilitation order has been breached "wilfully and persistently".

6.3 "Persistent offender" is not defined in legislation but has been considered by the Court of Appeal on a number of occasions.

17. primarily attaining the age of 12, 15 or 18

18. accordingly, when sentencing those convicted when aged 18 and above who have committed an offence whilst under that age, more general public policy considerations may play a greater part
19. Criminal Justice and Immigration Act 2008, s.1(4)(c)
20. Powers of Criminal Courts (Sentencing) Act 2000, s.100(2).

However, following the implementation of the 2008 Act, the sentencing framework is different from that when the definition was judicially developed, particularly the greater emphasis on the requirement to use a custodial sentence as "a measure of last resort".

6.4 A dictionary definition of "persistent" is "persisting or having a tendency to persist"; "persist" is defined as "to continue firmly or obstinately in a course of action in spite of difficulty or opposition".

In determining whether an offender is a persistent offender for these purposes, a court should consider the simple test of whether the young person is one who persists in offending. In most circumstances, therefore, the normal expectation is that the offender will have had some contact with authority in which the offending conduct was challenged before being classed as "persistent".

6.5 This conclusion may be derived from information about previous convictions but may also arise from orders which require an admission or finding of guilt – these include reprimands, final warnings, restorative justice disposals and conditional cautions; since they do not require such an admission, penalty notices for disorder are unlikely to be sufficiently reliable.

6.6 Even where a young person is found to be a persistent offender, a court is not obliged to impose the custodial sentence or youth rehabilitation order with intensive supervision and surveillance or fostering that becomes available as a result of that finding. The other tests continue to apply and it is clear that Parliament expects custodial sentences to be imposed only rarely on those aged 14 or less.

A young offender is likely to be found to be persistent (and, in relation to a custodial sentence, the test of being a measure of last resort is most likely to be satisfied) where the offender has been convicted of, or made subject to a pre-court disposal that involves an admission or finding of guilt in relation to, imprisonable offences on at least 3 occasions in the past 12 months.

Similarly, an offender is likely to be found to have "persistently" breached a youth rehabilitation order where there have been three breaches demonstrating a lack of willingness to comply with the order; the court must find the breaches to have been 'wilful' if it is to gain access to the extra powers.

G. Enforcing the responsibilities of parents and guardians

7.1 A significant difference arising from the procedures for dealing with young people who commit criminal offences is the importance attached to the presence of a parent, carer or appropriate adult at key stages, especially when sentence is imposed. In addition, specific provisions exist to enable a court to reinforce the responsibilities of a parent or guardian.

7.2 The statutory framework clearly envisages the attendance of an adult with a degree of responsibility for the young person; this obligation reflects the principal aim of reducing offending, recognising that that is unlikely to be achieved by the young person alone. A court must be aware of a risk that a young person will seek to avoid this requirement either by urging the court to proceed in the absence of an adult or in arranging for a person to come to court who purports to have (but in reality does not have) the necessary degree of responsibility.

7.3 Insistence on attendance may produce a delay in the case before the court; however, it is important that this obligation is maintained and that it is widely recognised that a court will require such attendance, especially when imposing sentence. If a court proceeds in the absence of a responsible adult, it should ensure that the outcome of the hearing is properly communicated.

7.4 Where a person under the age of 18 is convicted of an offence, the court is under a duty to **bind over a parent or guardian** if satisfied that such a course of action would be desirable in the interest of preventing the commission of further offences.[21] Such an order may not be made where the court imposes a referral order. Similarly, the court has the power to make a **parenting order** where it would be desirable in the interest of preventing the commission of any further offence.[22] Where the offender is aged 16 or less and the court considers that a parenting order would be desirable, there is a presumption in favour of the order being made and reasons must be given if it is not made.[23] In most circumstances, where an order is necessary it is more likely that a parenting order will be appropriate.

7.5 When considering whether to impose a parenting order, the court should give careful consideration to the strength of the familial relationships and to any diversity issues that might impact on the achievement of the purposes of the order. Such factors and issues arising may be documented in a pre-sentence report.

7.6 Particular issues may arise in relation to an offender who is, or who runs the risk of, experiencing familial abuse or rejection on the grounds of sexual orientation. In considering such factors, which may be documented in a PSR, the court must take care not to disclose facts about an offender's sexual orientation without his or her consent. Similar issues might arise in a family where racial tensions exist.

SENTENCES

A. REFERRAL ORDERS

8.1 Where an offender is being sentenced in a youth court or a magistrates' court, a Referral Order is a mandatory sentence in many circumstances in which a young person is to be sentenced for the first time and is discretionary in a wider range of situations. In particular, it is possible to make an order on a second conviction where a referral order was not made following the first conviction.

8.2 When an order is made, the court determines the length of the order (between 3 months and 12 months) but the action taken during that order is decided by a Youth Offender Panel consisting of members of the community supported by a member of a Youth Offending Team. Any victim of the offence may be invited to attend the meeting of the Panel at which the terms are agreed.

8.3 When determining the length of an order, although the needs of the offender are a factor, the primary consideration in most circumstances is the relative seriousness of the offence. Given the mandatory nature of the order in many circumstances, it is less likely that the needs of the offender will be considered in a pre-sentence report. This consideration is more likely to take place once the order has been made and in preparation for the Panel meeting since, within the period of the order, the Youth Offender Panel will agree what needs to be undertaken by the young person both in the light of the nature of the offence and of the young person's needs.

8.4 A court should be prepared to use the whole range of periods allowed; in general, orders of 10-12 months should be made only for the more serious offences.

8.5 Typically, the length of an order should be between 3-5 months for offences where the court assesses seriousness to be relatively low, between 5-7 months for an offence of medium level seriousness and between 7-9 months for an offence where the court considers seriousness to be relatively high. In determining which level applies, a court may find assistance in Section 2 of the Youth Court Bench Book issued by the Judicial Studies Board which provides indications of the level of seriousness of an average offence of the types described.[24]

B. FINANCIAL ORDERS

9.1 A court may impose a fine for any

21. Powers of Criminal Courts (Sentencing) Act 2000, s.150
22. Crime and Disorder Act 1998, s.8(6)
23. ibid., s.9(1)
24. www.jsboard.co.uk/downloads/ycbb/ycbb_section2.pdf

offence. In accordance with statutory requirements, where financial orders are being considered, priority must be given to compensation orders and, where an order for costs is to be made alongside a fine, the amount of the costs must not exceed the amount of the fine.

9.2 In practice, many young people who offend have few financial resources. Where a young person is in receipt of the *Education Maintenance Allowance* or a similar provision which is related to the means of the offender or those with whom the offender lives, a court will need to consider the extent to which making a deduction from the allowance would prejudice the access of the young person to education or training.

9.3 As a general rule, it will rarely be appropriate to take the allowance into account as a resource from which a financial penalty may be paid, especially where the recipient is a young person who is living independently or as part of a household primarily dependent on state benefit.

C. YOUTH REHABILITATION ORDERS

10.1 The Criminal Justice and Immigration Act 2008 provides for a single community sentence (the youth rehabilitation order) within which a court may include one or more requirements variously designed to provide for punishment, for protection of the public, for reducing reoffending and for reparation.

10.2 A youth rehabilitation order with intensive supervision and surveillance or with fostering is also provided but may be imposed only where a custodial sentence otherwise would have been appropriate (see 10.23 below).[25]

(i) Threshold and availability

10.3 In order for a court to be able to impose a youth rehabilitation order, it must be satisfied that the offence is "serious enough".[26] Even where an offence crosses this threshold, a court is not obliged to make a youth rehabilitation order.[27]

10.4 In determining the content and length of an order, the guiding principles are proportionality and suitability since statute provides that the restrictions on liberty within such an order must be commensurate with the seriousness of the offence[28] and that, taken together, the requirements within the order are the most suitable for the offender.[29]

10.5 In contrast to the provisions relating to adult offenders, a court may impose a youth rehabilitation order (other than one with intensive supervision and surveillance or fostering[30]) for an offence that is not imprisonable.

10.6 A youth rehabilitation order is not an available sentence where the "compulsory referral conditions" are found to exist; accordingly, the order will not be available in a youth court or other magistrates' court for a first time offender who has pleaded guilty to an imprisonable offence.

(ii) Effect of a guilty plea

10.7 Where a court is considering sentence for an offence for which a custodial sentence is justified, a guilty plea may be one of the factors that persuades a court that it can properly impose a youth rehabilitation order instead and no further adjustment to the sentence needs to be made to fulfil the obligation to give credit for that plea.

10.8 Where the provisional sentence is already a youth rehabilitation order, the necessary reduction for a guilty plea should apply to those requirements within the order that

25. Criminal Justice and Immigration Act 2008, ss.1(3) and 1(4); Criminal Justice Act 2003, s.174(2)(ca) and (cb) as inserted by Criminal Justice and Immigration Act 2008, sched.4, para.80(2); however, it may be imposed in other circumstances following "wilful and persistent" breach of a youth rehabilitation order: see para. 10.41 below

26. Criminal Justice Act 2003, s.148(1)
27. ibid., s.148(5)
28. ibid., s.148(3)(b)
29. ibid., s.148(3)(a)
30. such an order may be imposed following wilful and persistent failure to comply with a youth rehabilitation order imposed for a non-imprisonable offence: Criminal Justice and Immigration Act 2008, schedule 2, para. 6(13) and para. 8(12)

are primarily punitive rather than to those which are primarily rehabilitative.

(iii) Approach to determining nature and extent of requirements

10.9 In determining the nature and extent of requirements to be included within an order and the length of that order, the key factors are the assessment of the seriousness of the offence, the purpose(s) of sentencing the court wishes to achieve, the risk of re-offending, the ability of the offender to comply, and the availability of requirements in the local area.

10.10 Since a court must determine that the offence (or combination of offences) is "serious enough" to justify such an order, a court will be able to determine the nature and extent of the requirements within the order primarily by reference to the likelihood of the young person re-offending and to the risk of the young person causing serious harm. This is in accordance with the principal aim of the youth justice system, the welfare principle and the sentencing aim of "protection of the public".

10.11 Before making an order a court will consider a pre-sentence report. In preparing that report, (following national standards and practice guidance) the Youth Offending Team (YOT) will be seeking to identify an appropriate balance between the seriousness of the offence, the risk of harm in the future from any further offences the young person might commit and the needs of the young person.

10.12 In most cases, the assessment by the YOT will be undertaken by use of *Asset*[31] supported by professional judgement. An initial assessment will calculate the risk of re-offending; where necessary, an additional assessment will assess the risk of serious harm likely to be involved in further offending. Those assessments

will be reviewed by the YOT in the context of all other available information and the report will identify a level of intervention for the court to consider.

10.13 There are three intervention levels:

- Standard level - for those who show a low likelihood of reoffending and a low risk of serious harm; in those circumstances, the order primarily will seek to repair the harm caused by the offence – typically, this will involve interventions to meet the requirements of the order and the engagement of parents in those interventions and/or in supporting the young person;

- Enhanced level - for those who show a medium likelihood of reoffending or a medium risk of serious harm; in those circumstances, the order will, in addition, seek to enable help or change as appropriate – typically, this will involve greater activity in motivating the young person and in addressing the reasons for non-compliance with the law and may involve external interventions;

- Intensive level - for those with a high likelihood of reoffending or a high or very high risk of serious harm; in those circumstances, the order will, in addition, seek to ensure control of the young person as necessary to minimise the risk of further offending or of serious harm – typically this will involve additional controls, restrictions and monitoring.[32]

10.14 For the broad generality of offences where a youth rehabilitation order is to be imposed, this approach will enable the writer of a pre-sentence report to make proposals that match the obligations on the court to balance the various statutory obligations that apply.

10.15 Where a young person is assessed as presenting **a high risk of re-offending or of causing serious harm** despite having committed a relatively less serious offence, the emphasis is likely to be on requirements that are primarily rehabilitative or for the protection of the public. Care will need to be taken to

---

31. A "common, structured framework for the assessment of all young people involved in the criminal justice system" which is designed to "identify a multitude of factors and circumstances .. which may have contributed" to the offending behaviour: see www.yjb.gov.uk

32. YOUTH JUSTICE: The Scaled Approach, YJB 2009 www.yjb.gov.uk/scaledapproach

ensure both that the requirements are "those most suitable for the offender" and that the restrictions on liberty are commensurate with the seriousness of the offence.

10.16 Where a young person is assessed as presenting a **low risk despite having committed a relatively high seriousness offence**, the emphasis is likely to be on requirements that are primarily punitive, again ensuring that restrictions on liberty are commensurate with the seriousness of the offence. In relation to young offenders, the primary purpose of punitive sanctions is to achieve acknowledgement by the young person of responsibility for his or her actions and, where possible, taking a proper part in repairing the damage caused.

(iv) Length of order

10.17 When imposing a youth rehabilitation order, the court must fix a period within which the requirements of the order are to be completed; this must not be more than 3 years from the date on which the order comes into effect.[33] Where the order contains two or more requirements, the order may specify an earlier date for any of those requirements.[34]

10.18 The period specified as the overall period for the order will normally commence on the day after the order is made but, where the young person is already subject to a detention and training order, the court may specify that the youth rehabilitation order will take effect either on the day that supervision begins in relation to the detention and training order or on the expiry of the term of that order.[35]

10.19 It is not possible to make a youth rehabilitation order when the young person is already subject to another youth rehabilitation order or to a reparation order unless the court revokes those orders.[36]

10.20 The overall length of an order has three

main consequences:

• where a supervision requirement is included, the obligation to attend appointments as directed by the responsible officer continues for the whole period;

• where a young person is in breach of a youth rehabilitation order, one of the sanctions available to a court is to amend the order by including within it any requirement that it would have had power to include when the order was made;[37] however, that new requirement must be capable of being complied with before the expiry of the overall period;[38]

• a young person is liable to re-sentence for the offence(s) for which the order was made if convicted of another offence whilst the order is in force.[39]

10.21 In determining the length of an order, a court should allow sufficient time for the order as a whole to be complied with, recognising that the young person is at risk of further sanction throughout the whole of the period, but allowing sufficient flexibility should a sanction need to be imposed for breach of the order. Where appropriate, an application for early discharge may be made.

(v) Determining the requirements and the length of an order - summary

10.22 As set out in paragraph 2.1 above, the approach to the sentencing of a youth will be far more individualistic than with an adult offender. Where a court is satisfied that an offence has crossed the community sentence threshold and that such a sentence is necessary or has crossed the custody threshold but is an offence for which a youth rehabilitation order is nonetheless considered to be appropriate, taking account of the assessment in the pre-sentence report, the consideration process that the court should follow is:

i) what requirements are most suitable for

33. Criminal Justice and Immigration Act 2008, sched.1, para. 32(1)
34. ibid., para. 32(2)
35. ibid., para. 30
36. ibid., para. 30(4)

37. ibid., sched.2, para. 6(2) (magistrates' court) and para. 8(2) (Crown Court)
38. ibid. para. 6(6) and para. 8(6)
39. ibid. para. 18 and para. 19

the offender?

ii) what overall period is necessary to ensure that all requirements may be satisfactorily completed?

iii) are the restrictions on liberty that result from those requirements commensurate with the seriousness of the offence?

(vi) Orders with intensive supervision and surveillance or with fostering

10.23 Such orders may be made where:[40]

- the court is dealing with a young person for an offence punishable with imprisonment;

- that offence (or combination of offences) crosses the custody threshold; and

- custody would be an appropriate sentence.

  If the offender was under 15 at the time of conviction, such an order may be imposed only where the offender is a "persistent offender".

10.24 When imposing such an order, the court must give its reasons for concluding that the offence(s) cross(es) the community sentence threshold and that the requirements set out above have been met.[41]

(a) With intensive supervision and surveillance

10.25 A youth rehabilitation order with intensive supervision and surveillance is an order that contains an "extended activity requirement", that is, an activity requirement with a maximum of 180 days. As a result, there are further obligations to include a supervision requirement[42] and a curfew requirement.[43]

10.26 Where appropriate, a youth rehabilitation order with intensive supervision and surveillance may also include additional requirements, although the order as a whole must comply with the obligation that the requirements must be those most suitable for the offender and that any restrictions on liberty must be commensurate with the seriousness of the offence.

10.27 When imposing such an order, a court must ensure that the requirements are not so onerous as to make the likelihood of breach almost inevitable.

(a) With fostering

10.28 Where a fostering requirement is included within a youth rehabilitation order, it will require the offender to reside with a local authority foster parent for a specified period; that period must not exceed 12 months.[44] The court must be satisfied that a significant factor in the offence was the circumstances in which the young person was living and that the imposition of a fostering requirement would assist in the rehabilitation of the young person. It is likely that other rights will be engaged (such as those under Article 8 of the European Convention on Human Rights[45]) and any interference with such rights must be proportionate.

10.29 Before including this requirement, the court must consult both the young person's parent or guardian (unless impracticable) and the local authority; it cannot be included unless the offender was legally represented in court when the court was considering whether or not to impose the requirement or, having had the opportunity to be represented, the offender has not applied for representation or that right was withdrawn because of the offender's conduct.[46] This requirement may be included only where the court has been notified that arrangements are

---

40. though see the additional powers where an offender has "wilfully and persistently" failed to comply with a youth rehabilitation order; para. 10.41 below
41. Criminal Justice Act 2003, s.174(2)(ca) and (cb)
42. a requirement to attend appointments with the responsible officer (or any other person determined by the responsible officer): Criminal Justice and Immigration Act 2008, sched.1, para. 9
43. a minimum of 2 hours and a maximum of 12 hours on any one day which must fall within the period of 6 months from the day on which the requirement first takes effect: ibid., para.14. It is

likely that this curfew will be electronically monitored: ibid., para. 3(4)(b) and para.2
44. Criminal Justice and Immigration Act 2008, sched.1, para.18
45. right to respect for family and private life
46. Criminal Justice and Immigration Act 2008, sched.1, para.19

available in the area of the relevant local authority.

10.30 A fostering requirement cannot be included with intensive supervision and surveillance and it cannot be included in a youth rehabilitation order unless the higher criteria described above have been met. Where appropriate, a youth rehabilitation order with fostering may also include other requirements (and must include supervision) although the order as a whole must comply with the obligation that the requirements must be those most suitable for the offender and that any restrictions on liberty must be commensurate with the seriousness of the offence.

10.31 It is unlikely that the statutory criteria will be met in many cases; where they are met and the court is considering making an order, care should be taken to ensure that there is a well developed plan for the care and support of the young person throughout the period of the order and following conclusion of the order. A court will need to be provided with sufficient information, including proposals for education and training during the order and plans for the offender on completion of the order.

(vii) Breaches

10.32 Where a young person fails to comply with a youth rehabilitation order, the "responsible officer" must consider whether there was a reasonable excuse. If the officer considers that there was no reasonable excuse and this is the first failure to comply with the order without reasonable excuse, the officer must issue a "warning".[47]

10.33 The warning will describe the circumstances of the failure to comply, a statement that the failure is not acceptable and a warning that a further failure to comply may lead to the order being referred back to the court. In most circumstances, two warnings will be permitted within a 12 month period before the matter is referred back to court.

10.34 There is a presumption in favour of referring the matter back to court after a third failure to comply and a discretionary power to do so after the second failure to comply.[48]

10.35 10.35 Breach of an order brought before a court may arise from a failure to keep an appointment or otherwise co-operate with the responsible officer or may arise from a failure to comply with one or more of the other requirements of the order.

10.36 Even where a breach has been proved, a court is not obliged to make any order but may allow the youth rehabilitation order to continue as imposed. In contrast with the powers in relation to an adult offender, there is no obligation on the court to make an order more onerous. Where a court determines that a sanction is necessary, it has the power to:

- impose a fine (in which case the order continues in its original form);

- amend the terms of the order; or

- revoke the order and re-sentence the offender.[49]

10.37 If amending the terms of the order, the court may impose any requirement that it could have imposed when making the order and this may be in addition to, or in substitution for, any requirements contained in the order. If the youth rehabilitation order did not contain an unpaid work requirement and the court includes such a requirement using this power, the minimum period of unpaid work is 20 hours; this will give greater flexibility when responding to less serious breaches or where there are significant other requirements to be complied with.[50]

---

47. Criminal Justice and Immigration Act 2008, schedule 2, para. 3

48. ibid., para. 4; where a young person has attained the age of 18 since the order was made, except where the order was made in the Crown Court and no direction was made permitting breach proceedings to be dealt with in the youth court or a magistrates' court, breach proceedings will be dealt with in a magistrates' court other than a youth court: ibid., para.5(3). However, the powers of the magistrates' court are the same as those of a youth court: ibid., para.6

49. ibid., para. 6, 8

50. ibid., para. 6(7) and para. 8(7)

10.38 A court may not amend the terms of a youth rehabilitation order that did not include an extended activity requirement or a fostering requirement by inserting them at this stage; should these requirements be considered appropriate following breach, the offender must be re-sentenced and the original youth rehabilitation order revoked.[51]

10.39 Before imposing a custodial sentence as a result of re-sentencing following breach, a court should be satisfied that the YOT and other local authority services have taken all steps necessary to ensure that the young person has been given appropriate opportunity and support necessary for compliance.[52]

10.40 Where the failure arises primarily from non-compliance with reporting or other similar obligations and a sanction is necessary, the most appropriate response is likely to be the inclusion of (or increase in) a primarily punitive requirement such as the curfew requirement, unpaid work, the exclusion requirement and the prohibited activity requirement or in the imposition of a fine. However, continuing failure to comply with the order is likely to lead to revocation of the order and re-sentencing for the original offence.

10.41 Where the offender has "wilfully and persistently" failed to comply with the order, and the court proposes to sentence again for the offence(s) in respect of which the order was made, additional powers are available.[53] These additional powers include:

- the making of a youth rehabilitation order with intensive supervision and surveillance even though the offence is not imprisonable or a custodial sentence would not have been imposed if the order had not been available;

- the imposition of a detention and training order for 4 months for breach of a youth rehabilitation order with intensive

supervision and surveillance imposed following wilful and persistent breach of an order made for a non-imprisonable offence even though the offence is not imprisonable.

10.42 In considering whether the failure to comply is "persistent", account should be taken of the principles set out in paragraph 6 above.

The primary objective when sentencing for breach of a youth rehabilitation order is to ensure that the young person completes the requirements imposed by the court.

Where the failure arises primarily from non-compliance with reporting or other similar obligations, where a sanction is necessary, the most appropriate is likely to be the inclusion of (or increase in) a primarily punitive requirement.

A court must ensure that it has sufficient information to enable it to understand why the order has been breached and that all steps have been taken by the YOT and other local authority services to give the young person appropriate opportunity and support. This will be particularly important if the court is considering imposing a custodial sentence as a result of the breach.

Where a court is determining whether the young person has "wilfully and persistently" breached an order, it should apply the same approach as when determining whether an offender is a "persistent offender". In particular, a young person is likely to be found to have "persistently" breached a youth rehabilitation order where there have been three breaches demonstrating a lack of willingness to comply with the order.

D. CUSTODIAL SENTENCES

11.1 There is a statutory presumption that a person aged under 18 will be dealt with summarily, usually in a youth court; in such circumstances, the maximum custodial sentence will be a detention and training order of no more than 24 months.

---

51. ibid., para. 6(8) and para. 8(8)
52. cp Education and Skills Act 2008, s.45(5)
53. in accordance with paragraphs 6 and 8 of schedule 2 to the Criminal Justice and Immigration Act 2008

Such an order may be made only for the periods prescribed – 4, 6, 8, 10, 12, 18 or 24 months.[54]

11.2 The custodial sentences available in the Crown Court are:

- detention and training order of up to 24 months;

- long term detention - in relation to a young person convicted[55] in the Crown Court, under section 91 of the Powers of Criminal Courts (Sentencing) Act 2000;

- extended sentence of detention or detention for public protection - where a young person is sent for trial or committed for sentence to the Crown Court to be dealt with under the dangerous offender provisions. In each case, the minimum period to be spent in custody under the sentence must be two years.

- detention for life – for offences of murder

11.3 A detention and training order may not be imposed on an offender aged 10 or 11 years at the time of conviction; an order may be imposed in relation to an offender aged between 12 and 14 at the time of conviction only if the offender is a "persistent offender" (see paragraph 6 above).[56] However, the 'persistent offender' criterion does not have to be met before the Crown Court imposes long term detention or detention for life in relation to offenders who are under 15 years of age.

11.4 A pre-sentence report must be considered before a custodial sentence is imposed.

(i) Threshold and approach

11.5 Under both domestic law and international convention, a custodial sentence must be imposed only as a "measure of last resort";

statute provides that such a sentence may be imposed only where an offence is "so serious that neither a community sentence nor a fine alone can be justified".[57]

11.6 For a first time offender who has pleaded guilty to an imprisonable offence, in most circumstances a referral order will be the most appropriate sentence.

11.7 Since the minimum length of a custodial sentence in the youth court is 4 months (significantly in excess of the minimum available in relation to an adult offender) and since the term of a custodial sentence must be the shortest commensurate with the seriousness of the offence, it is inevitable that the custody threshold is higher in the case of a young person than in the case of an adult - any case that warrants a detention and training order of less than four months must result in a non-custodial sentence.

11.8 In relation to a person under the age of 18, in determining whether an offence has crossed the custody threshold a court will need to consider whether the offence has resulted (or could reasonably have resulted) in serious harm. In determining whether a custodial sentence is unavoidable, generally, a court will need to take account both of the seriousness of the offence (particularly the extent to which it caused (or was likely to cause) serious harm) and of the risk of serious harm in the future. A custodial sentence is most likely to be unavoidable where it is necessary to protect the public from serious harm.

11.9 In addition, a court must take account of:

i) the requirement to have regard to the principal aim of the youth justice system;[58]
ii) the requirement to have regard to the welfare of the offender and the evidence that the risks associated with young offenders in a custodial setting are high.[59]

11.10 Even where the threshold is crossed, a

54. although consecutive sentences may lead to different periods being imposed in total
55. on the implementation of provisions contained in Criminal Justice Act 2003, sched.3, this sentence is likely to be able to be imposed following conviction in a youth court also subsequent to an indication to plead guilty
56. Powers of Criminal Courts (Sentencing) Act 2000, s.100(2).
57. Criminal Justice Act 2003, s.152(2)
58. the reduction of offending (including re-offending); see para. 2.6 above
59. see part B above

court is not required to impose a custodial sentence.

11.11 In determining whether an offence has crossed the custody threshold,

Before deciding to impose a custodial sentence on a young offender, the court must ensure that all the statutory tests are satisfied - namely

(i) that the offender cannot properly be dealt with by a fine alone or by a youth rehabilitation order;

(ii) that a youth rehabilitation order with intensive supervision and surveillance or with fostering cannot be justified; and

(iii) that custody is the last resort

and in doing so should take account of the circumstances, age and maturity of the young offender.

11.12 When a custodial sentence is imposed, a court must state its reasons for being satisfied that the offence(s) is (are) so serious that no other sanction is appropriate and, in particular, why a youth rehabilitation order with intensive supervision and surveillance or with fostering cannot be justified.[60] This justification will need to be based on the principles and purposes of sentencing set out in the statutory framework.

Where the offence(s) has crossed the custody threshold, the statutory tests are likely to be satisfied only where a custodial sentence will be more effective in preventing offending and in achieving the other specified purposes. The obligation to have regard to the welfare of the offender will require a court to take account of a wide range of issues including those relating to mental health, capability and maturity.

(ii) Length of sentence

11.13 A court imposing a custodial sentence is required to set the shortest term

commensurate with the seriousness of the offence(s).[61] Offence specific guidelines do not generally provide starting points or ranges for offenders aged under 18 because of the wide range of issues that are likely to arise and the marked differences in the sentencing framework depending on the age of the offender. Where they are provided, they are for offenders aged 17 with a provision that, for younger offenders, a court should consider whether a lower starting point is justified in recognition of the offender's age and maturity.

11.14 Any approach needs to take account of the general sentencing rules that apply where there is more than one offence or more than one defendant. Where the offence has been committed by offender(s) aged 18 or over and by offender(s) aged under 18, the court will need to consider the role of each offender and the number of offenders involved.

11.15 Where the primary offender is under the age of 18, a court is likely to determine sentence for that offender first giving proper weight to the offender's age and maturity; that will provide a framework within which sentence for the offender(s) over 18 can be determined. Where the primary offender is over 18, a court is likely to determine sentence for that offender first; that will provide a framework within which sentence for the offender(s) under 18 can be determined giving proper weight to age and maturity.

11.16 Where an offence crosses the custodial threshold **and** the court determines that a custodial sentence is unavoidable:

• where the offender is aged 15, 16 or 17, the court will need to consider the maturity of the offender as well as chronological age. It may be appropriate, depending on maturity, to consider a starting point from half to three quarters of that which would have been identified for an adult offender.

It will be particularly important to consider maturity when the court has

---

60. Criminal Justice Act 2003, s.174(4B) as inserted by Criminal Justice and Immigration Act 2008, sched.4, para.80(3)

61. Criminal Justice Act 2003, s.153(2)

to sentence more than one offender. When the offenders are of different ages, including when one or more is over 18, the court will also need to have proper regard to parity between their sentences.

The closer an offender was to age 18 when the offence was committed and the greater the maturity of the offender or the sophistication of the offence, the closer the starting point is likely to be to that appropriate for an adult. Some offenders will be extremely mature, more so than some offenders who are over 18, whilst others will be significantly less mature.

For younger offenders, greater flexibility will be required to reflect the potentially wide range of culpability.

Where an offence shows considerable planning or sophistication, a court may need to adjust the approach upwards.

Where the offender is particularly immature, the court may need to adjust the approach downwards.

- where the young person is aged 14 or less, sentence should normally be imposed in a youth court (except in cases of homicide or where the young person comes within the "dangerous offender" criteria); the length of a custodial sentence will normally be shorter than for an offender aged 15-17 convicted of the same offence.

- an offender aged 14 years or less should be sentenced to long term detention[62] only where that is necessary for the protection of the public either because of the risk of serious harm from future offending or because of the persistence of offending behaviour.

11.17 In determining the term of a detention and training order, the court must take account of any period for which the offender has been remanded in custody or on bail subject to a qualifying curfew condition

and electronic monitoring.[63] As the available terms are specified, the proper approach in taking a remand period into account is to reduce, if possible, the sentence otherwise appropriate to reflect that period. Where a short custodial sentence was being considered, the court might conclude that a non-custodial sentence was appropriate.

11.18 On the implementation of the relevant parts of schedule 3 to the Criminal Justice Act 2003, a "plea before venue" procedure will be introduced for offenders under the age of 18 and will include a general power to commit for sentence where a court accepts jurisdiction following indication of a guilty plea. As with adult offenders, where a young person could have been dealt with in the Crown Court but the youth court has retained jurisdiction, where appropriate the maximum period of 24 months may be imposed following a guilty plea at the first reasonable opportunity where that plea was a factor in retaining a case for sentence in the youth court.

TRIAL AND SENTENCING OF CASES IN THE CROWN COURT

12.1 There is a clear principle (established both in statute and in domestic and European case law) that cases involving young offenders should be tried and sentenced in the youth court wherever possible. This section summarises the relevant statutory provisions and case law. [64]

12.2 It has long been recognised that the Crown Court should be reserved for the most serious cases, noting the greater formality of the proceedings and the increased number of people likely to be

---

62. Powers of Criminal Courts (Sentencing) Act 2000, s.91

63. Powers of Criminal Courts (Sentencing) Act 2000, s.101(8), (9); for these purpose, "remanded in custody" includes periods held in police detention and certain remands or committals to local authority accommodation: ibid. s.101(11)

64. see in particular R (H,A, and O) v Southampton Youth Court [2004] EWHC 2912

present.[65] These factors present additional obstacles in ensuring that proceedings in the Crown Court involving young offenders are conducted in accordance with international obligations.[66]

12.3 Accordingly, it is rare for a young offender to be tried or sentenced in the Crown Court and for a sentence beyond the powers of the youth court to be imposed, except where that sentence is very substantially beyond those powers.

12.4 A youth will appear in the Crown Court for trial and sentence only:

  (i) when charged with "homicide";
  (ii) when subject to a minimum statutory sentence;
  (iii) when charged with a "grave crime" and a youth court has determined that, if convicted, a sentence beyond its powers should be available; or
  (iv) when charged together with an adult offender who has been sent to the Crown Court and it has been determined that the cases should be kept together.

12.5 Where a sentence under the "dangerous offender" provisions is likely to be needed the youth may be committed for trial or for sentence.

(i) Homicide

12.6 An exception to the presumption that a person aged under 18 should be tried summarily arises where the young person is charged with an offence of "homicide". For a case falling within this description, there is no discretion and it must be sent to the Crown Court for trial. The meaning of "homicide" is not defined in statute.

(ii) Statutory minimum sentences

12.7 A further exception to the presumption in favour of summary trial arises where a young person is charged with an offence which has a statutory minimum custodial sentence and the criteria for that sentence would be likely to be satisfied

if the young person were convicted.[67] A sentence of long term detention[68] may be imposed following committal where these mandatory sentence provisions apply; before there can be a departure from the minimum sentence prescribed, a court must find that there are "exceptional circumstances".

(iii) "Grave crimes"

12.8 A further exception to the statutory presumption in favour of summary trial arises where a young person is charged with a "grave crime" and a youth court has determined that, if convicted, a sentence beyond its powers should be available. In such circumstances, a young person may be sentenced by the Crown Court to long term detention under section 91 of the Powers of Criminal Courts (Sentencing) Act 2000. At present, such a sentence may be imposed only by the Crown Court and only where the offender was **convicted** in the Crown Court, and that court considers that neither a community order nor a detention and training order is suitable.

12.9 An offence comes within section 91 where:

  • it is punishable with 14 years imprisonment or more for an adult (but is not a sentence fixed by law), or

  • is an offence contrary to sections 3, 13, 25 or 26 of the Sexual Offences Act 2003,[69] or

  • is one of a number of specified offences in relation to firearms, ammunition and weapons which are subject to a minimum term but in respect of which a court has found exceptional circumstances justifying a lesser sentence.

  When this sentence is imposed, it will be for a longer period than that available to a youth court.

---

65. ibid., [33]
66. see, for example, S.C. v United Kingdom (2005) 40 E.H.R.R. 10

67. Magistrates' Courts Act 1980, s.24
68. imposed under Powers of Criminal Courts (Sentencing) Act 2000, s.91
69. sexual assault, child sex offences committed by a child or young person, sexual activity with a child family member, inciting a child family member to engage in sexual activity

12.10 This general power should be used rarely since:

i) it is the general policy of Parliament that those under 18 should be tried in the youth court wherever possible;

ii) trial in the Crown Court under this provision should be reserved for the most serious cases, recognising the greater formality of the proceedings and the greatly increased number of people involved;

iii) offenders aged under 15 will rarely attract a period of detention under this provision and those under 12 even more rarely.[70]

12.11 Accordingly,

(i) a young person aged 10 or 11 should be committed to the Crown Court under this provision only where charged with an offence of such exceptional gravity that, despite the normal prohibition on a custodial sentence for a person of that age, a sentence exceeding two years is a realistic possibility;[71]

(ii) for a young person aged 12-17 (for which a detention and training order could be imposed), a sentence under these provisions should generally be imposed only where the shortest term commensurate with the seriousness of the offence(s) is substantially beyond the 2 year maximum for a detention and training order.

(iv) Dangerous offenders

12.12 There are rigorous statutory tests which must be satisfied before a court may conclude that a youth is a "dangerous offender" and requires sentence under the dangerous offender provisions in the Criminal Justice Act 2003 (as amended).[72] Such a sentence may be imposed only where an equivalent determinate sentence of at least 4 years would have been imposed. Criteria relating to future offending and the risk of serious harm must be assessed in the light of the maturity of the offender, the possibility of change in a much shorter time than would apply for an adult and the wider circumstances of the young person.

12.13 At present, the provisions by which a potentially "dangerous" young offender reaches the Crown Court are overlapping to some extent as a result of the only partial implementation of the provisions of the Criminal Justice Act 2003, which introduce a new section 51A to the Crime and Disorder Act 1998. This new section requires a young offender to be sent for trial where it appears that the criteria for imposition of a sentence under the dangerous offender provisions will be met on conviction. However, the power to commit for sentence following conviction in a youth court or magistrates' court is preserved.[73]

12.14 The nature of the offence is likely to be very significant in determining both whether the offender meets the risk and harm criteria and, even if so, whether a sentence under the provisions is necessary (given that there is now wide discretion).

Since a young offender should normally be dealt with in a youth court, where a young person charged with a specified offence would not otherwise be committed or sent to the Crown Court for trial, generally it is preferable for the decision whether to commit under these provisions to be made after conviction.[74]

(v) Jointly charged with an adult

12.15 A further exception to the presumption in favour of summary trial arises where a young person is charged jointly with a person aged 18 or over; if the court considers it necessary to commit them

70. see footnote 64; those who meet the criteria for "dangerous offenders" will be dealt with under separate provisions: see below

71. see R(D) v Manchester City Youth Court [2002] 1 Cr.App.R.(S) 373

72. see the review of statutory provisions and case law authority in Dangerous Offenders: A Guide for Sentencers and Practitioners at p.18 www.sentencing-guidelines.gov.uk

73. Powers of Criminal Courts (Sentencing) Act 2000, s.3C

74. see, for example, the statement that there is a strong presumption against sending young offenders to the Crown Court unless clearly required: R(W) v Southampton Youth Court [2002] EWHC 1640 per Lord Woolf CJ

both for trial it will have the power to commit the young person to the Crown Court for trial.[75]

12.16 Any presumption in favour of sending a youth to the Crown Court to be tried jointly with an adult must be balanced with the general presumption that young offenders should be dealt with in a youth court.

12.17 When deciding whether to separate the youth and adult defendants, a court must consider:

- the young age of the offender, particularly where the age gap between the adult and youth is substantial,

- the immaturity and intellect of the youth,

- the relative culpability of the youth compared with the adult and whether or not the role played by the youth was minor, and

- any lack of previous convictions on the part of the youth compared with the adult offender.

12.18 A very significant factor will be whether the trial of the adult and youth could be severed without inconvenience to witnesses or injustice to the case as a whole, including whether there are benefits in the same tribunal sentencing all offenders. In most circumstances, a single trial of all issues is likely to be most in the interests of justice.

(vi) Remittal from the Crown Court

12.19 Where a young person is convicted before the Crown Court of an offence other than homicide, there is an obligation to remit the young person to a youth court for sentence unless that is "undesirable".[76] In considering whether remittal is "undesirable", a court should balance the need for expertise in the sentencing of young offenders with the benefits of

sentence being imposed by the court which had determined guilt.

12.20 Particular attention should be given to the presumption where a young person appears before the Crown Court only because he or she is jointly charged with an adult offender. A referral order is not available in the Crown Court for a first-time offender and such orders may now be made following a second conviction in certain circumstances.

Annex A

Equality, human rights and areas of potential discrimination

1. These paragraphs summarise information gathered by the Sentencing Advisory Panel concerning the incidence and effect of issues relevant to equality and discrimination and the obligations regarding human rights. It is provided to assist those involved in the sentencing of young offenders. Fuller information is available in specialist documents.

General

2. A common thread running through many of the responses to the consultation undertaken by the Sentencing Advisory Panel was the high incidence amongst those coming before the court of a range of issues relating, in a broad sense, to mental health, learning disabilities and learning difficulties, physical disability and experiences of loss or abuse. Concerns were expressed about disadvantages experienced by "looked after" children and by those from communities poorly understood by the public at large.

3. Additionally, research has consistently identified a range of factors that are regularly present in the background of juveniles who commit offences. These tend to include low family income, poor housing, poor employment records, low educational attainment, early experience of violence or abuse (often accompanied by harsh and

---

75. the procedures around the transfer to the Crown Court of a young person charged with an offence will change on the implementation of the relevant provisions in the Criminal Justice Act 2003, sched.3

76. Powers of Criminal Courts (Sentencing) Act 2000, s.8(2)

erratic discipline within the home) and the misuse of drugs.[77] Whilst it is clear that these factors do not cause delinquency (since many who have experienced them do not commit crime), nonetheless there is a strong association and any response to criminal activity amongst young people will need to recognise the presence of such factors if it is to be effective.

4. There is also some evidence that those young people who are "looked after" are more at risk of being drawn into the criminal justice system than other young people acting in similar ways[78] not least because of the risks arising from mixing with offending peers, difficulties in management of challenging behaviour (and the possibility that a strict reaction to the "offender" will be seen in part to have a deterrent effect on others) and the lack of stability in care placements. It is estimated that 50% of young people in custody have lived in care or have had previous involvement with Social Services compared with 3% in the general population.[79]

Identification of issues

5. Responses to the Panel's consultation recorded the importance not only of good quality pre-sentence reports (PSRs) and specialist reports from mental health practitioners, children's services and addictions workers but also of a court having a good understanding of "normal" adolescent behaviour and of the influences of the changes that take place during adolescence, recognising that they can lead to experimentation and to low self esteem.

6. Concerns were expressed about the significant under-reporting not only of mental health issues but also of a wide range of learning difficulties, including learning disabilities, amongst young people in custody and subject to community orders. One respondent particularly urged the Panel to make explicit "the need to secure professional screening and assessment to inform court decision making" and that this should occur at the earliest possible opportunity in the "youth justice pathway".

7. Even where issues have not been identified by other agencies before a case comes before the court, the high level of reported incidence of these issues suggests that a court should be on notice that young offenders are more likely than not to present with at least one functional problem. Recognising and understanding these problems is likely to be key to understanding the causes of offending and, therefore, to the identification of a sanction that has a realistic chance of meeting the aim of preventing re-offending.

8. The Panel was also informed that speech and language difficulties are common; where they exist, they are likely to affect the ability of the young person to communicate, to understand court processes and sanctions and to complete requirements within community orders. As a matter of general principle, courts need to be alert to the need to ensure that the young person is able to communicate effectively within the sentencing process and understands what a court order requires; where a court is making an order aiming to reduce re-offending, this awareness will enable a court to gather sufficient information to enable a proper decision to be made and for the sanction to be appropriate in light of the limited abilities of the young offender. In particular, where a custodial sentence is likely to be imposed, a court should ensure that a full assessment, including a psychiatric report where appropriate, has been undertaken.

Incidence and effect

9. It is estimated that 83% of young people in custody have been excluded from school (compared with 6% of young people in the general population),[80] 86% have engaged in substance misuse (compared with 21%),[81] 38% have been diagnosed with Attention Deficit Hyperactivity Disorder (ADHD) (compared with 6%),[82] and 31% have a

---

77. See, for example, the range of approaches in the Youth Crime Action Plan 2008 Chapter 5: www.homeoffice.gov.uk

78. See, for example, Care experience and criminalisation The Adolescent and Childcare Trust, September 2008 www.tactcare.org.uk

79. Counting the cost, reducing child imprisonment Nacro, 2003

80. Juveniles in custody HM Inspectorate of Prisons, 2004

81. Substance misuse and the juvenile secure estate YJB, 2004

82. Youth Crime Action Plan Home Office, 2008

recognised mental disorder (compared with 10%).[83]

10. In addition, it has been reported that one in five young offenders have an IQ of less than 70[84] and that this is likely to make it more difficult to complete interventions within a sentence.

11. Some young people have general communication difficulties that may affect their behaviour in court, sometimes suggesting arrogance or indifference, and which can also impact on their ability to understand what is required of them.

12. Although responses to the Panel's consultation generally noted that there is little evidence suggesting inappropriate discrimination in the sentencing of young people, one respondent pointed out that young people may believe that they will be discriminated against; this might be for any of a wide range of reasons including ethnicity and sexuality. A court will need to be alert to the fact that such a belief may result in the young person responding to the court in ways that are not helpful.

13. More specifically, one respondent drew attention to the high levels of expectation of discrimination on the part of lesbian, gay and trans-sexual people who come into contact with the criminal justice system; courts should be aware that it is likely to colour the young person's response.

14. It is also recognised that there is a greater risk of self harm than exists in relation to an adult.[85] In 2008, 9% of all juvenile offenders were assessed as being at risk of self harm or of suicide; the proportion was 15% for female juvenile offenders. This is of particular concern when vulnerable young people are held in custody.

15. Additional issues arise about the impact of custody on both the offender and her child where an offender is the primary carer of a small child or is pregnant.[86]

16. Some responses pointed out that, at times, certain sentencing options can exacerbate fraught family relationships or even promote abuse (curfew orders); it was important both that good information was available and that courts are fully aware of the issue to ensure that restrictions are well informed before they are imposed. This may be particularly pertinent in relation to a parenting order or when imposing a requirement within a youth rehabilitation order that will result in a young person spending prolonged periods within a family unit.

Further information

17. Whilst the majority of responses indicated that no further guidance was needed from the Sentencing Guidelines Council on these issues (and it was clear that many considered they could rely on the PSR for relevant information), there were some requests for accessible and immediately available material. The topics on which this was sought included Attention Deficit Hyperactivity Disorder (ADHD), Asperger's and other diagnoses on the autism spectrum.

18. One response drew attention to guides being prepared by the British Dyslexia Association and the British Institute of Learning Disabilities and another believed that work was being done within HMCS to prepare a guide for the judiciary on young people and learning difficulties.

19. It is widely recognised that it is not always possible for issues related to mental health or other disabilities, including poor communication skills, to be identified at an early stage in the proceedings leading to sentence. As a result, the court needs to

83. Mental health needs and effectiveness of provision for young offenders in custody and in the community YJB, 2005

84. Chitsabesan et al., 2006

85. Self harm by young people in custody is reported as 2,635 incidents in the year to the end of August 2008. This will include incidents where no treatment was required as well as more serious incidents. The number of young people self harming will be smaller than the number of incidents. *Data supplied by the Youth Justice Board from administrative systems through a self reporting system from secure establishments*

86. The Corston Report – a review of women with particular vulnerabilities in the Criminal Justice System, March 2007, Home Office, www.homeoffice.gov.uk

be constantly mindful of the nature of the issues that might arise, the possibility that they may have avoided identification prior to appearance before the court and the fact that they may affect the ability of a young person to understand or complete requirements imposed by a court.

Conclusion

20. A court will wish to aim to ensure that any young person is able to take a proper part in the court proceedings, is able to understand what the court requires as a result of the sentence imposed and that that sentence properly takes account of any likely difficulties in compliance.

21. Similarly, a court needs to be alert to the possibility that an adult accompanying the offender may have similar needs to those identified above.

Index

A

absconding 115
absolute discharge 148, 158, 201
abuse xvi, 188
  abuse of process 113
acceptable behaviour contract (ABC) xi, 79, 80, 87
accommodation 56, 190
accountability 21
  accountability of parents 36
achievement 77, 86
action plan order 161
activity 174
  extended activity requirement 165
'acute' services 86
admission 109
'admonishment' 108
adult xii
adversarial system 61
advocacy services 189
affirmation 201
'age-appropriate' expectations 87
age-related aspects xii, xvii, 32, 36, 122, 134, 136
  age and understanding 132
  criminal capacity 85
  custody 179
  reaching 18 during the proceedings 122
  sentencing 140
  YRO 162
aggravating factor 201
aiding, abetting adult, etc. 117
aims 86
alcohol 56, 107, 177
alternative
  to custody xv, xvi, 99, 182
  to prosecution 107
ancillary order 153, 201
anger management 107
anti-social behaviour (ASB) 33, 50, 52, 62, 82, 197
  annual review of ASBOs 97
  Anti-Social Behaviour Act 2003 75, 78, 83, 111
  anti-social behaviour order

(ASBO) 79, 89, 118, 129
  'badge of honour' 80, 92, 226
  ASBO 'action squad' 91
  ASBO Concern 80
  discharging an ASBO 97
apology 63, 149
appeal to the Crown Court 137
appropriate adult 54, 57, 59
  'Guidance for Appropriate Adults' 104
  PACE 102, 103
arrest 101
arson 120
assessment 154, 189, 201
  YOT by 109
ASSET 57, 67, 71, 154, 168
attendance centre 99, 162, 175
  enforcement of order 137
attitude 71, 168, 190
Audit Commission 76
authority
  youth view of 147

B

'badge of honour' 80, 92, 226
bail 48, 113, 115
  Bail Act 1976 115, 133, 224
  bail notice 115
  bail support 54
  conditional bail 134
  electronic tagging 134
  general presumption in favour of 133
  'street bail' 101, 115
balance 148
Balls, Ed 92, 195
Barnardos 58, 187, 188, 194
Beijing Rules 40, 88
Belgium 31
Bench Training and Development Committee (BTDC) 128
benefits 190
Bentley, Derek 24
best practice 202
binding-over 118, 129
  parental bind-over 156
biological influences 30
black and minority ethnic people 28
borstal (former) xvi, 32, 202, 224
breach 202
  YRO 168

Notes

Notes

The
Magistrates' Court

An Introduction

by Bryan Gibson
Consultant Mike Watkins

A simple speedy summary.

This fully revised 2009 Fifth Edition takes account of the wide scale changes which have affected the work of Justices of the Peace and their courts in recent years.

- A unique handbook
- Consistently rated excellent by reviewers
- Especially useful for newcomers to the topic

A most useful introduction that can be used alongside other training materials or as an ideal self-study guide.

Also includes a **Timeline** and an extensive **Glossary of Words, Phrases, Acronyms and Abbreviations** - the language of the system - which will be of particular use to people wishing to quickly get to grips with the terminology of the magistrates' courts.

Pages 192
Format Paperback
Published 18/05/2009
ISBN 9781904380528

The Penal Crisis

and the

Clapham Omnibus

Questions and Answers in
Restorative Justice

by David J Cornwell

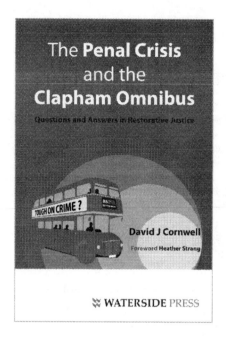

What is restorative justice ... and does it work?

These are just two of the many questions posed by David J Cornwell in this incisive work. Based on a lifetime of research and experience it deals with the concerns about crime and punishment of that most vivid of judicial creations, 'The Man or Woman on the Clapham Omnibus'.

Cornwell dismantles the traditional arguments for 'locking people away' and undermines the idea that it is necessary to be 'tough on crime'. The book credits people with a higher level of intelligence. It provides them with proper answers and explanations based on sound data, copious research and an in-depth analysis of existing trends. It is a work for people who value credibility rather than politically-driven excuses with their increasingly damaging effects.

Foreword Heather Strang
Pages 256
Format Paperback
Published10/07/2009
ISBN 9781904380474

More details at WatersidePress.co.uk

☙ WATERSIDE PRESS

Sir

William Garrow

His Life, Times and Fight for Justice

by John Hostettler and Richard Braby

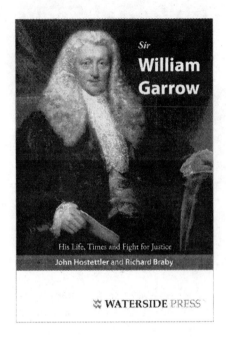

The full and real account of William Garrow's life, including his legal career and family story.

'Without the pioneering work of William Garrow, the legal system would be stuck in the Middle Ages': **Radio Times**

Having only been dramatised in BBC1 TV's 'Garrow's Law', the true story of Sir William Garrow's life, including his unique contribution to the development of English law and its processes is so far little known by the general public.

This book tells the real story of the man behind the drama.

Foreword Geoffrey Robertson QC
Pages 272
Format Hardback
Publication 30/11/2009
ISBN 9781904380559

❈ **WATERSIDE** PRESS